SOME PARADOXES
OF PAUL

SOME PARADOXES OF PAUL

by

EDMUND B. KELLER

PHILOSOPHICAL LIBRARY

New York

Copyright, © 1974, by Philosophical Library, Inc.,

15 East 40th Street, New York, N. Y. 10016

Library of Congress Catalog Card Number: 74-75085

SBN 8022-2144-0

Manufactured in the United States of America

For JOHN, PAUL,
MARLENE, and EARL

TABLE OF CONTENTS

PREFACE

The original impulse for this book came from the study and observation of the followers of "the Way" in the New Testament, and the development of early Christianity. It occurred to me that there was a tendency to superimpose structures of thought from later generations upon the primitive or archaic environment.

The more immediate reason for this publication was the desire to consider the Pauline paradoxes from another perspective. In consequence of that desire this work was submitted originally in partial fulfillment of the requirements for the degree of Doctor of Philosophy in Boston University Graduate School.

My grateful acknowledgements are due to all the scholars whose work I have consulted and where authority is quoted at the proper place, as well as to the publishers and institutions who have kindly given permission for the use of materials quoted. I wish to express thanks to my typist, Mrs. E. Lee Bothast, whose untiring and thoughtful help brought to completion the manuscript which is the substance of this book.

There are those toward whom I have special thoughts of gratitude. I have in mind especially Dr. L. Harold DeWolf in Systematic Theology, and Dr. Nils Ehrenstrom in Ecumenical Studies, both of whom supervised my graduate study program in Boston. Dr. Thomas Kepler in New Testament at Oberlin Graduate School of Theology, brought insights and inspiration to the Pauline studies of the New Testament.

I would also like to acknowledge the helpful experience in partnership with the Philosophical Library Publishers to bring this book to publication.

Above all, there is a debt of gratitude to my wife, Beatrice, whose companionship and encouragement has made it possible to accomplish this present work.

Cleveland, Ohio

Edmund B. Keller

xi

SOME PARADOXES
OF PAUL

CHAPTER I

INTRODUCTION

A. *The Purpose of this Investigation*

The title of this work indicates that what is being attempted is not a comprehensive treatise on paradox but a study of some of the paradoxical themes of Paul. The purpose is to discover their true relationship to one another and to determine the quality of truth which is expressed. The investigation includes some general background materials on the subject of paradox but specifically the aim will be to understand the connection between Paul's paradoxical statements which have been selected for this purpose.

The printed materials on the subject of paradox clearly indicate that men have employed this literary manner of expression across the years. Jesus made frequent use of paradox in his discourses as shown by the New Testament. Plato and Socrates used this figure of speech on many occasions as revealed by their extant writings. But for what reasons does Paul resort to paradox? What is the relationship of his ideas when thus expressed? In order to answer these questions some specific Pauline paradoxes will be considered.

Several alternatives may be visualized at this stage: (1) Paul may have used paradox as a rhetorical contrivance to arrest attention and stimulate action. (2) He may have wanted to show that preliminary concepts must be enlarged to accommodate new truth. (3) He may have become involved in real logical contradiction because he could not find a way to resolve some particular paradox. (4) He perhaps moved from one level of being to another resolving his paradoxes within himself. These are a few possibilities and others might well be forthcoming as the study progresses.

The definition of paradox will be reserved for the next chapter which is to follow. However, it may be noted here at the outset that in general no definition is ever adequate because the subject defined constantly overflows the bounds and limits set by the definition. There is also the fact that all attempts at definition reveal lines and tendencies in the character of the person proposing the definition.[1]

B. *The Previous Studies of the Subject*

There are shelves upon shelves of books in the various libraries covering topics which relate to the life, letters, and interpretation of Paul. Yet when it comes to the matter of his paradoxes there has been no organized presentation of them. Several years ago there appeared a book of sermons by William L. Watkinson[2] on a few of the moral paradoxes of Paul. The aim of these sermons was homiletical. Ralph W. Sockman[3] wrote a book on Jesus' use of paradox with reference to some similar ideas in Paul's letters. This has been true of a number of publications on the subject. There are some older works on the general teaching of the Bible on the subject of paradox, but they are not especially helpful. The articles which appear under the heading "paradox" in the encyclopedias and reference works offer some useful ideas, but are necessarily limited and brief.[4] Some of the journals and periodicals show a varying degree of interest in Paul's paradoxes. The standard commentaries contain the most valuable work done in recent Pauline research.

C. *The Timely Relevance of the Study*

The subject of paradox has become popular and is likely to appear in newspaper editorials, syndicated columns, and religious magazines. Some of the religious journals have shown an interest in paradox in such articles as, "Theology Beyond Paradox" by Arnold B. Come.[5] Clarence H. Hamilton had an article published under the heading "Encounter with Reality in Buddhist Madhyamika Philosophy" in which he discusses a number of its inherent paradoxes.[6] Robert Lawson Slater made a study of Hinayana Buddhism in modern Burma, which resulted in the publication of a book entitled *Paradox and Nirvana.*[7] Erich Fromm wrote a book on the love of God from the viewpoint of "paradoxical logic."[8] Kermit Eby and June Greenlief made a sociological study of the paradoxes of democracy.[9] William Ernest Hocking has commented on the paradoxical impotence of the modern state by reason of its "deficiency in the field of motivation."[10] Much of the contemporary theological interest in paradox has come about through the discussion of writings by Søren Kierkegaard.

There is a growing awareness today of strange inconsistencies of thought and action which need to be resolved. There is a general desire for peace, yet within and among the nations there is preparation for war. Some of the conveniences of modern life have a tendency to separate people while also pulling them together. In the moral and religious realm with the increased religious interest there has also been a decreasing moral sensitivity, with the increase of physical and technological power there has also come a progressive insecurity. The subject of paradox has appeared in these different relationships making it of timely relevance. A study of Paul's paradoxical themes will be in keeping with this interest.

D. *The Literary Sources Mainly Biblical*

The primary literary sources of information for this volume are the letters of Paul. The most trustworthy of these according to most scholars at the present time are nine letters composed or dictated by Paul. These include the following: Romans, I and

II Corinthians, Galatians, Philippians, Colossians, I and II Thessalonians, and Philemon. Ephesians, I and II Timothy, and Titus are considered to be Pauline only in a secondary sense, along with the Book of Acts. In passing it may be noted that it is a recognized fact that some Pauline letters have been lost and are not available for consideration.[11] It is not the purpose of this investigation to determine authorship or authenticity of the secondary sources mentioned above. Except for purposes of comparison, the paradoxes of Paul which are the concern of this study will be limited to the nine letters considered to be genuine.

With respect to the general secondary materials to be used on the subject of paradox, the object is to project and analyze the nature of thoughts and conclusions of men in several fields with the hope that this will provide a broader base of information and understanding. The chief goal, however, must not be lost sight of and that is to see the relationship of some of Paul's own paradoxes in the New Testament letters previously mentioned.

Paul's critics at Corinth would gladly have derided the letter writer Paul if there had been any grounds for doing so. On the contrary they were compelled to say: 'His letters are impressive and forceful."[12] Their qualitative judgment on the primary source material is important, yet it should be kept in mind that the Paul behind the letters is the real Paul. Undoubtedly Paul would have elaborated and clarified some of his ideas further were it possible now to have him do so. Yet even with the letters we have he reveals much of himself and his thought.

After the footnote below all the passages quoted in this work from the Old and New Testaments, unless otherwise designated, are from the 1946 and 1952 editions of the Revised Standard Version of the Bible and are used by the written permission of the publishers, Thomas Nelson and Sons.

F. *The Procedure to be Followed*

In principle the experiential way of dealing with matters of belief and practice has been employed in every vital and living pattern of existence especially since New Testament times. But in most cases it has been implicit rather than explicit. Christian experience has been tacitly assumed.

The position taken here is that religious faith which is rationally justified must be considered no less valid than the faith expressed in the hypotheses of the sciences, each being open to empirical verification when made the basis of action. This is not to say that the sole criterion of truth is subjective experience. Such a position would be unwise in view of the related facts in the objective world. Both the subject and objective aspects must be included in any sound appraisal of life. The significance of this procedure will be made clear as the work proceeds.

As a working hypothesis it will be maintained that Paul's paradoxical themes are best understood in terms of their divine and human relationships. The gospel is communicated by the method of relationship. The different kinds of paradoxes such as the psychological, rhetorical, ethical, and religious help to clarify the nature of this relationship.

Having stated the main concerns of this dissertation in the introductory chapter, it is possible now to give attention to the first major task, which is to discover the general nature of paradox (Chapter Two). Upon the completion of this, the next major undertaking will be to consider the historical background of Paul (Chapter Three). The third major task will be to examine some of the specific paradoxical themes of Paul (Chapter Four). After that is done the fourth major task will be to study the general nature and purpose of the Pauline paradox (Chapter Five). Finally, the results of the investigation will be summarized and the conclusions will be stated (Chapter Six).

CHAPTER II

THE NATURE OF PARADOX

A. *The Meaning of Paradox as a Literary Form*

The preceding chapter indicates that the purpose of this investigation is to try and determine the relationship of certain Pauline paradoxical themes as to their nature and meaning. Such an investigation involves a general as well as a specific understanding of the nature and the function of paradox. This will be pointed out in Chapters Four and Five. To understand these chapters it will be helpful to point out that the term "paradox" has a variety of meanings. Such is the purpose of the present chapter which begins with the definition of paradox.

1. *Definition.* The dictionaries recognize several meanings of the word "paradox." In the *Oxford English Dictionary* the following definitions are given: "A statement or tenet contrary to received opinion or belief; often with the implication that it is marvelous or incredible;" "A statement or proposition which on the face of it seems self-contradictory, absurd, or at variance with common sense;" "Often applied to a proposition or statement that is actually self-contradictory, or contradictory to reason or ascertained truth, and so, essentially absurd and false."[1] In these three definitions the connotation of the term paradox may be that of a proposition of surprise, a seeming contradiction contrary to current conventions, a deliberate logical contradiction of incompatible assertions.

The etymological meaning of the word "paradox" stems from two Greek words $\pi\alpha\rho\alpha'$, beyond, beside, contrary to expectation, and δόξα, opinion, belief, the latter coming from δοκεῖν, to seem.[2] From this usage it readily passes into the meaning of wonderful, admirable.[3] The disciples in Luke's gospel comment on Jesus' words and say in amazement, "We have seen strange things today."[4] In New Testament Greek these words are literally, "We have seen paradoxes today." (ὅτι εἴδομεν παράδοξα σήμερον.)[5] The word was so used in Greek until the eighteenth century when in English the idea of self-contradiction gradually came into usage.[6]

The Greeks found it necessary to make a differentiation in their use of the word paradox. They used the term "paralogism"[7] (παράλογος, reason) instead of paradox in the case of some illogicality. Another term that was used whenever a real contradiction was intentionally placed was "contradox."[8] Still another word "oxymoron" meaning "pointedly foolish" was suggested in the place of paradox when a real contradiction was intended. A word of contrary signification was added to an epithet, thereby the incongruous terms would give point to the statement.

In the French language the word *paradoxe* is used to mean, "Ce qui est contraire à l'opinion généralement admise, á la prévision ou à la vraisemblance."[9] This usage of the word paradox coincides with the Greek mentioned earlier. In German a similar meaning of the word is expressed in these words, *wider Erwarten, wider das Gewohnte.*

It is thus apparent that "paradox" is used in several diverse senses as a literary form. Its divergent usage will become even more obvious in a later discussion of recent theological positions. At this stage it will prove helpful to consider some of the different kinds of paradoxes alluded to in Chapter One. There is no intent to set up a standard rule by which to judge all paradoxes, but rather to offer suggestions which may serve as guides to different levels of experience and communication. It may well be that several "kinds" of paradoxes accommodate each other or overlap. However, a brief analysis of seven will be made.

8

As a rhetorical device, a paradox is a short, vivid statement made without qualification or explanation which arrests sudden attention. It presents a dramatic contrast by which truth may be discovered leaving the mind to do the rest for itself. Very often the subject matter is of some neglected aspect of life. L. Harold DeWolf[10] and Henry Nelson Wieman[11] both recognize the legitimate use of this kind of paradox.

The names of several authors are cited in *The Dictionary of Philosophy* in connection with the distinction that is made between paradoxes which involve the use of a name (word) relationship or the semantic concept of truth and those who do not. It is claimed that the semantic paradox can be "solved by the supposition that notations for the name relation and for truth (having the requisite properties) do not occur in the logistic system set up — and in principle, it is held, ought not to occur."[12] In the semantic paradox words may be coined or borrowed to express the meaning of Christian faith. If there is any disparity between the words and their referents it can hardly be called paradoxical. Words never fully comprehend God yet common words can lead to a depth of spiritual meaning. There are also nonlinguistic, visual and auditory forms, by which truth may be communicated.

Paradox may be in a form by which religious truth can be apprehended and loved. Josiah Royce spoke of the dependence of man's capacity for divine revelation upon his admission of ignorance and unworthiness as "the religious paradox."[13] The awareness of God on the borderline between knowing and not knowing is taken here to mean knowledge about and acquaintance with God. Gustaf Aulén has used "religious paradox"[14] with a similar yet different connotation. He holds that God forgives the sinner, receives the sinner, but this is not rationally motivated and cannot be contained in rational categories. Some of the profoundest truths may be found in religious paradox — life through death, joy through suffering, love through severance, peace through conflict, victory through surrender, self-realization through

9

self-renunciation, conquest through cross.[15] Devotion and integrity hold a high place in religious paradox.

Another kind of paradox is psychological. Here the emphasis is on the person himself, upon inner sentiments and motivation. In the case of Jesus it was not a matter of simple mental equivocation; it was a matter of placing himself in juxtaposition to the Samaritan and all that Samaria stood for that enabled Jesus to remove those differences which appeared as unsurmountable barriers.[16] It is not only important to think the truth, what is of greater importance is the willingness to do the truth.

This introduces the next kind of paradox, namely, the ethical. Certain ethical principles may become paradoxes in theory or in ideal which are to be acted upon. Ethics is related to life. Jesus makes it clear that losing life in a physical and spiritual sense has its rich reward. William Ernest Hocking has commented on this fact as follows:

> 'He that loseth his life for my sake, the same shall save it.' In this expression, the words for my sake' indicate an essential factor of thought; namely, the affirmation power of a purposeful devotion, without which the blank formula "Die to live" gropes for foothold in the will.[17]

This will serve as one illustration of similar dictums which Jesus formulated in his teaching.

Still another kind of paradox appears to be contradictory. Edwin Lewis once said: "A paradox is a truth by way of an apparent contradiction."[18] He illustrated the point with a list of seeming contradictions which included the Bible as the word of God, yet it comes to us in the words of men. Gustaf Adolf Deissmann likewise has noted such passages of Scripture, for example, Paul's declaration of strength and weakness, great humility and majestic self-confidence.[19] Deissmann claims there is no internal contradiction involved in such paradoxes.

The term "paradox" is, however, also used for a real, not apparent, contradiction. Evidence of logical paradox in that sense may be seen in the claim that any human attempt at the expression of Christian experience can produce only "contradictory, logically incompatible" assertions.[20] So speaks Donald M. Baillie, and he is joined by Emil Brunner who believes that logical absurdity is the hallmark of Christian faith.[21]

What then, is the logical status of paradox? Is the status that of real logical contradiction? Gustaf Aulen rejects the idea that God's reception of the sinner is a "logically contradictory proposition."[22] His reasons for holding this view are similar to those given by Paul Tillich who states that "paradox points to the fact that in God's acting finite reason is superseded but not annihilated; it expresses this fact in terms which are not logically contradictory."[23] L. Harold DeWolf would go farther in giving status to logical paradox, for he believes that rational synthesis must go beyond paradox to a deeper level of meaning.[24]

This section began with attempts to define paradox. The discussion led to the consideration of seven different kinds of paradox involving a number of scholars who will be given further opportunity to state their views later on. The analysis of their positions was limited for this reason, yet the illustrations will serve the purpose of showing different lines of comprehension and communication.

As a provisionary guide for the road ahead this definition of paradox is suggested. A paradox is an apparent or real logical opposition of words, statements, or propositions which point the way to an inherent meaning deeper than is directly articulated. In the event that the words, statements, or propositions are not opposites the particular paradox may have a hidden truth in one experience with different applications, for example, "When I am weak, then I am strong."[25] The distinction here is between being physically weak in oneself and spiritually strong in God. The "inherent meaning" of paradox needs to be sought on different levels of being and in different relations.

When Jesus explained that He had kept nothing back, and

yet had more to give, He was making a distinction between the substance and the development of truth. It could be said with accuracy that the seed contains the plant[26] — stem, ears, full corn — and that when the seed is given all is given. Yet this is not the denial of the spring, the summer, and the autumn time.

In summary it may be said that paradoxical thoughts arise out of the endeavor to express a relationship of apparent opposites. The kernel of truth may lie in knowing what application to make and at what level of experience. A number of reasons have been stated for the use of paradox in previous paragraphs. In the final analysis the communication of the gospel takes place in terms of relationships.

2. *Relation to Other Literary Forms.* The relation of paradox to other literary forms will further illustrate its nature. Among the most outstanding possibilities for such a comparison are the following: hyperbole, irony, antithesis, epigram, parable, parallelism.

While it is essential to distinguish paradox from hyperbole, it must also be remembered that they are related.[27] The dictionary describes a hyperbole as a literary form or statement so obviously exaggerated as to be self-corrective. It serves the purpose of added emphasis. It surprises or startles the hearer into interest. It puts an improbable or impossible case to persuade belief in the more probable case of real life. Jesus made frequent use of hyperbole. He spoke of the power of faith to uproot trees and remove mountains, of the camel passing through the needle's eye. He also spoke of hating father, mother, wife and children, of the dead burying the dead. Perhaps his most sweeping hyperbole was this: "If your right hand causes you to sin, cut it off. . . . If your right eye causes you to sin, pluck it out."[28] Giovanni Papini has claimed that Jesus' hyperbolic statements and paradoxes were the saving of truths which might otherwise have passed into oblivion. Thus he says:

Jesus was the greatest overturner, the supreme maker of

12

paradoxes, radical and without fear. This is His greatness. His eternal freshness and youth, the secret of the turning sooner or later of every great heart toward His gospel. No other revaluation will ever be so divinely paradoxical as His.[29]

Paul also used hyperbole, but he was not a literalist in his use of it. For example, he states "I can do all things through Him that strengthens me," and "In humility count others better than yourselves."[30] He commends his hearers in Rome for their faith which "is proclaimed in all the world."[31] Obviously such a hyperbolic sweep cannot mean the great official world. Still none can deny the sedate truth which is conveyed. Such use of hyperbole is intended to give emphasis to some point. In another part of the letter to the Romans a motto of striking images is used which closes with a hyperbole "put on the Lord Jesus Christ."[32]

Irony was another literary form which Paul used, and its relationship to paradox is a close one. Irony consists in saying one thing and implying another, or in making a statement which expresses one's meaning by language of an opposite tendency. In other words, the meaning intended is contrary to that seemingly expressed. In some instances it may be a gentle irony, at other times it may have a cutting edge. It would be unfair to conclude that Paul used only the latter from some of the references we have. For instance, in his Corinthian correspondence his irony plays on the heads of the pagan sophists like summer lightning.[33] He speaks out against some of the Jewish scribes with whom no business is done unless some miracle is offered.[34] There is an undertone of irony in his reproach against the idea of "favorites" among the apostles.[35] Even the chief apostles provoked his irony by their weak attitude over the Gentile question, those "reputed to be something."[36] Paradox also has this feature of using opposites to express its meaning.

Another literary form which is related to paradox is antithesis. The latter may be described as consisting of contrasted or opposed ideas which are emphasized by the way the contrasting words or opposing words are placed, as for example, darkness and light. The Hebrew religion has a strong tendency toward antithesis.[37] This is especially evident in the poetic literature in which the theme is illustrated by contrast with its opposite.[38] Jesus made frequent use of such contrasting ideas as hearing and doing, seeing and believing, building and destroying. Certain references in the New Testament further show the antithetic form of literature.[39] Paul frequently balances one thing with another for comparison or contrast, for example, "afflicted . . . but not crushed; perplexed, but not driven to despair.[40] Carl von Weizäcker, in his treatment of the apostolic church, has noted a strong antithetical inclination in Paul:

> Everywhere we find certain antitheses which are stated by him in all their sharpness of outline: these he seeks to solve, or rather he applies to them a great solution which he had discovered once for all. It was the great antithesis through which he made his own way to his faith that was constantly reflected in it in argument after argument, determining his whole treatment of human history.[41]

In both antithesis and paradox use is made of opposite words or statements. However, in the latter of these two forms of literature the opposite words or statements are joined, mingled, or identified. In practical usage these two — paradox and antithesis — do meet.

Still another literary form which has a close affinity to paradox is the epigram. The epigram as it often appears in writing has in it a bright or witty remark briefly expressed. The element of self-contradiction may be real or apparent in epigram. Usually the epigram has in it a suggested truth or half-truth the user wishes to convey as in the case of this searching and irresistible epigram:

'Tis with our judgment as our watches, none
Go just alike, yet each believes his own.[42]

Yet it is equally well known that people and watches are in need of adjustment in life and correction from time to time.

It is often an epigram which gives the higher turn to the argument, and ends it at the same time. For instance the long talk by Paul about speaking in tongues and its tendency to disturb the regular services in church, is crowned by the remark, "God is not a God of confusion but of peace."[43] A look at another of his epigrams will show how he made or constructed an epigram.[44] Paul rarely leaves an argument without saying something better than all that has gone before it. Even the passage on "Love" is greatest in its close, "but the greatest of these is love."[45]

The parable as a literary form has a similarity to paradox, but the latter should not be made a class of the former. W. J. Moulton calls attention to this in his article in which he cites Bugge's proposal to regard paradox as a class of parable. Moulton states that such a proposal has been confronted by a wide divergence of views, and that expositors have generally declined to make paradoxes a distinct group in their treatment of parables.[46]

In both the Hebrew and the Greek languages the word "parable" means resemblance. The essential part of its meaning is the bringing together of two different ideas so that the one helps explain or emphasize the other. The Old Testament offers at least five passages which might be classified, in the technical sense, as parables.[47] In terms of the New Testament parables, G. M. Mackie has given this helpful explanation:

In the parable two different planes of experience were brought together, one familiar, concrete, and definite, the other an area of abstractions, conjectures, and possibilities. At the point of contact it was possible for those who desired to

15

do so to pass from the known to the unknown. Imagination was exercised and the critical faculty appealed to, and sympathy was enlisted according to the merits of the case presented.[48]

A striking similarity between paradox and parable lies in the fact that the meaning of both may be found on the borderline between the known and the unknown. It is generally understood that Jesus' parables try to drive home one main point and that the parables were drawn from such occurences as were possible or may actually have belonged to the experience of the hearer. The interpretation of the parables, however, is not subject to an inflexible method since the parables differ from each other.

Parallelism presents another literary form which was commonly used in Hebrew literature. It was in 1753 (although it had been noticed before) that Robert Lowth subjected Hebrew poetry to careful scrutiny and put forth the thought that the fundamental characteristic of Hebrew poetry was not rhyme but parallelism. The parallels were employed as an illumination of the unknown by its exact consonance with a truth previously perceived or known.[49] Arthur J. Culler offers the following definition of parallelism:

> By parallelism is meant the correspondence in sense between two or more units of expression which serve either by confirmation, contrast, or amplification to emphasize their common subject matter. This means that the rhythm we should seek as we read Hebrew lines is to be found in the balance of the thought rather than in the beat of the syllable.[50]

In his letters Paul had occasion to use parallelism for the more forcible exhibition of some single truth he wanted to have recognized.[51] His mind was built up on contrasts: slavery and freedom, law and grace, life and death, visible and invisible, temporal and eternal. All of his great affirmations are at the same time denials of some opposite, just as his life in Christ was a denial of the life he tried to live without Christ.[52]

Generally parallelism makes use of such psychological principles as: deep calling deep, life to life, thought to thought. Some writers have held that parallelism is the fundamental characteristic of paradox, as for example, Gilbert K. Chesterton whose views will be examined in conjunction with other writers in a later section of this work. But as a rule paradox and parallelism are considered as related forms of literature though each standing in its own right.

The examination of other forms of literature in the preceding paragraphs has led to the thought that paradox has several close relatives. The next discussion will pertain to the place of paradox in literature, for example, in poetry, in science, in the Bible.

B. *The Place of Paradox in Literature*

Paradox is as ancient as literature itself. John Wright Buckham refers to Hui Sze (C. 350 B.C.) in China who taught his "ten paradoxes" to the dialecticians of his day, as for example: "All things in the universe are similar to one another and differ from one another; the South has no limit and has a limit."[53]

Long before Intertestamental times paradox was latent in Hebrew thought. Some Old Testament statements lent themselves to paradoxical expression. Since a number of Biblical paradoxes will be pointed out shortly, they will be omitted here. The topic which will now occupy attention has to do with paradoxical statements in poetry.

1. *Paradox in Poetry.* The attempt to investigate ancient or medieval poetry will not be made here, but rather a cursory examination of recent paradoxical poetry. It may be borne in mind, as Edward Chauncey Baldwin has stated that "Poetry is among every people the earliest form of literary expression."[54]

It was Robert Browning who noted in a poem that life's success lies in its failure, and that the divine verdict, in contrast to the world, is passed, not upon the paltry sum of man's deeds and attainment, but upon the visions of goodness which were his own recognition of defeat:

> For thence, — a paradox
> Which comforts while it mocks, —
> Shall life succeed in that it seems to fail:
> What I aspired to be,
> And was not, comforts me:
> A brute I might have been, but would not
> sink i' the scale.[55]

Such a passage must be read with understanding. The question is not the inoperative casual wish, or the formal acknowledgment of the more excellent way, on the part of those confirmed in self-indulgence. It is rather a question of the vision of goodness which has pierced a man with a sense of his own unworthiness, the ideal after which he has painfully limped — it is of these things that Browning speaks.[56]

In his critical biography of Emily Dickinson, the writer George F. Whicher states that she was keenly aware of the subtle transformation involved in the replacing of a fact by the idea formed by it. She had learned by experience not merely to induce suspension of belief which would be favorable to the imaginative dramatization of abstract ideas, but to test what her mind had brought by active disbelief. The part of caution was to check the exuberant mind by a constant deference back to experience.[57] Invariably Emily Dickinson discovered that these two aspects of experience failed to correspond. She gave heed and walked in a disciplinary path with a precarious gait rather than take a walk on air. The dream and fact often present a wide divergence which she clearly recognized. In one of her poems she expresses her paradoxical sentiments concerning the complicated discipline which she recognized in man. She saw that in his experience man is some-

18

times compelled to choose what he thought in his mind he had previously rejected.[58]

Edwin Markham was writing poetry in the early dawn of the twentieth century when men turned for inspiration to the common side of life. In the following paradoxical poem his main interest was freedom.

> And this freedom will be the freedom of all.
> It will loosen both master and slave from the chain.
> For, by a divine paradox,
> Where there is one slave
> There are two.
> So in the wonderful reciprocities of being,
> We can never reach the higher levels
> Until all of our fellows ascend with us.
> There is no true security for the individual
> Except as he finds it
> In the security of all.[59]

James Russell Lowell, in an earlier day at the time of the Civil War when freedom was brought to social consciousness, wrote in a similar vein.

> Men! whose boast is that ye
>   Come of fathers brave and free,
> If there breathes on earth a slave,
>   Are ye truly free and brave?[60]

The human predicament which the above two poems illustrate with respect to freedom is well known. The demonstration of positive freedom is the test and crux of the problem, and therein is hope and security.

Alfred Lord Tennyson was vexed by another problem. After seeking an abstract and philosophical expression of his conception of God as "Infinite Ideality, Immeasurable Reality, Infinite

19

Personality, Hallowed by Thy name," he concludes in lines that glow with reverence and humility of spirit:

> We feel we are nothing — for all is Thou and in Thee;
> We feel we are something — that also has come from Thee;
> We feel we are nothing — but Thou wilt help us to be.
> Hallowed by Thy name — Halleluiah![61]

This was Tennyson's answer from the viewpoint of his own speculative philosophy to the materialism of his day. He is attempting to communicate the kind of life which can be lived when men realize their dependence upon God and are aware of His help. Thus the poet resolves the paradox in a vital synthesis, "but Thou wilt help us to be."

Another poet known for his symbolic paradoxes is Francis Thompson. In his searching poem which is perhaps the best known, he relates a succession of paradoxes growing out of the interplay of the divine and the human. He tells of his own unsuccessful attempt to run away from God. In the last lines he asks:

> Halts by me that footfall:
> Is my gloom, after all,
> Shade of His hand, outstretched caressingly?
> 'Ah, fondest, blindest, weakest,
> I am He Whom thou seekest!
> Thou dravest love from thee, who dravest Me.'[62]

After many crucial and trying situations in his own life, Thompson thus found his refuge and help in God.

More recently Virginia Taylor McCormick has published a paradoxical poem which shows the simplicity and complexity of life, and the wonder of finding true riches in unexpected places.

> Life is a strange comingling of reality and dreams,
> More simple, yet more complex, than it seems,

20

I have felt the beast triumphant in a man
Preaching Jesus and his love;
From a tramp asking bread
Wisdom of Solomon I have heard.
Felons have looked to me as kind
As Mary's husband when they smiled,
And once I saw upon a Naples street
A harlot die to save a stranger child.
In unaccustomed places I have known
Sleep pillowing upon a stone
Fireless, without shelter, I have warmed
My heart by beauty of cold stars.
In my small garden I have found
All heaven in the larkspur's blue,
God in a violet's drop of dew.[63]

It may well take considerable imagination to see as this poet does "all heaven" in the blue of a larkspur, but the essential issue of resolving the discrepancies between good intentions and accomplishments is clearly indicated.

Paradox holds a significant place in poetry as has been shown by the selections which have been cited thus far. The poets have found in this literary form a medium for the expression of their experiences and hopes. They know it as an instrument which awakens interest, stimulates thought, and lingers in the memory.

2. *Paradox in Scientific Thought.* — Men who are familiar with the instruments of experimentation and verification in science have come to recognize a certain paradoxical aspect of their work. In the early part of this century, William Hampson attempted some explanations of the how and the why of things which appeared to contradict general experience or scientific principles. He states this interesting feature about Nature in the preface of this book:

Nature is a great conjurer. With many of her tricks we are

21

so familiar that they do not astonish us; but on giving them a little consideration we often find that they are really very puzzling performances, and we become as eager to learn the explanation as children at a Christmas conjuring party to hear the performer's account of how he does it.[64]

Hampson then proceeds to deal with mechanical paradoxes, paradoxes of the physical state, chemical paradoxes, and psychological paradoxes in succession. He cites convincing laboratory illustrations to prove his points, as for example, the mechanical paradox of repulsion and attraction by the same agent.[65]

Sir Oliver Lodge, a notable physicist, made this pertinent observation concerning science. In a published article on physics[66] he noted that Heisenberg established the impossibility of determining both the speed and position of an electron within the atom. To deal with these indeterminates he formulated a "law of uncertainty" or principle of indeterminacy, by which the product of two uncertainties is equal to a definable constant. This famous Uncertainty Principle underlined what every psychologist knew in his heart, namely, that no one person could ever make exactly the same experiment, nor could two different people ever make exactly the same measurement. Indeed, as the anatomists were showing, all our brains, though similar in general construction, were different in detail, so that every man was bound to see things differently from his neighbor, and consequently no truth could be exactly the same for any two people. One reason why no measurement could be repeated, with exactly identical results, was that the act of measurement, whether in psychology or physics, altered the system measured. The observer was not, and could never hope to be, independent of the thing that he observed.

In 1900 Max Planck advanced his Quantum Theory to explain certain problems which had resulted from his studies of radiation. The implications of his work did not become apparent until further studies had been made by other scientists. This accentuated the physicists' willingness to use two apparently paradoxical theories of light: the corpuscular theory of Newton and the wave theory of Huygens. For over two centuries scientific experiment and theory had claimed that light must consist of waves. In 1905 Albert Einstein carried the Quantum Theory into a new domain. He postulated that all forms of radiant energy actually travel through space in separate and discontinuous quanta. As a result of his experimentation a new principle or photoelectric law was put into operation in television and other devices which use a photoelectric cell.[67]

The physicist who is forced to admit several theories of light, each demonstrably true, yet seemingly inconsistent with one another, and who therefore accepts each separate phenomenon as somehow significant even though he cannot fit them all into any unified scheme, suggests at least that a similar solution may be found in areas of man's moral and spiritual life. Nevertheless the growth of factual knowledge continues, together with the striving for a unified theoretical conception comprising all empirical data. A recent study in nuclear physics has demonstrated that submicroscopic particles do not behave symmetrically. This may lead to a goal which eluded Einstein, that is, a Unified Field Theory, which would encompass all the laws of matter, energy, and the universe.

But even with all these advances there remains much uncertainty about the choice of basic theoretical concepts. Hence extreme caution must be exercised in deciding whether an alleged phenomenon hitherto unknown is possible or not. David G. Moses took special note of this fact with reference to both religion and science. He stated:

No scientist who is worth the name ever pretends to have discovered all that is to be known about the material world. . . . At any particular time he may not be able to decide between two hypotheses that seem to explain equally satisfactory (sic) a set of facts, but he never relinquishes the effort to prove one of them to be more satisfactory than the other.[68]

Along a similar line of thought, Sir Oliver Lodge expressed this futuristic sentiment:

We are not stagnant, but in a state of flux; our ideas are those of the modern era, but there is no finality, no absolute completeness, even about our most fundamental conceptions. We creep from thought to thought, we delight in the findings of our day and generation, we hold up a gem or two for admiration, but no material explanation can be ultimately satisfying. When, for a moment, after a long day's survey of of the field, we lift our eyes and gaze towards the spiritual horizon, we perceive a region beyond the scope of science, where measurements fail, where explanations cease, and we catch a glimpse of an unfathomable glory.[69]

The history of physical science is partly the history of paradoxes becoming commonplaces — the motion of the earth, the pressure of the atmosphere, the circulation of blood, the electrical phenomena produced by Galvan's experiments, and other comparable paradoxes which seemed to be unsoluble. What the future will bring forth remains to be seen.

In Chapter One reference was made to a book in the field of social science which deals with certain paradoxes. In that book, Kermit Eby, professor of social science at the University of Chicago, and June Greenlief, offer a penetrating study of social forces which threaten democracy and individuality. One example must suffice to indicate the nature of their work.

It is paradoxical that in a country which puts so much emphasis on liberty and freedom as the keynote of national idealism and national goals, the nonconformist is treated openly with the harshest social brutality. The paradox lies in the fact that this man of 'modern society' who has freed his material ego, his individuality, in more ways than ever before, is also more obviously unhappy than ever before. Likewise, the American, the most 'socialized', the most over-organized man, is at one and the same time the loneliest of men.[70]

In order to resolve inconsistencies such as these the authors of the above book suggest some ways along the principled paths toward preserving democracy and at the same time individuality.

In yet another field there exists an awareness of paradox. It is an accepted fact in medicine today that the emergence of psychosomatic theories signals the breakdown of the simpler concepts of the body-mind relationship of previous physical theories. The body, mind, spirit, are so interrelated as to make it impossible to treat one without touching upon the others. The more that is known about the world within the more profound the world without becomes. Not everything written by Sigmund Freud is acceptable, yet he has done pioneer work in helping his readers to understand human nature. Freud made the observation that there was a positive desire for life which he chose to call "libido" and a negative impulse toward death which he called "mortido." In his study of psycho-analysis he discovered that man wants both life and death; he affirms and he vetoes. Neither of these sides of the paradox can stand alone, but must be considered together for the complete meaning of life.

In both fields of human endeavor, social and scientific, it is made clear that paradoxes have a place in literature and in life. There are different kinds of paradoxes and different authors suggest different ways of resolving paradoxical statements or situations. Some paradoxes are of an ethical nature, some psychological, some seemingly contradictory, to mention only three kinds.

Attention must now be diverted to a consideration of paradox in the Bible. It has long been recognized that the literature of

25

the Bible contains paradoxical statements or words which imply a meaning deeper than is directly expressed.

3. *Paradox in the Bible.* There are fewer paradoxes in the Old Testament than in the New Testament. This may in part be explained by the fact that in the Old Testament the concept of religion has more to do with compact and bargain and therefore does not lend itself readily to the paradoxical. Robert Lawson Slater has presented the idea that the Old Testament writers were mainly concerned with the mighty acts of God and what was revealed and known than with what was not known. The paradoxical relationship involving God and man is expressed, but the writers express this paradox without being aware of it.[71] Another reason for the lack of paradox in the Old Testament may have been that as a literary expression it did not lie in the genius of the Hebrew language.

Some of the references to be cited shortly from the Old Testament will support the thought that paradoxical statements were nevertheless used. Solomon ponders:

> Will God indeed dwell on the earth? Behold, heaven and the highest heaven cannot contain thee; how much less this house which I have built![72]

Still Solomon built and dedicated his Temple. In the Book of Job the problem of evil reaches the level of speculation but does not go beyond. Zophar asks,

> Can you find out the deep things of God?
> Can you find out the limit of the Almighty?[73]

And Job says, "I desire to argue my case with God,"[74] yet he exalts the Majesty of God. Further on in this dramatic story the writer has Job say to his comforters, "miserable comforters are you all."[75]

The Book of Psalms reveals spiritual conditions that are paradoxical in nature. In the passages which follow, the absence of God from life does not mean the absence of God from knowledge.

Why dost thou stand afar off, O Lord? Why dost thou hide thyself in times of trouble?[76]

I say to God, my rock; 'Why hast thou forgotten me?'[77]

The stone which the builders rejected has become the chief cornerstone.[78]

Such passages as the preceding ones from the Psalms easily lend themselves to paradoxical usage, for there is in them different layers of meaning in human experience. Paul makes use of the latter text to indicate the rejection of Christ who nevertheless became the foundation and chief "cornerstone" of the Christian faith.

The Old Testament book which comes nearest to the New Testament in paradoxical thinking is Isaiah. The approximate relationship can be seen in these passages:

Hear and hear, but do not understand; see and see, but do not perceive.[79]

Hear, you deaf; and look, you blind, that you may see![80]

Come, buy and eat! Come, buy wine and milk without money and without price.[81]

For my thoughts are not your thoughts, neither are your ways my ways, says the Lord. For as the heavens are higher than the earth, so are my ways higher than your ways and my thoughts than your thoughts.[82]

Yet in the same chapter the prophet gives this counsel:

> Seek the Lord while he may be found, call upon him while
> he is near.[83]

In the fifty-third chapter the writer comes closest to the New
Testament mood of the blessing of affliction in the suffering
servant theme which sets forth victory out of defeat as the
inmost secret of God's plan.

An examination of the Old Testament Apocryphal books reveals several passages in which the word "paradox" is literally
used or some synonym put in its place by the translator. Scholars
believe that IV Maccabees comes later than I Maccabees, perhaps early in the last century B.C. Moses Hadas has translated
the Greek word for paradox literally as shown in this passage from IV Maccabees:

> Nor must you regard it as a paradox that reason is able
> to bear rule even over enmity.[84]

In II Maccabees the redactor wants to show that the providence
of God ruled over his people. Sidney Tedesche has translated
paradox as "contrary to expectation,"[85] rather than using the
Greek word.

In the Wisdom of Sirach (Ecclesiasticus) the writer praises
the work of the Creator in the universe. He uses the word paradox, yet in his translation of this book Edgar Goodspeed chose
the word "strange" as is usually done in the English translations.
Thus we read: "There are strange and wonderful works in it."[86]

The Book of Judith also shows the work of the translator in
substituting the word strange for paradox.[87]

It is useful to make note of these passages from the Apocrypha
for they demonstrate the use of the word "paradox" or its English derivation. The effect of the unknown or unexpected is
reflected in such paradoxical expressions. There are at least

28

rhetorical and religious connotations which must be taken into account in dealing with such texts.

Before leaving this discussion of the Old Testament and the Apocryphal books and taking up the New Testament, it may be helpful to note that it was customary in those days to cultivate the old *mashal* or proverb for the sake of stimulating further thought. This may have something to do with Jesus' use of paradox, though this was not the only reason he used paradox. In the Beatitudes He ascribed blessedness to just the opposite qualities from those which are generally accounted blessed — the poor in spirit, the mourners, the meek, the maligned and persecuted. Russell Henry Stafford offers the following comment on the Beatitudes:

> They are so paradoxical, indeed, that one is tempted to suppose that their purpose was simply to elicit interest by their startling quality, without regard for accuracy. But our acquaintance with the entire sincerity of Jesus keeps us from yielding to that temptation. It often happens, as here, that a clear statement of principle bears the aspect or paradox . . . the statement that the earth revolves about the sun seems paradoxical. Nevertheless, it happens to be true.[88]

The Sermon on the Mount likewise has paradoxical statements, sometimes in a form so different as to arouse vigorous protest in the hearer's mind, until the meaning is subjected to a test. The following passages represent some of the paradoxes in the first four books of the New Testament.

> Whoever exalts himself shall be humbled, and whoever humbles himself shall be exalted.[89]

> He who finds his life will lose it, and he who loses his life for my sake will find it.[90]

29

If anyone would be first, he must be last of all and servant of all.[91]

For to him who has will more be given, and he will have abundance; but from him who has not, even what he has will be taken away.[92]

Do not be anxious about your life, what you shall eat or what you shall drink, nor about your body, what you shall put on. Is not life more than food, and the body more than clothing . . . do not be anxious about tomorrow, for tomorrow will be anxious for itself.[93]

But it shall not be so among you; but whoever would be great among you must be your servant.[94]

Love your enemies and pray for those who persecute you.[95]

But many that are first will be last, and the last first.[96]

So if the Son makes you free, you will be free indeed.[97]

This is why I speak to them in parables, because seeing they do not see, and hearing they do not hear, nor do they understand.[98]

The hour is coming . . . when you will be scattered every man to his home, and you will leave me alone; yet I am not alone, for the Father is with me.[99]

And Jesus said, 'Father, forgive them; for they know not what they do.'[100]

In such declarations as these Jesus seems to delight in confronting his hearers with statements which seem to them impossible, but they are not so since "with God all things are possible."[101] It almost seems that Jesus deliberately takes the risk of scorn and misunderstanding, trusting to men's saner second thoughts. His appeal is to men of spirit like his own who will try to understand what paradoxical words alone cannot convey. He is speaking of observations and actual experiences in life, and such matters are difficult for one person to translate to another.

Some of the Pauline paradoxes are to be studied later in this work so will be passed over in this section. In summary of the preceding paragraphs it may be said that paradox finds a significant place in the Bible. It serves as an instrument of moral inspiration and reform.

C. The Expression and Interpretation of Experience

1. *Changes in the Meaning of Words.* The findings of semantics and linguistics have amply shown that words not only change in their meanings, but also that words have different meanings at different times and places. When the Gileadites intercepted the Ephraimites at the passage of the Jordan, the use of a single word served to detect the tribal affiliation of the fugitives.[102]

The Bible translators across the centuries have been keenly aware of changes in the meaning of words. Luther A. Weigle, one of the translators of the Revised Standard Version of the Bible, states the problem as follows:

> There are words which have so changed in meaning or acquired such new meanings, that they no longer convey to the reader the meaning which they had for the King James translators and were intended to express. Most of them were accurate translations in 1611; but they have now become misleading.[103]

31

This matter of translation is further established by Ronald Knox, a British scholar and Roman Catholic. In a wise and witty book he discusses the difficulty of enabling the Bible to address contemporary man in living speech and in such a way as to convey its full-dimensioned meaning and vitality. This, he insists, a translation that is merely literal cannot do. He reflects on the special problem of the "consecrated phrases" — the rendering that has been so sanctified by familiarity or by liturgical usage that any change provokes cries of outrage no matter how inaccurate or inadequate the piously approved translation may be.

Commenting on two words that are commonly translated "let him deny himself" (*arneito heauton*) Ronald Knox writes:

> This has become a consecrated phrase, and for years, now, nuns have been encouraging schoolgirls to give up toffee, during Lent and write the fact down on a card as a record of 'self-denial.' For years Salvation Army lasses have picketed us with demands for a half-penny because it is 'self-denial week.' The whole glorious content of the phrase *arneito heauton,* let him obliterate himself, let him annihilate himself, let him rule Self out of his world-picture altogether, has become degraded and lost. That is what happens to consecrated phrases.[104]

Perhaps it would be better to follow Weymouth with "let him renounce self" and Goodspeed with "he must disregard himself" rather than the translation "let him deny himself." But essentially this points up the problem of changes in the meaning of words.

Not long ago there appeared a book by William Barclay of Glasgow University dealing with thirty-seven words which have either changed or degenerated in meaning. The word "eritheia" will serve to illustrate the nature of his work. As Barclay says in his own words:

It had nothing to do with *eris* which means 'strife.' *Erithos* was originally a spinner or weaver, and *eritheia* was a perfectly respectable word meaning 'labor for wages'. Then it sank to signify work done for motives of pay and nothing else, work which has only one question, What can I get out of it? It went on to mean 'Canvassing and intriguing for place and power,' and ended up by meaning 'selfish ambition.'[105]

In view of the foregoing statements concerning both changes and degeneration in the use of words, it may be well to consider that such a possibility exists with regard to the word "paradox." William Shakespeare, in his dramatic play "Hamlet" uses paradox in the old sense when he remarks "this was sometime a paradox, but now time gives it proof." But as C. T. Onions has stated, Shakespeare also uses paradox in terms of self-contradicton and the latter usage is commoner in his works.[106] Some light may be thrown upon this double usage of paradox by Augustus DeMorgan who states that after looking into books of paradoxes for over thirty years he discovered that a depravation of meaning had taken place. He states his findings in this way:

Many of the things brought forward would now be called *crotchets,* which is the nearest word we have to the old paradox. But there is this difference, that by calling a thing a *crotchet* we mean to speak lightly of it; which is not the necessary meaning of *paradox.* Thus in the sixteenth century many people spoke of the earth's motion as the paradox of Copernicus, who held the ingenuity of that theory in very high esteem, and some, I think, who even inclined toward it. In the seventeenth century, the depravation of meaning took place, in England at least. Phillips says paradox is 'a thing which seemeth strange'— here is the old meaning: after a colon, he proceeds — 'and absurd, and is

33

contrary to common opinion,' which is an addition due to his own time.[107]

Assuming that the above statement is correct in tracing the history and meaning of paradox, it helps to understand what has likely happened down to the present time. In fact much of the ambiguity surrounding the word "paradox" today has resulted from different definitions and uses of the word. The usage of a word generally determines its acceptability according to popular standards. The use Paul made of paradoxical themes will be closely examined upon reaching Chapter IV.

It is believed that Paul used words and ideas which were available to him in his day, some of which were extraneous to his own interests and natural way of thinking. Paton J. Gloag has commented upon this fact in the following statement in which he says:

> Paul was reduced to the necessity of employing old words to express new ideas, and he often could not avoid using them in a sense differing considerably from their popular meaning; a number of words of this kind occur which appear to have been used by the apostle with some variation in their meaning, so that a very strict attention to the context is necessary to reproduce the ideas which they are employed to express.[108]

This is not an unnatural situation in life, for this would be true of people today who use words or phrases of others but have in mind a different meaning. One of the leading problems in Pauline study has to do with whether or not he adopted certain terms or phrases which were currently used with certain qualifications expressed or unexpressed in his letters. Still another matter involved concerns the transmission of words. Have those who wrote Paul's letters rightly understood and faithfully reported his paradoxes, for instance? Have his words and their application in the oral tradition and in writing been preserved? Such questions as these along with matters of translation are ever present to the mind of Bible scholars.

2. *Factors Preceding Experience.* In the laboratory, as also in life, it frequently becomes necessary to go out ahead of the facts. M. Louis Pasteur, the great French scientist, became convinced in his mind that rabies, the dreadful disease that follows the bite of a mad dog, was a bacterial disease. He was unable to isolate the fatal germ, but he did perfect an antitoxin which, when injected into the bloodstream of a sufferer; cleared out the poison and saved his life.

Having the data or facts about any particular thing is essential in any serious research. But it is possible to accumulate a great number of facts without ever coming to know those facts in any real personal way. The meaning of the preceding sentence is brought to light in the French words *savoir* and *connaitre* which have the twofold meaning of knowing in a formal sense and knowing in the sense of having a personal acquaintance with something. In German the same holds true in the use of the two words *kennen* and *wissen.* Such a differentiation helps to recognize, especially in a religious frame of reference, that personal experience is preceded by events and records of previous ages. It is pertinent in matters of faith to have an affirmative attitude, but that is not enough. There must also be a body of belief, a reason for faith. These two aspects of faith are just as essential in religion as they are in science. Some years ago Charles Grandison Finney was disturbed about the position of some who held a very limited view of "faith" in respect to religion. He wrote:

No one can believe that which he does not understand. It is impossible to believe that which is not so revealed to the mind, that the mind understands it. It has been erroneously assumed, that faith did not need light, that is, that it is not essential to faith that we understand the doctrines or facts that we are called upon to believe . . . any fact or doctrine not understood is like a proposition in an unknown tongue; it is impossible that the mind should receive or reject it, should believe or disbelieve it, until it is understood.[109]

This statement amplifies the main contention under discussion, namely, that recorded facts provide knowledge, but this knowledge must be understood in experience personally to have a meaning on a different level. Thus again "doctrines of facts" which come before having a bearing on what follows after.

In somewhat different terms, but along the same line of thought, Hugh R. Walpole made the observation that people turn to the dictionary to find "the meaning" of a word, forgetting that the meaning depends on the setting of the word, and what is more important, that the meaning of words is not in the words but in the people.[110] In other words, people want to communicate sentiments and ideas in one form or another, but words at best are symbols. When someone attempts to tell about an experience something has already transpired about which the statement attempts to tell. The matter of conveying experience and the difficulty involved will be discussed shortly. It will be of further help here to bear in mind some of the manifold factors which precede and become a part of experience. Alfred North Whitehead has identified the meaning of experience in the following paragraph:

In order to discover some of the major categories under which we can classify the infinitely various components of experience, we must appeal to evidence relating to every variety of occasion. Nothing can be omitted, experience drunk and experience sober, experience sleeping and experience waking, experience drowsy and experience wide awake, experience self-forgetful, experience intellectual and experience physical, experience religious and experience sceptical, experience self-conscious and experience self-forgetful, experience intellectual and experience physical, experience anxious and experience care-free, experience anticipatory and experience retrospective, experience happy and experience grieving, experience dominated by emotion and experience under self-restraint, experience normal and abnormal.[111]

Such a comprehensive view of experience has the virtue of being inclusive, but it is included here mainly to point up situations in life which provide a basis for experience which, in the words of Whitehead, is "evidence relating to every variety of occasion."

Alfred Lord Tennyson has captured a similar thought and has put it into poetic expression:

> I am part of all that I have met;
> Yet all experience is an arch wherethrough
> Gleams that untravelled world, whose margin fades
> For ever and for ever when I move.[112]

The part of his thought which would apply in particular in this discussion is in the words, "all that I have met" for this suggests a world of meaning previous to personal knowledge of it which yet becomes part of experience but fades with passing time and circumstance while yet providing the basis for moving forward into the untravelled world. So much of life is preconditioned that often the person himself cannot distinguish clearly between experience and description.

3. *The Difficulty of Conveying Experience.* — The expression of experience can never fully convey all that is experienced. Whenever men try to communicate their ways of experience and apprehension of truth expressed in terms of one age by means of terms which are relevant in a successive age there is always an uncertain element involved. This is partly because no two persons can have an identical experience since environmental conditions vary and also because truth can be seen from different

angles. There is also the fact which was noted earlier that words are symbols — signs and sounds — there is a semantic or word relationship which depends upon the particular situation or person.

Throughout this work there is an awareness of the basic issue or problem of trying to establish the relationship between experience and expression, between apprehension and communication. Kirsopp Lake comments on this problem and suggests a reasonable interpretation:

> It is clear that we have to deal with a mixture of experience and expression. One of the main difficulties of all study of religion is this inevitably recurring confusion. No means has yet been found of, as it were, *filtering out expression* so that we shall have a residum of *pure experience*. All that we can do is to express the experience in a variety of ways, and try to eliminate or to allow for such parts of our experience as are closely due to ourselves and not to the experience.[113]

Scholars have wrestled with the recorded accounts of Paul's "calling" on the Damascus road in chapters nine, twenty-two, and twenty-six in the Book of Acts, as well as with his accounts about this event in his life.[114] The fact of his calling is there, but the surrounding details do not agree. Paul could not find words adequate to express its significance. Once he spoke of it in terms of "utterances" heard "unutterable" in words.[115] It may be true as some have maintained, that the deeper men go into religion the less likely they are to find words with which to tell others about it. Perhaps the unique sense of direction of Paul's life defies expression, even while the realization of that direction is dependent on the social life which in turn rests upon expression. The fruits of his labor attest to the genuineness of his Christian faith.

In a tribute to poetry, Evelyn Underhill has written of a

certain mystic quality of life which in terms of love and adoration moves the human mind. To quote her own words:

> Poetry both enchants and informs, addressing its rhythmic and symbolic speech to regions of the mind which are inaccessible to argument, and evoking movements of awe and love which no exhortation can obtain.[116]

The foregoing quotation suggests an element of experience on the level of inspiration and aesthetic appreciation which can never be completely defined but which evokes "movements of awe and love" and deeds of human service.

One other related aspect to this present discussion of the difficulty of conveying experience is a language barrier. In the attempt to communicate meanings there is always an inadequacy (not disparity) of language. For instance, the "rationalization" of the universe as a task, from the nature of the case, can never be achieved. The apparent consequences might be stated epigramatically in this fashion — there are "irrationalities" which are not unreasonable. If this sounds like a paradox, the paradox is only apparent and arises from what Plato calls, Τῶν λόγων ναʼο θενεʼς, the inadequacy of language to convey the whole of the speaker's meaning and nothing beyond the meaning.[117] Elsewhere Plato addresses himself to a discussion of the instability of definitions.[118] He prefers the spoken word in place of the fixed written word.

D. *The Use of Paradox as a Literary Tool*

The patterns of human thought and the forms used as literary tools are many and varied. One of these tools is the paradox. It has been used as an effective way of changing the scenery or formulating new and different ideas.

1. *A Way of Getting Attention.* — One of the most common uses of paradox has been that of getting attention or riveting at-

tention on some hidden or neglected truth. It serves the purpose of stimulating tired or sluggish minds to some new conception by introducing something strange or surprising. Jesus apparently found it useful to speak in paradox and the record indicates that he aroused the curiosity of his hearers sufficiently to keep them thinking. They had faith, but what Jesus wanted them to consider was a different kind of faith. Christian faith must be nourished by verification in experience.

R. G. Collingwood has presented a thought which may serve to illustrate why Jesus considered getting the attention of men an important teaching device. The first requisite as always was an appeal to faith which would lead to value differences. Here are Collingwood's own words:

> The faith that sets out in search of understanding is a faith already endowed with sufficient understanding to recognize its need for more. And in searching for more understanding, it is searching not for an extraneous addition to itself, but for a development and confirmation of its own nature. If we wholly believed, if we did not feel the need for help for our unbelief, we should not need to think we could rest wholly satisfied with our faith.[119]

The preacher, the pioneer, and the poet have all used paradox as a literary tool to awaken faith and to focus attention on some neglected aspect of truth. One truth which is often overlooked has to do with unfinished condition of human knowledge.

2. *Indication of Truth Transcending Human Knowledge.* — Again and again man has been confronted by the incompleteness of human knowledge. The sum of his ignorance is greater than the sum of his knowledge. The more he learns, the greater becomes the unknown world about him. Several reasons may be given for the partial condition of man's knowledge. One reason is that man is constitutionally limited. He is born with certain

limitations in spite of his attitude to the contrary. Alfred North Whitehead has remarked:

> Nothing is more curious than the self-satisfied dogmatism with which mankind at each period of its history cherishes the delusion of the finality of its existing modes of knowledge. . . . This dogmatic common sense is the death of philosophic adventure. The Universe is vast.[120]

Truth transcends human knowledge, but truth must also be believed and followed. In the last paragraph of one of his volumes L. Harold DeWolf makes a statement which is a classic:

> If he (the Christian) is wise he will not mistake the horizon of his knowledge for the limits of his world. God and truth and human destiny are not bounded by the horizons of our ignorance. Yet by faith we can claim them all as the God-given heritage of our everlasting careers.[121]

Another reason for the incompleteness of knowledge is that men allow one particular bent they are born with or have acquired to assert a certain despotism over them. It may be the limitations of the historical period in which they live, or the method of earning a livelihood, or the scheme of values with which they grow up that is responsible for certain limitations. In respect to such limitations Paul Arthur Schilpp quotes from Albert Schweitzer as follows:

> Christianity has need of thought that it may come to the consciousness of its real self. For centuries it treasured the great commandment of love and mercy as traditional truth without recognizing it as a reason for opposing slavery, witch-burning, torture, and all the other ancient and medieval forms of inhumanity. It was only when it experienced the influence of the thinking of the Age of Enlightenment that

it was stirred into entering the struggle for humanity. The remembrance of this ought to preserve it forever from assuming any air of superiority in comparison with Thought.[122]

This is a revealing insight on social and religious limitations, but it should also be noted that in spite of such handicaps Christianity made some important advances.

Still another reason which may be given for the limited condition of knowledge is that by a deliberate act of his own will man can and does veto the truth. He refuses to listen to truth, or barricades the way to truth, or chooses not to follow the truth. The statement from Paul which says, "we cannot do anything against the truth, but only for the truth"[123] must be taken in an ultimate sense since history amply illustrates how men have successfully barricaded the way to truth until some means was devised to open the way for truth. Charles Grandison Finney was aware of the problem which man's will presents for faith. Here are the words he used to describe the situation:

> Faith is the will's reception, and unbelief is the will's rejection, of truth. . . . Unbelief is the soul's withholding confidence from the truth and from the God of truth. It is the heart's rejection of evidence, and refusal to be influenced by it. . . . for if the mind knows, or supposes that light may be had, on any question of duty, and does not make honest efforts to obtain it, this can be accounted for only by ascribing it to the will's reluctance to know the path of duty. In this case light is rejected. The mind has light so far as to know what more is proffered, but this proffered light is rejected. This is the sin of unbelief.[124]

This penetrating statement deserves careful thought for not infrequently does man refuse truth. In the parable of the Sower, Jesus spoke about the various conditions of soil and then proceeds to relate the different kinds and hearts of men.[125] How well

He knew the ability of his hearers to reject the truth at the price of unfulfilled talents and neglect of the needs of men.

To summarize what has been stated in this section it may be well to note that in any given age truth may be beyond the present level of understanding. Yet the essential nature of the spiritual is life and truth so that any advance in these areas means ultimately something won.

3. *Incapacity of Reason to Grasp Life's Mysteries.* — In the development of scientific thought and research, one fact has become impressively clear. There is no mystery of the physical world which does not point to a mystery beyond itself to something else. Astronomy has infinitely extended man's conception of the Universe. The microscope has lengthened his range of observation no less than the telescope. Still there remains much mystery about life and its surroundings. In some instances the mysterious is again being recognized by the very sciences which were once supposed to be the implacable enemies of all insoluble mysteries.

The point to be remembered is that just as science accepts as facts, things the ultimate constitution of which presently transcends human conception or explanation, so also in the higher realm of Christian faith, there are facts or truths that transcend the current level of understanding. What is above man's finite, limited, fallible reason is not necessarily impossible. Time and history have amply provided evidence to mention only a few important persons as Heraclitus, Galileo, and Newton. The late Albert Einstein was fascinated by the element of mystery and willingly conceded that in spite of many scientific advances each new discovery has led to further evidence of man's ignorance. He expresses this fact in saying:

> The most beautiful thing we can experience is the mysterious. It is the source of all true art and science. . . . To know that what is impenetrable to us really exists, manifesting itself as the highest wisdom and the most radiant beauty which

our full faculties can comprehend only in their most primitive forms — this knowledge, this feeling, is at the center of true religiousness.[126]

Religion is truly man's greatest adventure in mystery. He wants to know. He yearns to understand. He cares to penetrate mystery. Man is able to reason, to dream, to adventure because he has the incentive to do so. The sense of wonder calls to man, as to the child Samuel through the darkness of the temple. But it was light and not darkness that made the experience a mystery. The prophet said, "Truly, thou art a God who hidest thyself, O God of Israel, the Savior."[127] Yet God is hid in light, writes the Psalmist.[128] The human mind and heart answers the call to light. Man cannot live very long on a diet of question marks and avoid spiritual malnutrition. He knows that he has to make decisions even at times when the basis upon which he decides is insufficient. Apart from the vastness of the universe, man's problem of trying to understand life is increased because he does not fully understand himself. He needs light on many of life's mysteries including such experiences as suffering and pain, sin and death, duty and disappointment. Scientific knowledge and discovery has helped man to understand some facts about heredity and environment in these matters, but the matter of individual personality eludes the scientific grasp. George Santayana expressed the sentiment suggested here in one of his revealing poems:

O world, thou choosest not the better part!
It is not wisdom to be only wise,
And on the inward vision close the eyes;
But it is wisdom to believe the heart.
Columbus found a world, and had no chart
Save one that faith deciphered in the skies;
To trust the soul's invincible surmise
Was all his science and his only art.
Our knowledge is a torch of smoky pine

44

That lights the pathway but one step ahead
Across the void of mystery and dread.
Bid, then, the tender light of faith to shine
By which alone the mortal heart is led
Unto the thinking of the thought divine.[129]

The Bible uses the word "mystery" on various occasions although in recent times the word "secret" has sometimes transplanted it. Jesus, for example, said to his disciples: "To you has been given the secret of the kingdom of God, but for those outside everything is in parables."[130] Nevertheless he expected his hearers to decipher the meaning of what he was saying to them. Sometimes he related stories or parables as in the thirteenth chapter of Matthew to show what he thought concerning the kingdom of God. The purpose seems to have been to get men to consider and to enter into the proper relationship with God. To be sure there might be some mystery connected with such an experience, but as the poet Santayana in the preceding verse has stated, "the tender light of faith" can lead to thoughts divine. Man must prepare to make the adventure. As the old preacher (Mr. Deshee) in Marc Connelly's play "Green Pastures," said: "De Book ain't got time to go into all de details. . . . You know sometimes I think de Lawd expects us to figure out a few things for ourselves."[131]

Thus it can now be affirmed that mystery in religion can be understood by means of parable and by means of person. The Christian believes in Jesus Christ as light for the way, truth by demonstration, and life which is eternal. Paul knows in whom he has believed[132] and clings to that conviction with all his might knowing that God will sustain him in moments of doubt. He knows the meaning of the love of God in Christ which nothing can take away from him.[133] This assurance of both knowledge about and acquaintance with God as revealed in Jesus Christ,[134] was partly a mystery for Paul but also the rock foundation to build on. In a true religious sense he might have accepted what Amelia

Josephine Burr has said in a different context but with an emphasis on the personal. She acknowledged that there were many material things of which she was uncertain, but on the level of human relationships she had

> . . . certainty enough
> For I am sure of you.[135]

This assurance of knowing a person gave her confidence and hope. In the final analysis Christian faith centers in Jesus Christ as a person whose way, truth, and life can be a vital, living experience. It was that for Paul and thus he engaged himself in the great ministry of reconciliation.

The discussion which has been carried on in this section regarding the incapacity of reason to grasp life's mysteries must be terminated with a brief summary. It has become apparent that mystery is connected with many aspects of man's life and likewise with the universe in which he lives. Will the day come when all mystery will disappear? The present answer seems to be that each new discovery opens the way for wider, but sometimes dangerous possibilities.

In the section which precedes this one it was learned that paradox has various usages as literary tool. The present aim is to show how the term "paradox" is currently employed in theological thought.

E. *Paradox in Recent Theological Thought*

It will not be feasible within the purpose and scope of this study to undertake a detailed, critical examination of the great variety of positions which are held in respect to paradox in theology. Nevertheless an attempt will be made to state and to clarify some of the different ways in which the term is used today. In Chapter Two recognition was given to the fact that there are at least seven different kinds of paradox even though

46

some of these may overlap in actual experience. Any realistic delineation of paradox must therefore recognize variations as well as different methods of interpretation. The plan here calls for a differentiation of meaning along these lines: (1) The Rejection of Paradox, (2) The Affirmation of Paradox, and (3) Other Possibilities. These will be taken up in order.

1. *The Rejection of Paradox.* Not all men agree that paradox is a legitimate means of expressing ideas. Some have looked upon the term as savoring too much of the unexplained and the unexplored. Others see no significance in paradox whatever. Bertrand Russell at one time favored the use of paradox, but later dismissed all such modes of thinking with the assertion that "paradoxes arise from the attribution of significance to sentences that are in fact nonsensical."[136] Susanne Langer in a published article on paradox had this to say: "The laws of logic have not produced it; the world does not contain it. The presence of a true paradox in any proposition is essentially an index of nonsignificance."[137] Both of these writers represent a clear rejection of paradox. While it may be true that paradoxes have been formulated which were in reality nonsensical, it would hardly be correct to place them all in that category. Surely the examples of Jesus cited earlier do not fit this description of paradox.

The next two scholars to be considered reflect a qualified rejection of certain meanings attributed to paradox and to that extent they reject paradox. Henry Nelson Wieman became particularly concerned over the proposition offered by some theologians that paradox points beyond the realm in which the finite reason is applicable. He challenged those who hold "that human inquiry cannot get knowledge of any specific character which will identify with assurance the essential nature of the ultimate referent of our faith and our ultimate concern."[138] He claimed that such a position is fatal to man, and it may be added that it would likewise be fatal to man's life of prayer in which a two-way communication is necessary. As Wieman sees it, paradox is "not in itself an instrument of truth"[139] but a means by which

47

truth may be discovered by the scientific process of observation and verification to be presented in vivid and dramatic terms in paradox. Albert C. Knudson followed a similar line of thought in his rejection of paradox "as currently employed by dialectical theologians and others under their influence."[140] He argued that the doctrine of divine grace and providence, for instance, instead of excluding the independent action of the human will, presupposes it. In his book on Christian ethics he describes the adherents to a frank irrationalism as belonging to the "cult of the paradoxical."[141] His primary aim was to reject paradox as understood by such proponents.

Henry Churchill King acknowledge a kind of legitimacy in the "paradoxes of the great church creeds," but he insisted that present day theologians could not be content with them. He gave his view in this fashion:

> The presence of these paradoxes in the creeds is quite justified, for our well-founded convictions must often outrun our power to complete intellectual expression of them. We are more than intellect. But the theologians nevertheless cannot be content to leave them simply as paradoxes.[142]

Edwin McNeill Poteat rejects paradox in the human situation and he suggests the term "ambivalence" should be used. The significance of this word may be seen in his own remarks:

> Only within recent years has it become clear that the psyche responds to life by what is known as ambivalence, defined simply as "simultaneous conflicting feelings toward a person or thing, as love and hate.' . . . Life, deeply seen, is not bothered so much by the illusions of peace or strife, security or calamity, success or failure, as a dialectic movement between extremes, or paradoxically, as a compound of what appear to be opposites.[143]

48

There have been scholars across the years who have rejected paradox in one form or another. Some of the forms called "paradox" which are accepted as such may upon closer investigation actually prove to be otherwise. This is a thought to bear in mind in studying the relation of paradox to other forms of literature. It is also a thought which may have a bearing upon the study of Paul's paradoxical themes in Chapter IV.

The discussion that will follow covers a considerable range of theological ideas having to do with the affirmation of paradox. Perhaps in no previous generation has there been such a lively interest and attempt made to speak on this subject with such different points of view.

2. *The Affirmation of Paradox.* Much of the theological interest and discussion of paradox in recent times may be attributed to Søren Kierkegaard. The publication of his views on the subject produced mixed or sharp reactions. He based his thoughts above all else on the "absolute paradox"[144] by which he means the Incarnation, God's appearance in Christ. Yet he states, "No knowledge can have for its object the absurdity that the eternal is the historical."[145] To say, as he does, that Christ is the paradoxical in bodily form raises the question how the eternal came to be recognized in the historical person of Jesus Christ. Kierkegaard's own view of apprehension reveals that the historical includes the fact of its becoming "in the presence of some content."[146] The Incarnation was paradoxical, "negatively by revealing the absolute unlikeness of sin, positively by proposing to do away with the absolute unlikeness in absolute likeness."[147] On the basis of such statements it is questionable whether the self-revelation of Christ was able to bring light.

Kierkegaard also based his thought on the paradox of despair.[148] He chose the way of the absurd[149] and thus put himself on the horns of a dilemma with respect to credibility. To quote his own words: "The supreme paradox of all thought is the attempt to discover something that cannot think."[150] Such a remark may suggest human limitations, but surely thinking is going on even at the point of the denial of thought. In fact he appeals to reason to rule against itself. He believes reason is competent to observe its own limits. He asserts its usefulness to observe when its own bounds are passed.[151] Again he says, "the eternal essential truth is by no means itself a paradox; but it becomes paradoxical by virtue of its relationship to an existing individual."[152] If this be true, then it is difficult to understand how he can claim an unbridgeable gap between the infinite and the finite.

Karl Barth followed the lead of Søren Kierkegaard, although the former has shown an independence of thought. His affirmation of paradox is expressed in "that strange abyss which we call a paradox."[153] A key issue in theological discussion has been Barth's idea of revelation which he considers to be the sole and absolute action of God, coming direct and unmediated from without.[154] God is 'impossible-possibility'; that is, he is beyond human possibilities.[155] "The Gospel is not a truth among other truths. Rather it sets a question-mark against all truths. Human experience and human perception end where God begins."[156] Reason cannot reach certitude in anything, least of all in religion. Man in his native state cannot know God.[157] Only faith, which is transcendental, can guarantee truth and certitude. But one may rightly ask whether faith is not itself obedience and trust. Is not reasoning used to refute reason? The big question Barth left unanswered in statements like the above has to do with revelation. How does revelation take place? He put up both sides of a paradox without finding a way across the chasm. Does God stand "over against the man and everything human in an endless qualitative difference?"[158] The evidence is to the contrary. In fact, Barth himself appeals to the faith of the early New Testament Church which faith was itself based on faith in Christ.[159] If a man is a vessel of wrath, as he says, "incapable of thinking of God" or obeying God[160] surely this makes the ministry of Jesus seem of little consequence.

Emil Brunner likewise raised the issue whether God is knowable. He contends that the only way to comprehend truth is in the incomprehensible of a moving coming Deity.[161] Just how the infinite becomes finite is not made clear, nor is it evident how the God who is claimed to be "wholly other" can be made responsible for the "wages of sin."[162]

Brunner offers this definition of paradox: "A genuine paradox only exists where there is a real contradiction between two necessary ideas."[163] Elsewhere he states that the paradoxes of faith are not accidental but "necessary contradictions in themselves and therefore also contradictions against the fundamental law of all knowledge, the law of contradiction."[164] "The object of faith is something which is absurd to reason, i.e., paradox, the hall-mark of logical inconsistency clings to all genuine pronouncements of faith."[165]

The following two statements have been made by Brunner with respect to the Church. The logical contradiction is seen in the conflicting views he presents. First he remarks:

> The Body of Christ is a pure communion of persons without institutional character . . . as the body of Christ the church has nothing to do with an organization and has nothing of the character of the institutional about it.[166]

Then a few pages later he writes:

> To this ecclesia the existing churchly institutions are related as means . . . an instrument for the growth and renewal of the (ecclesia).[167]

One thing is certain, if Christ's Church is related to churchly institutions by means of growth and renewal the first statement above is incorrect.

A similar logical conflict may be seen in several statements by Frederick C. Grant. For instance, he says in relation to the church and Scripture, "it was not the sacred society . . . which gave authority to scripture" and on a later page, "it is the church use of these books which gave them their sacrosanct character."[168] Or the gospel "is simply not concerned with politics at all"; nevertheless it is "the greatest agrarian protest in all history."[169] Such ambiguous remarks may sound paradoxical but they are in reality incompatible.

Donald M. Baillie holds a view of paradox similar to that of Barth and Brunner. The expression of Christian experience is said to be paradoxical "because God cannot be comprehended in any human words or in any of the categories of our finite thought," so any attempt to analyze and describe experience can produce only "contradictory, logically incompatible . . . assertions."[170] The paradoxes of faith are inevitable,

> not because the divine reality is self-contradictory, but because when we objectify it all our judgments are in some measure falsified, and the higher truth which reconciles them cannot be fully expressed in words, though it is experienced and lived in the 'I-and-Thou' relationship of faith towards God. . . . A paradox is a self-contradictory statement, we simply do not know what it means or what we mean by it unless it has the direct connection with the faith which it attempts to express.[171]

In support of the thought expressed in the last line above Baillie cites Sergius Bulgakov whose preference is the term "antinomy" rather than "dialectical contradiction". He insists they mean different things. He states what he means as follows:

> An antinomy simultaneously admits the truth of two contradictory, logically incompatible, but ontologically equally necessary assertions. An antinomy testifies to the existence of a mystery beyond which the human reason cannot penetrate. This mystery nevertheless is actualized and lived in religious experience. All fundamental dogmatic definitions are of this nature.[172]

The point of agreement between Baillie and Bulgakov seems to be that while mystery cannot be stated in words without contradiction, it is actualized and lived in religious experience, that is, in direct faith — relationship towards God. It is difficult indeed to fathom how faith can be altogether the work of God, but at the same time man's choice and decision. Baillie does not adequately clarify this relation of faith. In brief, his position on paradox is that of logical contradiction.

The next point of view to be considered is that of Reinhold Niebuhr. Although not in agreement with much that Barth and Brunner have written, he shows an inclination toward their views on paradox but differs from them sharply in his interpretation. He accepts the designation "biblical realism".[173] It is his contention that dialectic statement does not express a solely vertical relation between God and man, thinkable only from God's side. It has no actual original existence and yet it always presses toward a solution. The dialectic is essentially a form of expression required by the perverted and unreal human view of God-man relatedness. Every apparent contradiction requires critical examination according to Niebuhr. In reference to the two affirmations of a particular paradox, he states, "Both are unqualifiedly true, each on its own level. Yet either affirmation becomes false if it is made without reference to the other."[174]

In what is perhaps his clearest statement concerning paradox with special regard to faith and reason, he comments thus:

> Faith is not reason. . . . This faith in the sovereignty of a divine creator, judge, and redeemer is not subject to rational proof, because it stands beyond and above the rational coherences of the world and can therefore not be proved by an analysis of these coherences. But a scientific and philosophical analysis of these coherences is not incapable of revealing where they point beyond themselves to a freedom which is not in them, to contradictions between each other which suggest a profounder mystery and meaning beyond them.[175]

53

Elsewhere Niebuhr asserts that certain experienced realities and facts of human nature which point beyond themselves can be fitted into a framework of meaning only if the meaning has a penumbra of mystery. "The mystery consists of a power and a love beyond our comprehension which overrules these various historical dramas."[176]

In his use of paradox in anthropology Niebuhr shows man in his paradoxical unity of opposites. Man is at once organism and spirit, impulsive and rational, determined and free.[177] Speaking of freedom he insists that man is unable to "comprehend himself in his full stature of freedom with a principle of comprehension which is beyond comprehension."[178] This statement implies that he does not recognize freedom as a power of contrary choice or the misuse of power, nor that freedom implies the possibility of sin and guilt which in turn presupposes the reality of freedom. Niebuhr sees the usefulness of reason for adjustment in the natural world, but he insists on transcendence of reason by faith in dealing with God and His grace. Thus he actually leaves the problem of the reconciliation of God's otherness with His action in the world unsolved. The *Anknüpfungspunkt*, the point of contact remains in doubt.

Niebuhr stands on the battle line between the gospel and human action. He has been a radical critic of Christian social strategy. His proposed method has been to create character by a balance of tensions of the ethical life.[179] In the final round it must be said that whatever mystery or meaning may be associated with paradox it must be intelligible enough for men to accept or reject. Human reason, aware of its own limitations, is always superior to human reason which condemns itself to incompetence, for the latter has to be demonstrated by rational argument.

In presenting the points of view of several scholars on the affirmation of paradox thus far the outstanding feature has been their contention that God cannot be comprehended in any human words, that experience cannot be communicated in categories of human thought. Such men as Baillie and Brunner insist that the attempt to use reason to communicate experience only leads to real logical contradiction. The basic issue which is giving theologians concern today is thus set in clearer perspective. The issue is to determine the relationship between comprehension and communication.

Are there real logical contradictions in paradox? This question is answered by Gustaf Aulén in his use of "religious paradox" which he suggests "is a fruitful tension between seemingly opposed ideas, which ought not to lead to irrational contradiction."[180]

> When, for example, God in forgiveness receives the sinner into communication with himself, this is a paradoxical act, but it is not at all a logically contradictory proposition. . . . It is this event which is reflected in the conception of faith. There is nothing of absurdity in this tension. It is rather a question of content which cannot be rationally motivated and which is so abundant that it cannot be contained within rational categories.[181]

Aulén believes that paradox lies at the very core of Christian religious experience, as a permanent and not just a temporary apologetic element. He opposes the premature elimination of all paradox from the Christian idea of God, when both sides of the paradox are deeply rooted in Christian revelation.[182] It is better to trust that in God all apparent contradictions will be finally resolved, and to try and show the consistency between power and justice, justice and love, love and holiness, as partial confirmations of this ultimate trust.

The part that is not clear is just how Aulén aims to show the nature of the response in Christian experience. What is the part of the human will? Granted God forgives man while he (man) is yet a sinner, how is this made a matter of personal assurance? Christian experience, he states, is paradoxical in that its substance is "contrary to what we might intend or expect."[183] But Christian living is not the work of grace alone. Divine grace must somehow be related to the physical and spiritual life of man. The Bible insists that man must choose, consider, and pursue a proper course of conduct.

Aulén holds that experience can be expressed in "a paradoxical act" which is not logically contradictory, but his depreciation or limitation of reason raises a question about the nature of the content of faith.

Paul Tillich has probably formulated "theological dialectic" with more thoroughness from the standpoint of philosophy than any other scholar. He takes the position that paradox is not against logic, but that paradox projects beyond the reach of finite reason.

> Theological dialectic does not violate the principle of logical rationality. When Paul points to his situation as an apostle and to that of Christians generally in a series of *paradoxa* (II Corinthians), he does not intend to say something illogical; he intends to give the adequate understandable, and therefore logical expression of the infinite tensions of Christian existence. . . Paradox points to the fact that in God's acting finite reason is superseded but not annihilated; it expresses this fact in terms which are not logically contradictory but which are supposed to point beyond the realm in which finite reason is applicable. . . .[184]

The problem of comprehension is recognized in this statement made by Tillich. He maintains that experience, relative to paradox, is "against the opinion of finite reason," and that God's acting transcends "all possible human expectations . . . and preparations . . . and possibilities."[185] He takes note of confusion in recent theological dialectic. He makes this observation:

> The confusion begins when these *paradoxa* are brought down to the level of genuine logical contradictions and people are asked to sacrifice reason in order to accept senseless com-

binations of words as divine wisdom. . . . Paradox in religion and theology does not conflict with the principle of logical rationality. Paradox has its logical place.[186]

This statement makes it clear that reason finds a place in the thought of Tillich. Religious expression of the paradoxical life situation is not something contradictory and illogical, it is rather the acknowledgment of a realm beyond which finite reason applies, according to his view. If the mind of man is empowered to think or envision possibilities as Jesus did in respect to the Kingdom of God one may wonder why Tillich rules out finite reason in such matters.

It will be seen that both Aulén and Tillich have in common the intention of putting a solid foundation of experience under the construction of their thought regarding paradox. Both of these scholars have taken exception to the thought that the communication of experience leads to real logical contradiction. In their views they both hold that in God's relation to man a place is reached beyond which finite reason can not go.

Turning now to other affirmations of paradox, it may be noted that Nicolas Berdyaev has expressed some of his views in terms which are paradoxical. One of the captivating features of his thought is the working of "dialectic". He learned it first from Hegel and then from Marx, yet his dialectic is different because it is essentially Christian. He was never imprisoned by it. For him the dialectic quality of life and of experience, or the relations between God and man, necessity and freedom and so forth was never something inexorable. He saw to it that his dialectic did not become determinism. Berdyaev maintained that both God and man are free and regarded all true creativity as a divine-human process, a divine call and a human answer. In brief, it was a divine-human response out of unlimited freedom to a divine-human summons. "God expects from me a free creative act," he said.[187]

Spiritual experience rather than discursive reason is the pat-

tern Berdyaev chose to follow. He believes God gives a proposi-
tional revelation of Himself as shown by this statement:

> Divinity cannot be rationally determined and remains out-
> side the scope of logical concepts. . . . All the dogmas of
> Christianity giving expression to the facts and events of
> spiritual experience have a supra-logical and supra-rational
> character and are above the law of identity and contradic-
> tion.[188]

In this and similar passages his dialectic is evident. He acknowl-
edges his debt to Kant in respect to dualism, but criticizes him
for obscuring "the path of knowledge of the authentic world of
existence as distinct from the world of phenomena, for the category of spirit is almost entirely lacking in his philosophy."[189]

Berdyaev speaks of contradictions in the Christian era such
as Christianity without human creation, and human creation without Christianity, God without man, and man without God. But
he goes on to this hopeful statement.

> When Christianity has reached its full development this an-
> tithesis will be resolved and there will be a positive revela-
> tion of God-Humanity, the union of the two movements, the
> uniting of Christianity and creation.[190]

The dialectic of Berdyaev is resolved on the level of existence
or spiritual experience. The place of reason in determining action
is left without objective reference. This puts an undue emphasis
on the subjective. He thinks of God as the subject of experience
rather than the object of thought. In Christian faith, both sides
are needed, the subjective and the objective.

L. Harold DeWolf identifies himself with those who accept
the position of "both-and" in dealing with the pull of opposing
forces or interests. His dialectic leads to a higher rational synthesis. In order to see his approach to paradox the following
quotation is given:

Undoubtedly there is a sense in which the gospel is paradoxical. It is wonderful. It passes the bounds of our experience and understanding that there should exist a Being able to create us and the world in which we live. It is even more wonderful that such a creator should love us and tenderly care for us, even suffer for us, while we are in sinful rebellion against Him. Yet there is nothing in the gospel which contradicts the principles of reason nor the data of our experience. The argument that Christian teaching is essentially paradoxical, that is, self-contradictory, assumes gratuitously some irrational doctrines. If, for example, it is maintained that the infinite God who is absolutely other than man became man while He continued to be absolutely other than man, one has indeed asserted self-contradiction.[191]

These lines contain several different meanings of paradox. DeWolf aims to express the thought that experience may be articulated in logical communication. In this connection he gave two illustrations to clarify his own position and to show how a deeper meaning of paradox may be obtained.

When Heraclitus says that the 'way up and the way down are the same,' his effort at communication fails completely unless the reader understands that, regardless of the question whether matter is being transformed from earth to fire or from fire to earth, an orderly change is taking place, and that Heraclitus is insisting that change and its laws alone truly exist. When Socrates declares he is the wisest man in Athens because he knows that he knows nothing, communication fails unless the reader goes on to reason that Socrates is not contradicting himself but giving a new insight into a love of wisdom and a critical method which count the little already gained as but loss, as compared with the vast realm of indefiniteness and mystery which yet remains.[192]

DeWolf summarizes his own position with these words: "Paradoxes, in short, are useful so long as we look for the truth, not in them, but in a new rational synthesis beyond them."[193] The opposing propositions or words of a paradox partially state what each demands from the other for a synthesis on a higher level of truth.

Willard L. Sperry calls attention to the fact that "The human mind is so constituted that when it is confronted by a duality of experience the mind can distinguish opposites, but life insists on working out some kind of harmony."[194] Continuing this line of thought he goes on to state that the main antithetical concerns of every truly simple religion revolve around the best idea of oneself and second the best idea about the universe around oneself. Each of these objects of thought seem at first to be self-sufficient, but life makes it impossible to keep them apart. "So long as our hold is not broken on either side we feel the physical sensation of 'reality' in our taut members."[195] Sperry regards the mind of man, normally speaking, as being in somewhat the same position. The solution offered here for paradox in religion is not one which goes beyond paradox as in the case of DeWolf. Rather the solution is to be sought somewhere at the middle between the two poles or opposites.

Walter Marshall Horton contends that the ultimate affirmations of religious faith always involve an element of paradox. He puts the thought in this manner:

> In the realm of faith, balance and proportion are more significant than exactness and consistency; and the best way to hit the bull's eye of theological truth is by affirming both sides of a paradox that stretches halfway across the center of the target — not by yielding to the pull which either end of the paradox exerts . . . this issue of logical inconsistencies is rooted in our highest human experiences; and when it is put into poetry, the language of religion, it warms us with a sense of its comprehensive adequacy.[196]

It may seem as if Studdert-Kennedy and Baron von Hugel were in complete opposition to one another, says Horton, but a closer look will reveal that they are simply defending opposite poles of a paradox.

> Both, in the last analysis, find God best revealed in the Cross of Christ. . . . One thinks of God as the Absolute Being, above the vicissitudes of time and change; the other thinks of God as Holy Will. One leans toward pantheism, the other toward dualism; but each is held back by a dim intuitive consciousness of the truth which the other represents.[197]

Sperry, Horton and Finegan have similar points of view in looking for the meaning of paradox at the center between the two opposite sides. Jack Finegan has given a definition of paradox which includes this thought.

> A paradox is something which is seemingly contradictory but may yet be true in fact. It is indeed often between the poles of an apparent contradiction that truth is found. The logical position found at either extreme is not to be adopted. Thus one is driven to a position in the center between the two, even though the central position appears superficially to be logically inconsistent or impossible.[198]

Another viewpoint which resembles the meaning of paradox as it is being discussed here is that of Robert L. Calhoun. He says:

> A paradox is the putting together of two propositions which, for their full meaning, cannot stand alone, in isolation. It is therefore not a uniting of contradictions, for in contradictions the components can be distinguished and can stand alone. It thus does not stop the process of thought before it gets started, but rather leads thought on.[199]

61

Calhoun thus recognizes that it is essential in the process of thought not to introduce real logical contradictions. Thought is action which is another way of saying that communication takes place.

Harris Franklin Rall advocates the use of the term "polarity" as meaning something more than paradox. He makes a distinction between "polarity" and "paradox" which can be seen in this following statement.

> Paradox moves in the realm of thought and is settled, if at all, by reason. Polarity is a dynamic term; it deals with a duality of movement, or forces, and the problem which it poses is met by attitude and action rather than argument.[200]

Somewhat later in the same connection Rall adds a further clarification between these two terms.

> Paradox belongs to a form; the essential matter is the fact of the polarity of life. It is not that life is irrational or that we have a contradiction of mutually exclusive principles; it is rather that there is in all concrete existence, from lowest to highest, a certain duality of movement or of forces. If there were direct opposition it would mean a deadlock; actually, though it involves a certain tension, it is rather the condition of life and growth.[201]

It is "the pull of forces remaining in tension, going to constitute that life of man at whose heart is the need of constant decision and action."[202] Paradoxical statements may seem to contradict each other but each may be true in its own right. By comparison it may be noted that the polarity which Rall is suggesting is not the dialectic of Hegel, the immanent and unceasing process in which the opposition of thesis and antithesis is constantly being resolved in the unity of a higher synthesis. Nor is Rall in favor of the "both-and" formula or the process of "alternation" which is advocated by Hocking. The latter view is yet to be examined. The position taken by Rall is that of tension between opposites which requires constant decision and action.

It will be useful to sum up the trends of paradoxical thought in this presentation which began with Søren Kierkegaard. Many issues were raised by him but the one bearing on this discussion concerns the matter of comprehension and communication. Following some of his remarks it soon became evident that scholars were sharply divided on whether experience of a Christian nature could be communicated by means of reason and the categories of human discourse. It was noted, on the one hand, that scholars such as Barth, Brunner, Baillie, and Niebuhr insist God cannot be comprehended in terms of human words or by the categories of thought. Such attempts, they say, to express the paradoxes of Christian faith lead to real logical contradiction and logical inconsistency.

On the other hand, it was pointed out that scholars like Aulén, Tillich, and Berdyaev take exception to the proposition that Christian faith as it is experienced finds expression in "irrational" or logical contradictions. However, Tillich and Aulén agree that faith in terms of a paradoxical act of God cannot be motivated by reason nor can such faith be contained within rational categories. The substance of Christian experience is contrary to what man may intend or expect (Aulén). In God's acting reason is superseded — paradox points beyond the realm in which finite reason may be applied (Tillich). Paradoxical dialectic is to be resolved on the level of spiritual experience, not on the level of discursive reason (Berdyaev).

The next transition in the development of this subject came at the point where scholars like DeWolf, Sperry, Horton, Finegan, Calhoun, and Rall were introduced. These men, while representing different views of paradox, have a common interest in attempting to arrive at an understanding of the relation between comprehension and communication. How is experience to be expressed? Each of these theologians whose name was mentioned above is of the opinion that paradoxes are resolved in further thought or in decision and action as the case may be (DeWolf, Rall).

In retrospect it may be seen that in general all of the positions which have been examined in relation to the affirmation of paradox give recognition to different reaches of experience. There are many different levels of life to be taken into account. While no attempt has been made to fit all of the views into the seven different kinds of paradox suggested in this work under the section dealing with the definition of paradox, it is recognized that many different relations and levels of life are being discussed.

3. *Other Possibilities.* The work proceeds to a presentation of some other possibilities which have been proposed as a way to resolve religious or theological paradox. There may be others besides these which could be included but even these additional views will add to the diversity of interpretation.

Arnold B. Come made a study of four types of paradox; namely, the apologetic, the ontological, the semantic, the logical. He rejects the last three in favor of the first or apologetic paradox because "it exists at the border line between the non-Christian and the Christian lives."[203] However, life must be lived "beyond paradox". He makes clear that his objection to dialectical theology as it regards paradox is not because it offends human dignity or the demands of finite reason. He states his objection in this fashion:

> We object to the persistent paradox because it stops short of giving adequate place to the real, actual presence and activity of God as Holy Spirit among us and within us, and through us into all the world around us. Theology beyond paradox will be theology of the Holy Spirit. Not a theology about the Holy Spirit, although that is a crying need, but rather a theology as an understanding of our Christian faith — relationship with God in terms of our ac-

64

tual personal union with him and in terms of his actual presence with us and activity through us.[204]

Come calls for something additional in terms of "Divine Disturbance" which gradually brings about the firmness and strength and warmth of a life together. This life together brings forth an understanding which results not in being servants but friends. This, then, suggests Come, is the "experience and the knowledge of God the Holy Spirit."[205]

Without a doubt more needs to be said concerning the Holy Spirit, and more place must be given to the presence and ministry of God as Holy Spirit. But what shall be the test as to whether the claims men make in terms of the possession of the Holy Spirit are genuine or not? What is going to be the depth and meaning of this relationship of God as Holy Spirit to man? The New Testament has something to say to such questions as these.

Beloved, do not believe every spirit, but test the spirits to see whether they are of God.[206]

Do not quench the Spirit . . . but test everything; hold fast what is good, abstain from every form of evil.[207]

Walk by the Spirit, and do not gratify the desires of the flesh.[208]

But the fruit of the Spirit is love, joy, peace, patience, kindness, goodness, faithfulness, gentleness, self-control; against such there is no law.[209]

Thus you will know them by their fruits.[210]

These are some of the better known references which indicate that human reason is not by-passed or disregarded in matters which require verification and evaluation. In fact, there is good reason to doubt that unless man responds to the appeal and guidance of the Holy Spirit man will ever be a follower of the Christian way of living. God is calling[211] but not all men will take time to listen. "To each is given the manifestation of the Spirit for the common good,"[212] says Paul but this is no guarantee that sin and selfishness will not thwart what the Spirit wishes to accomplish. The solution offered by Come goes beyond paradox but he has not shown what an understanding of faith involves in terms of actual content.

Gilbert K. Chesterton, as a metaphysical moralist, made a study of the paradoxes of Christianity. He applied to life what he chose to call the "Christian paradox of parallel passions.[213] He claimed that paradox in the deepest mysteries of life drives man to paradox in language in statements of what he sees. The meaning Chesterton attaches to his idea of "parallel passions" is made clear in this composite statement:

> The real trouble with this world of ours is not that it is an unreasonable world, nor even that it is a reasonable one. The commonest kind of trouble is that it is nearly reasonable, but not quite . . . its wildness lies in wait. . . . Everywhere there is this element of the quiet and incalculable. . . . Paganism declared that virtue was in balance; Christianity declared it was in conflict; the collision of two passions apparently opposite. . . . Take, for instance, the matter of modesty, in the balance between mere pride and mere prostration. . . . Christianity separated the two ideas and then exaggerated them both. . . . Christianity got over the difficulty of combining furious opposites, by keeping them both, and keeping them both furious.[214]

Commenting on the position of Chesterton in a book of sermons on Christian paradoxes, Gerald Kennedy pays him tribute for showing that heresy always attempts to overemphasize one aspect of the gospel.[215] Chesterton insists that "orthodoxy" feels the pull of the opposites, but keeps them from flying apart, and thus keeps them true. The opposites are not really inconsistent, but their nature as two impetuous emotions makes it difficult to hold them simultaneously. Yet in the view of Chesterton they must both be kept, and they must both be kept furious.

The conclusion which would seem to follow from this brief examination of Chesterton's view of paradox is that the opposites run parallel to each other, but this begs the question whether there can be any communication between the two. What, if any, is the point of contact? What effect do the "furious" emotions have upon each other? These questions suggest a weakness in his position.

William Ernest Hocking has offered a different solution in handling opposites when he put forth the idea or "principle of alternation". He declares that man must choose both sides of paradox in relation to the demands of action and rest in religion and these must be chosen alternately. He affirms in his own words:

> The life of knowledge as well as the life of action swings, I believe in irregular rhythm or alternation, between this pole of certainty and the region of exploration, tentativeness, probability, hypothesis.[216]

In another reference he indicates how the principle he holds functions. Contrasting the two aspects of alternation he states the following:

> On the one hand the peace of the hermit, the silence of the forest, the exaltation of sacrifice, the mightiness of simplification and unity, the joy of self-abandonment, the calm of absolute contemplation, the vision of God. On the other hand, the variety and stress of life, the zest of common ends, the mastery of means, the glory of infinite enterprise, the pride of creativity and self-possession.[217]

67

Such a view of man as participant and critical spectator seems necessary in practical life whenever alternative commitment are present which themselves imply the denial of one or the other. But in regard to paradox it would seem that something more is needed which Hocking's view does not supply. "Opposition" may well be, as Josiah Royce held, "a necessary step in the search for the whole truth."[218]

In presenting a variety of theological viewpoints on the subject of paradox in the preceding pages the primary object has been to learn what, if any, is the relation between comprehension and communication. In the process of this endeavor it was apparent that scholars have used and explained the meaning of paradox in several diverse ways. Attempts have been made to resolve paradox along the different lines suggested by these words: (1) outright denial, (2) ambivalence, (3) irresolvable logical contradiction, (4) contradiction, (5) antinomy, (6) antithesis, (7) both-and rational synthesis, (8) polarity, (9) beyond paradox, (10) parallel passions, (11) alternation, (12) or any one of the other views put forth in this volume.

It may be said that in the examination of all these views something has been gained for an understanding of present-day theological discussion. The conclusions which were drawn at various points along the way are tentative evaluations and impressions. It is hoped that what has been accomplished will set in clearer perspective some of the questions which will be at issue in the investigation of Pauline materials.

CHAPTER III

HISTORICAL BACKGROUND FOR THIS STUDY

A. *The Factors Influencing Paul*

Those who have made a study of human nature and the manner in which the mind functions are inclined to agree that the milieu and impressions of youth play a great part in the development of personality and social attitudes. It is, therefore, significant to note some of the background which likely influenced Paul. James Iverach observed that the mercantile life of Tarsus made a profound impression on Paul's young mind as evidenced by his thought, and that almost all of his metaphors and illustrations are drawn from it.[1] John S. Howson, with reference to Paul's metaphors, supports this point of view.[2]

If Paul was born in Tarsus instead of Jerusalem, and the prevailing tendency is to say he was, then some further word of description about the capitol of the Province of Cilicia in southeast Asia Minor may prove to be helpful.

Tarsus stood only a few miles from the coast of the Mediterranean and was connected with this great body of water by a navigable stream. The town stood in the midst of a fertile plain, and was built on both sides of the river Cydnus, which descended to it from the nearby Taurus mountains. On these neighboring mountains herds of goats were kept. The atmosphere was relatively cold and thus the animals grew long fine-haired coats which became famous for strength and durability. In antiquity Paul's birthplace was noted for its tent cloth, or *cilicium,* as it was called, after the Province of Cilicia; an interesting memory of this has survived in the French word for hair-cloth, *cilice.* A tent maker in this area was known as a weaver of tough fabric. The New Testament indicates that in part Paul found employment as a tent maker, which was a source of income along the shores of the Mediterranean.

Tarsus was also known as a trade center; for behind the town there was a famous pass, the Cilician Gates, which led up through the mountains to the central countries of Asia Minor. As a boy, Paul may have watched the rafts of timber which, cut from the mountains and floated down the river, were sent to the dry-docks and other designated places. No doubt he saw bales of goods, with the names of the owners on them, from the east and the west. Tarsus was also a university center, but not on a par with Athens and Alexandria. Although the town was under Roman rule, it enjoyed self-government. Paul took great pride in pointing to Tarsus as no mean city. But there were other formative influences which must be taken into account, apart from the direct revelation of God and the primitive Christian community, which contributed to Paul's language and ideas. The principal ones to note in this connection are the Jewish, the Hellenic, and the Roman. These will now be taken up in their turn.

1. *Jewish.* The proportionate amount of influence which is exerted upon any one person is a very difficult thing to determine. This fact has been demonstrated in the case of Paul as scholars have wrestled with the problem of his background. Shirley Jackson Case, in his appraisal of the Tübingen scholars and their followers with respect to Paul, states that in making him so emphatically

> the advocate of an absolute religion for the gentile world at large, [they] have passed too lightly over the Jewish leanings of Paul. They turned the spotlight effectively upon his controversy with the legalists, but unfortunately they

left other important aspects of the apostle's thought and interest quite too much in the shadow.[3]

Paul was an heir of several national characters as many people are today. His relation to Jewish life and thought must be assessed in the light of this fact. William D. Davies has published a work which advances the view held earlier by Thackeray, namely, that Paul was greatly influenced by the doctrines and beliefs current among the Jews of his day. Both of these writers hold that Paul stood in the main stream of first century Judaism and derived many ideas from it ordinarily labelled Hellenistic. They contend that Hellenism made a contribution to Paul's religious thought, but that in all essentials the sub-structure is Jewish.[4]

A number of years ago an illuminating article appeared on Paul. In it Morton Enslin made the attempt to question the probability of Paul's rabbinical training, although he cites Montefoire's suspicion of the tutelage under the eminent Gamaliel. But Enslin goes on to prove convincingly that Paul's training under Gamaliel is an assumption rather than an established fact. He thinks that Paul had no contact with Jerusalem until after his Damascus road experience.[5] This is an open question, whether Paul had been in Jerusalem prior to this time, for which there is no clear evidence. Samuel Belkin, along with others, recognizes the problem presented by the Book of Acts with regard to Paul studying at the feet of Gamaliel,[6] and questions the reliability of the source material. Yet on the other hand Belkin offers Paul's own words claiming to have surpassed his friends in Jewish studies, owing to his great devotion to the traditions of the fathers.[7] In his letters Paul claims he was well acquainted with Jewish laws and customs. He considered himself educated as a Pharisee, and his own home was Pharisaic.

Otto Pfleiderer put forth the idea that the two streams of thought, the Pharaisic and the Hellenistic, met in Paulinism in one bed without coalescing.[8] This view is emphatically rejected

71

by Albert Schweitzer who believes that it is impossible to conceive of Paul as thinking Judaically with half his mind and Hellenistically with the other half and still be considered as a single integral personality.[9] The position Schweitzer takes is to think of Paul exclusively in Jewish terms. It is almost inconceivable to imagine that Paul was not influenced by other cultures in view of his contacts with them. The observation which Thomas Wilson makes comes close to the historical situation. He comments as follows:

> No one questions the supremacy of Shakespeare in the field of dramatic art and creation. But none can deny that he employed material already at hand, some of it, e.g. *King Lear* and *Julius Caesar,* very old. St. Paul, equally great as a genius of the religious and moral life, in like manner can be understood in the light of the religious and moral traditions and ideas of his own and previous day.[10]

Paul actually belonged to three worlds or more and derived some influence from each.

In recent times considerable speculation and research has been going on as the result of the discovery of the Qumran literature. The first Qumran manuscripts were found in 1947 by Arab shepherds in a cave near the Wadi Qumran on the northwest shore of the Dead Sea. This discovery led to the excavation of an Essene library in that area. The Essenes, up until that time, had not attracted much scholarly attention. James Moffatt summarily dismissed them with these words:

> They appear and disappear in a mist, leaving hardly a clue to their existence. None of their sacred books has survived. We do not even know whether they were written in Greek or Aramaic. . . .[11]

The archeological excavation of the Qumran Scrolls has shown that the texts were all written in Hebrew except the Genesis Scroll which was in Aramaic. Scholars have been working to analyze Bible expressions which correspond to the writings of Qumran. The endeavor to record similarities between the two has also led to striking differences.

Several books and magazine articles have dealt with the possibility that the Qumran literature may have made an ideological contribution to the Pauline letters. Charles T. Fritsch, for instance, writes:

> Many of the terms and ideas in the Pauline literature are closely paralleled in the sectarian documents from Qumran.[12]

This point of view is disputed by other scholars who insist that parallel words and phrases do not necessarily indicate borrowing or that the connotations are the same for the user. Oscar Cullman has said that the writings of Qumran teach that various elements in Christianity, once attributed to the influence of Greek Culture and Hellenism, can now be explained as the outcome of trends within Judaism itself.[13] This sounds plausible but the fact must not be overlooked that the Judaism which prevailed in the days of primitive Christianity may already have appropriated aspects of other cultures.

One of the key issues in studying Paul revolves around his early training and the new way of the primitive Christian community. Belkin, for instance, insists that the transition involved did not bring about a complete break with his former Pharaisic doctrine.[14] Auguste Sabatier takes the opposite view that after the turning point referred to in the letter to the Galatians,[15] Judaism was wholly vanquished in Paul.[16] In opposition to this view Donald W. Riddle says that in essence Paul regarded himself as a Jew and that under no circumstances either before or after his revolutionary experience did Paul ever repudiate Judaism.[17] In support of this view just given, Gustaf A. Deissmann offers this representative statement:

The most genuine characteristics of the Jewish nature were preserved by Paul when he became a Christian. . . . . In opposition to mechanical discoveries of the Jewish and the Christian elements in him, we need not hesitate to call him the great Jew-Christian of the earliest age.[18]

A brief summary of the Jewish aspects of Paul's background might include his Jewish birth, his sense of continuity with the past coupled with the recognition of his people. He was all things to all men that he might win them to his new found faith which helped him understand the old.

2. *Hellenic.* For a period of years there was a revolt against Paul by those who claimed he betrayed the Judaic tradition and went over to the Hellenic. Wilfred Knox went so far as to indicate the exact turning point and departure from the Judaic to the Hellenic. He claimed it was Paul's speech at Athens.[19] The tendency to say that Paul forsook Judaism has persisted down through the years with varying degrees of emphasis. Claude G. Montefoire, who is usually more sympathetic toward the Christian faith than Joseph Klausner, nevertheless agrees with Klausner in regarding Paul as a Jew of the Dispersion and consequently unacquainted with the best of rabbinic Judaism of Palestine.[20] Paul himself claims to be a Hebrew[21] which suggests at least that his opponents were trying to deny his affinities with Aramaic speaking Judaism by making him a Hellenist. A recent interpretation by Martin Dibelius and Georg Kummel deals with the Hellenistic strain in Paul.

The fact that the Jews of today, coming directly from rabbinism, feel that there is something strange and un-Jewish about Paul's letters, is connected with the Hellenistic part of his inheritance.[22]

Such an interpretation may be illuminating but what about the un-Jewish aspects of Jesus' teaching in his day? It was thought

74

that he advocated ideas that were different and sometimes un-popular. No doubt Paul employed thoughts which originated in the Hellenic world, but objections to his message cannot be limited to that part of his inheritance. He dared to identify him-self with the Christian movement and helped to keep this move-ment from becoming a Jewish sect.

William Ramsay, after some thoughtful consideration about Paul's Hellenic background, had this to say:

> The influence of Greek thought on Paul, though real, is all surely external. Hellenism never touches the life and es-sence of Paulinism which is fundamentally and absolutely Hebrew; but it does strongly affect the expressions of Paul's teaching.[23]

Henry Wheeler Robinson suggests a different line of thought in this matter. He admits that Paul may have used some Greek terms, but that he remains psychologically Jewish. The state-ment which follows makes clear the relationship of these two aspects of Paul's formative background.

> His modifications of Jewish thought are primarily due to his personal experience, and such Hellenistic influences as were inevitable in his period were unconsciously imbibed by Paul and subordinated or assimilated to his Jewish psy-chology.[24]

It was pointed out earlier that Albert Schweitzer takes an extreme position with respect to the Jewishness of Paul. The following quotation amplifies his contention in respect to Hel-lenism.

> Paulinism and Hellenism have in common their religious terminology, but in respect to ideas, nothing. The apostle did not Hellenize Christianity. His conceptions are equally

distinct from those of Greek philosophy and from those of Mystery Religions. The affinities which have been alleged cannot stand an examination which takes into account of their real essence and of the different way in which the ideas are conditioned in the two cases.[25]

In contrast with some of these views which have been cited to show how scholars have dealt with the problem of Paul's background, William Ramsay asserts that Pauline thought is "wholly inconceivable in a mere narrow Hebrew, and wholly inexplicable without an education in Greek philosophy."[26] Such a statement is unwarranted. There was a flourishing Greek academy, sometimes called university, in Tarsus which Ramsay does not rate with the schools in Athens and Alexandria.[27] Still Tarsus had its athletes, rhetoricians, and at least five eminent Stoic philosophers among whom was Athenodorus. How far the presence of this academy influenced Paul cannot be determined, but it is fairly certain that his parents would not have permitted him to attend a pagan school. Paul knew common (Koine) Greek and wrote extensively in it. He probably learned some colloquial Greek on his travels. He was familiar with Stoic terms but this does not prove that he had either studied Stoic writings or had been taught by their teachers. He knew some lines of Greek poetry, but it is not necessary to assume that he had read from the Greek poets themselves.[28] The acquaintance he betrays occasionally with Roman law does not at all pass beyond the most common legal relations, and cannot be called jurisprudence. After making a study of the Greco-Roman environment of Paul, Charles A. A. Scott was convinced that while Paul uses the terminology current in the pagan world of his day this does not mean that he adopted the ideas which the terms were to express.[29] The active mind of Paul was not content to remain ignorant of the philosophical ideas of his day, but this may simply mean that his own mind had a philosophical turn. His knowledge of the Scriptures in Greek (the Septuagint) has caused considerable speculation. It is unlikely that a copy of the Septuagint was in his home where it could have been used as a manual for instruction. Still Arthur Nock makes the bold statement that "There is not a paragraph in Paul's writings which does not include subconscious recollections of the Greek Old Testament."[30] Albert Schweitzer offers this idea that there should be no rigid separation between Judaism of the Dispersion and that of Palestine particularly in the case of Paul whose home may have been a bit of Jerusalem outside of Palestine.[31] William Davies in his work on Paul and Judaic Rabbinicism writes as follows:

> It is wholly artificial to make too sharp a dichotomy between the Hebraic and the Hellenistic elements in Paul's thought, and that any Hellenistic elements which may be found in his thought do not imply that he was therefore outside the main current of first-century Judaism.[32]

A radical departure from this point of view can be seen in the demythologizing attempt of Rudolf Bultmann. He tries to divest the New Testament of all so-called unnecessary accoutrements and to present the original message in its primitive milieu. But on occasion he will ascribe certain texts to reductional gloss which do not agree with his own existentialist philosophy.[33] But rather than dealing with this aspect of his work, it will serve the purpose of this section of the present study to turn to his treatment of the Hellenistic background of Paul. Bultmann's own words may be cited to show where he would place the theology of the apostle.

> The historical presupposition for Paul's theology is not the kerygma of the oldest church but of the Hellenistic church; it was the latter that mediated the former to Paul.[34]

Granted there was a pre-Pauline church and that he was

influenced by Hellenistic ideas, it would be well nigh impossible to ignore his personal contacts with the disciples who had been with Jesus. Paul's encounter with Peter and James and others surely gave him some insights of the life and teaching of Jesus. To say that Paul was not concerned with Jesus beyond the fact that he became a man and lived on earth as Bultmann says is untenable. He goes on to say, "But beyond that Jesus' manner of life, his ministry, his personality, his character play no role at all; neither does Jesus' message.[35] How is one to regard such a view when the New Testament itself presents the faith of the early church, including Paul who wrote some of the earliest letters, as a continuity of that faith which the life, teaching, and work of Jesus made possible? Ironically, in his attempt to understand man in a purely historical way Bultmann has denied the decisive significance of the Cross for all history by defining its meaning only in terms of human decision. Moreover, he appeals to the faith of the early church as he attempts to reconstruct the scriptural setting and message thus in effect denying his own right to say that Paul and others were not so influenced.

Bultmann declares that from the beginning the Christian message was couched in mythological thought patterns of the ancient world. Thus, for example, Paul is supposed to have naively combined the Gnostic myth of a dying and rising deity with the Jewish myth of an atoning judge and redeemer.[36] This, according to Bultmann, has obscured the true Christian message right from the start. His solution is to do away with this mythological framework in favor of the relevant message of the early Church as he interprets that message with the tool of form criticism, as well as subjective analysis.

Perhaps it may throw some light on the preceding paragraph to make some reference to mystery-religions. No doubt Paul had some acquaintance with Greek mysteries, or heard about them in his travels. He uses the word "mystery" various times in his letters,[37] but again this does not imply necessarily that he accepted the original meaning or setting of the term. In the opinion of Gustaf A. Deissmann, after studying Paul's teaching of baptism and the Last Supper,

> the utmost that we can say is that in formulating his Christian doctrine, the mysteries may have helped him to realize more vividly that all the wealth of spiritual blessing at which they aimed was to be reached in the mystery of Christ alone.[38]

H. A. A. Kennedy in his volume admits that Paul may have done some borrowing, but insists that in the two areas just mentioned above, Paul did not think in terms of magical sacraments, but rather in terms of symbolic pictures of the death of sin and the new life in Christ which the believer had already experienced.[39] Thus it would appear that great caution must be observed in ascribing anything more than illustrative material to Paul's understanding of mystery-religions. The same might also be said in respect to the myths which were circulated in his time. In any case the paramount issue is whether Paul correctly understood and presented the historical Jesus as the foundation of faith for all time. Later on there will be opportunity to look at the relationship of Jesus and Paul so that discussion will be passed by now.

In summary it must be said that the proportionate amount of influence exerted on Paul from either the Jewish or Hellenic side cannot be conclusively determined. At the outset of this section of the dissertation it was stated that for many years Paul was regarded as a Hellenist. The tendency today is to think of him as a Jewish Rabbi. It almost seems to be the genius of Paul that he could be so many things to so many people. The evidence that is available in the New Testament suggests that he was nearer the Jewish than the Hellenic side, but both sides must be taken into account in studying the shaping influences of his character and his work. But this is not all there is to be included. Consideration must also be given to another world in which Paul lived, namely, the Roman world.

3. *Roman.* In the words of William Ramsay, "Paul grew up at once a Roman and a Tarsian and a Jew."[40] In view of this fact it is remarkable that so much time has been spent in books and periodicals on the Jewish and Hellenic sides of Paul's background and so little on the Roman.

At the time of the birth of Paul the conquest of the world was not the problem of Imperial Rome, but rather organization, consolidation, and civilization of areas already conquered. Well built roads, an imperial post, the denarius and the Roman gold piece as legal tender were provided throughout the Empire. There was an enormous production of inexpensive books. Two public libraries were established by Augustus in Rome, and others by his successors. Roman business methods and economic planning helped put trade on a better standing.[41] Considerable freedom was given to the provincials who enjoyed many of the benefits unknown before. Roman law brought about a greater justice, barring the rule of some of its emperors.

In respect to religion the Romans were noted for greater religious toleration than had been extended by other countries. They showed a willingness to learn from other religions and actually rediscovered some of their own deities, under different names, in the divinities of other nations. The following quotation from Gustaf Deissmann deserves to be included since it provides evidence to support the religious tolerance of Rome during this period, as well as to show the expansion of Judaism. To quote Deissmann's words:

> These modest Jewish synagogues up and down the Hellenistic world was a silent and, the history of religion tells us, extremely effective protest against the worship of images by the polytheistic pagans. More than a hundred and fifty Jewish congregations of the imperial period are already known to us within the olive zone of the Mediterranean

basin; their actual number was no doubt considerably
greater.[42]

There is little doubt that Paul would have visited in a number
of these synagogues. Their presence fortified his own faith.

In his discussion of religion in the imperial period of Rome,
Franz Cumont makes the interesting observation that the Hellenistic religion was essentially the product of oriental influences
pressing into the Mediterranean world from the East. He cites
M. Krumbacher to support the view that in the first three centuries the history of the empire may be summarized as a 'peace-
ful infiltration' of the Orient into the Occident.[43] He understands
the term "Hellenism" as not only a Grecizing of the oriental
elements, but much more the orientalizing of Greek culture. If
this be true then the Greek influence upon Paul would at least
be minimized.

When Rome turned persecutor of Christianity it was essentially
because the latter was not a national faith, and was thus considered as a denationalized sect. Rome feared private associations
though of a harmless nature since various uprisings did occur.
The Christians were considered unpatriotic and intolerant of
other religions, to say nothing of the Jewish protests and per-
secutions which even Paul helped to direct against the Christians.

The time came when Paul saw things differently and from a
new vantage point. As a Christian he found it helpful to be a
Roman citizen protected by Roman soldiers and the right to
appeal his case to Caesar. He prized his Roman citizenship.
How he came to get it is uncertain. Tarsus was a free city by
the grant of Augustus; it was neither a colony nor a "munici-
pium" and therefore birth did not convey this distinction. Such
citizenship for a provincial was usually conferred for some special
service or goodwill shown to the imperial house. Paul's father
may have obtained his citizenship by some distinguished service.
It has been thought that he may have purchased it in affluent
circumstances. Joseph Barber Lightfoot tells of the importance

of having Roman citizenship to the individual Roman, and what he has to say might equally well apply to persons such as Paul. Lightfoot puts it like this:

> To the Roman his citizenship was his passport in distant lands, his talisman in seasons of difficulties and danger. It shielded him alike from the caprice of municipal law and the injustice of local magistrates.[44]

Speaking of the missionary efforts of Paul and the effects of the Roman Empire upon him, William Ramsay went so far as to characterize Paul as statesman.[45] In another work of his Ramsay has paid Paul this tribute:

> There had passed into his nature something of the Roman constructiveness, the practical sense of economic facts, the power of seeing the means to reach an end of the world of reality and humanity, the quickness to catch and use and mold the ideas and ideals of the citizen of the Empire.[46]

Such a view tends to moderate Paul's abbreviated remark about pagan morals in the first chapter of his letter to the Romans. It is true that gladiatorial shows, depravity, laxity, and gross self-indulgence were all too common, but as Ludwig Friedlander has pointed out, it is easy to exaggerate this side of Roman life.[47] There was another side which expressed sympathetic interest in the poor and sick. Slaves were considered goods and chattels, yet those who were born in the home (vernae) often were treated as members of the household. Other factors on the positive side were mentioned in some of the earlier paragraphs on Roman society and should be kept in mind.

Paul presents himself as a many-sided person with a diversified nature. This may help to explain how it is possible for scholars to present various views concerning him. Amos N. Wilder has summarized this point of view in these lines:

It is the many sidedness, the completeness of Paul's Christianity which is the stumbling-block. It is human nature to wish to conform others to our own limitations; if we have gifts and insights corresponding to one segment of the full circle on Christian experience we have a blind spot for the other segments. Note that in Paul we find all the types and emphases of New Testament religion: ethical, mystical, apocalyptic, philosophical, administrative, ecstatic. He speaks with tongues more than they all! After he was gone, various schools borrowed of him, this one, one legacy, another, another. But he had encompassed them all.[48]

To the above statement may be added the observation of Kirsopp Lake who took into account that Paul was in a world of differing opinions, and being emotionally highstrung and intellectually active, it was certain that he would take sides warmly.[49] Thus even though his letters do express many different ideas one must try to balance them with the realization that he may have additional testimony.

Paul as he lives before us in his Epistles, writes Andrew Martin Fairbairn, is a man who holds many men within him — so many — that we may describe him as the most unintelligible to the analytical reason of a critic who has never warmed to the passion or been moved by the enthusiasm of humanity; but the most intelligible of men to the man who has heard within himself the sound of all the voices that speak in man.[50]

This presents another aspect in the shaping influence that is sometimes overlooked in Paul. To be sure there are contributions from the Jewish, the Hellenic, the Roman sides but as Alexander Balmain Bruce has wisely cautioned Paul's dependence upon others has been greatly overrated.[51] Paul is also creative, and to a discussion of his creative experience attention is now devoted.

4. *Creative Experience.* Paul's heredity and environment together or alone do not explain who he was and what he accomplished. Some have tried to explain his experience by tracing out the origin of certain elements and then to put together what they claimed to have found. Some have sought to give a single explanation for his background and legacy. Still others have imposed their own viewpoint or main interest on Paul's thought for the ideas they wished to communicate. Any explanation of Paul which neglects to take into account his profound, personal religious experience misses the main point. Paul Wernle went so far as to say that the "decisive factor in the genius of St. Paul's theology was his personal experience, his conversion on the road to Damascus."[52] William Ralph Inge believes that the phrase "Christ in me" is the overmastering experience which was "unquestionably the core of his religion."[53] Statements such as the life and work of Paul, particularly in connection with the these deserve careful consideration for a basic understanding of Christian Way.

One of the finest descriptions of the experiences of Paul, with well-documented Scripture references, was given some years ago by W. J. Conybeare and J. B. Howson.[54] The first pages of the introduction are filled with a variety of particulars concerning Paul. This source of information supports the view of those who believe that Paul is a complex person who has distinguished himself as a thinker, a man of executive ability, and a creative personality. All of these factors were in his equipment and each played a significant part.

The creative experience of Paul deals with both the tangible influence of life. It is therefore much easier to observe some of his ideas at work than it is to note how the ideas crystalized in his own experience. The creative genius is there in its formulating power as in the case of religious art and music but the product is human personality. R. Birch Hoyle comments on a similar thought when he says:

> There is of necessity much guess-work when any attempt is made to trace the sources of phrases, quotations, and echoes of quotations in Paul. There is no way of determining that the fine, delicate allusions which a keen literary taste may detect were actually present to Paul's mind when busy dictating letters. Some passages which seem like quotation may be but coincidence — similar thoughts out of similar situations without any direct connection between the authors of the same expression. In addition to this there are the remarkable and unanalyzable elements of personality. Ordinary experience cannot catch up with the genius (Paul would say 'the spirit') when in full career, nor explain the fusion of materials into a new product.[55]

In summary, then, this portion of the work has shown that the Jewish, Hellenic, Roman, and creative experiential factors helped shape the mind and work of Paul. But the greatest of these to the Christian was his creative religious experience.

B. *Paul as a Letter Writer*

1. *Dictation of Letters.* Apparently there is only one letter which Paul actually wrote.[56] It was his custom to dictate to an amanuensis as in the case of Tertius.[57] or as Peter used Silvanus.[58] The letters of Paul contain a variety and vivacity of style running all the way from exalted to barren prose. In certain parts the reader may find didactic and polemic statements interspersed with exhortation and warning. He sets out to comfort, strengthen; he defends himself against adversaries; settles doubtful questions; speaks of his personal experiences and intentions; adds greetings and messages of greetings; generally without any anxiety concerning subject matter passing from one thing to

another, often indeed jumping, and in the longer letter showing clearly abrupt changes of mood while he was dictating.[59]

Nowhere perhaps will there be found a parallel so close to the matter under discussion as in the case of the letters and speeches of Oliver Cromwell. He entertained the best and truest thoughts about England and her complicated affairs of his day, but in Cromwell's efforts to express them in speech or letter the reader is met with the most extraordinary mixture of exclamations, questions, arguments lost in words, unwieldy parenthesis, beautiful pathos, and subduing eloquence. Yet in the midst of these amazing utterances there is the heart and soul of the Puritan Era — the events and ideas of the time are in the very process of birth.

The difficulty of understanding the letters of Paul arises from different sources. In a considerable degree the variation in style may be due to the employment of different amanuenses. Part of the difficulty is in the problem of not knowing the arguments of his opponents to which he replies, arguments not necessary to restate because they are known to his readers. Part of the difficulty accrues from what appear to be italicized words or whole sentences which were supplied to complete and clarify his thought.[60] In part the difficulty comes from the various Bible translations which do not permit the reader to see clearly the older conceptions which may have existed.[61] Yet another difficulty may be traced to the difference between the figurative manner of speech in the Orient and the prosaic and philosophical way of thinking in the Western world. Arthur Darby Nock, for instance, affirms that Paul's style was full of second-hand Semitisms which came from the Septuagint, but that Paul also had some acquaintance with the Old Testament in Hebrew and seems to have had some knowledge of the original connotations which underlie the Greek as he quotes it. And "This stylistic phenomenon," writes Nock,

corresponds to a fact of the greatest importance in the

86

whole writing and thought of Paul in the whole development of early Christianity. The expression is externally Hellenic, but inwardly Jewish.[62]

In two instances Paul disavows any pretensions as a letter writer.[63] He was opposed to a certain kind of rhetorical "persuasiveness of speech,"[64] but his speech was nonetheless persuasive. Henry Thatcher Fowler offers this tribute to Paul in saying that,

> though the rushing stream of Paul's thought sometimes overflows its bounds and cuts for itself a new channel quite other than that in which it had started, and, at other times, the implications of an idea so stirred his emotional nature that he left his argument for rhapsodic flight of poetic apostrophe, still Paul was fundamentally a reasoner. He loved to unfold the implications of his basic conceptions to their issue in a satisfying theory of life or history.[65]

Apparently Paul found difficulty in getting his own letters to his intended readers. He mentions putting his own signature at the close of a letter as proof of its genuineness.[66] From this it would appear that forged letters were being circulated under the name of Paul.

The idea is widely accepted that Paul's letters were not intended for publication, but were designed to meet particular occasions or needs. Following his earthly ministry, the letters were collected and published. Some of his letters, according to the New Testament, must have gotten misplaced or were lost.[67]

The reasons Paul had for writing letters to various churches or to individuals are finally more important than any discussion as to how he wrote those letters. Paul was constrained by the love of Christ to perpetuate the gospel as it became known to him.

2. *Lack of Systematic Thought.* One thing which has be-

come clear in Pauline study is that he is not a systematic theologian with a definite plan before him, but rather that he is a versatile and capable letter writer whose theological reflections and ideas appear but are not directed by any system. Traditionally Pauline scholarship has tended to take another line, so that basically there was little difference in the bias or objective between the work of Marcion, Augustine, Luther, C. F. Bauer, Pfleiderer, Wrede, Schweitzer, Karl Barth and Loisy. All of these men have shared the assumption that Paul was a theologian, that his system of theology constitutes the essential content of his letters. Heinrich Julius Holtzmann has discussed this problem giving a variety of views over the years.[68] In the same volume Holtzmann declares that "scarce another writer of antiquity has left his commentators with such puzzles to solve as Paul."[69] This would seem to bear out the contention that systematic precision in Paul's work is conspicuous by its absence. The closest he comes to some kind of organized thought is perhaps in his letter to the Romans, but even this may not have been a conscious effort on his part. If he had known that his letters would some day be collected and published he might have organized and revised some of the material, as well as include additional thoughts.

John Locke, who was himself a capable thinker, is quoted by James Freeman Clarke as saying this about Paul:

> I think there is not anywhere to be found a more pertinent, close arguer, who has his eye always on the mark he drives at.[70]

Clarke continues the foregoing quotation by Locke with these words:

> I do not say that he is everywhere clear in his expressions to us now, but I do say he is everywhere a coherent, pertinent writer.[71]

Statements such as these present convincing testimony that the attempt to introduce system into Paul's letters is misleading. This does not mean that he did not make plans in teaching and social organization as will be shown later, but rather that he was not a systematic theologian. Just here James S. Stewart has a relevant word:

> It is when we have learnt to cease to look for this superficial consistency in Paul, this standardized, rigid system of thought and doctrine, that we begin to discover in him what is far more important — the deep, inner consistency of the man's religion, and the fundamental unity of all he wrote and thought.[72]

Along this line of thought it will be of interest to note two important aspects which are directly involved in the present discussion. There is first the matter of teaching or influence and persuasion, and secondly the matter of social organization. In respect to the first of these, Paul's letters assume that the readers have in their possession the Christian tradition. Readers of the New Testament are aware of the fact that there were scattered churches throughout Asia Minor before Paul engaged in missionary work as a Christian. Besides it was not until Paul had behind him a score of years of Christian activity and time for reflection before his extant letters began to appear. Even in the letter to the Romans, where presumably the people and not heard Paul's presentation of the Gospel, a substratum of Christian teaching is assumed. Paul takes for granted that the Gospel is known by those to whom he writes.[73] It would be extremely unsafe to build an argument as to the way Paul taught upon his silence, but fortunately he has left some indications of his manner of teaching.

Paul knew how to turn an argument on principle to some keen reference to personal character, which would require the disputant to reexamine the ground of his difficulty.[74] He was not deceived into a separation of man's opinion from man's true self, and he deemed it fair in argument to produce in court the personal characters which were back of the positions in issue. His views ran straight to conduct and life, from the principle of conduct to the conduct it enjoined, "you then who teach others, will you not teach yourself?"[75] This balance is essential in Paul's search and love of truth. In I Corinthians chapter thirteen he puts love above knowledge. Yet he knew that true knowledge was an attainment of growth.[76] His teaching is filled with equipoise, and checks which are pungent and personal.[77] His questions provoked answers as shown by several references.[78] He knew how to speak in "human terms" because of the natural limitations of men, and fitted his teaching to their spiritual needs.[79] He moved from one city or town to another and simply tarried and taught. His personal testimony "in demonstration of the Spirit and power,"[80] he considered to be of outmost importance in proclaiming the Gospel message.

While there is not extant a single fully reported sermon which Paul preached, some sketches and fragments of several discourses have survived and appear in the New Testament. These are likely presented to miscellaneous audiences. Paul, like Jesus, took occasions to teach or preach as he found them, or as they were thrust upon him, not in formal discourse, but often in the colloquial. And often no doubt with interruption in the form of some question, challenge, or dissent from his hearers. This manner of presentation suggests some of the difficulty an amanuensis might have encountered in taking notes and making the presentation suitable for reading.

The second aspect which is related to Paul's letter writing is social organization. Paul was a persuader of men, a moulder of life. His executive and statesmanlike ability is shown throughout his letters. This is not to say that he did not make mistakes in judgment or in dealing with his fellow men, but that he showed remarkable adaptability and willingness to learn. The churches he served had a simple organization, most of which was functional. This may have partially been caused by the fact that Paul travelled a lot as an itinerant messenger of the Gospel, and therefore was unable to provide the churches with detailed organization. Still there was a sense of continuity in the life and faith of the churches and an interdependence which Paul strengthened with challenging letters and visits. He thought and planned ahead and whenever possible enlisted volunteers in the service of Christ. But his chief concern was not teaching for the sake of teaching or to present the church as a social organization with official sanction. He made it his aim to present the "good news" of the life and work of Jesus Christ. Once this becomes clear his letters take on new meaning.

3. *Main Concern with the Gospel.* Being the kind of person he was, Paul had many concerns of a personal and social nature. But his main concern dealt with the Gospel which he admitted was understood and preached in various ways. In the early stages of his ministry he took time to learn about the apostolic preaching of those who had known Jesus in the flesh. He knew and probably listened to some sermons which were preached in churches he helped persecute. He spent time in the homes of some of the followers of Jesus that he might know more about Him. Out of all this there was something distinctive to Paul's Gospel. Rudolf Knopf has expressed the thought that Paul is not to be judged by what he had in common with his environment, but by what is peculiar to him. Knopf puts his idea this way:

> He who knows how to read and understand will ever be charmed anew by the power of personally experienced religion in the very refined, spiritual, and imperishable form in which it meets us in the Pauline letters. That which constitutes the greatness and value of the gospels — inwardness, belief in the Father, the worth of man's soul, love, and the close union of religion and ethics — all this is vitally experienced by Paul and is freely and insistently expounded.[81]

Many who have been bound by the thought that Paul was the great corrupter of Christianity will be reluctant to appreciate such a view or to take seriously the treatment of Paul's gospel by Archibald M. Hunter.[82] Yet there is much to be said in favor of the position that Paul was essentially true to the spirit and meaning of the Gospel. One of the finest evaluations of the centrality of the Gospel in Pauline thought is this one by Ernest F. Scott:

> One might infer from some modern commentators that Paul was little more than a man of multi-farious and ill-digested learning. Every verse is illustrated by parallels from ancient authors, Jewish and Hellenist, and the impression is left on us that he merely turned over his note-books and so patched up his Epistles to the Romans and the Corinthians. This was certainly not his method. *His whole interest was in the Christian message and what it meant to him.* The ideas were all subordinate, and he knew and cared little where they came from, so long as they helped him proclaim the gospel.[83]

In support of the positions which have been given by Knopf and Scott in this discussion of Paul's main concern, Harry Bulcock offers this thought. He cites Reinhold Seeberg to the effect that Paul did not create a "unified system" but that his thought moved amid a number of different sets of ideas which were held together by "religion as an experience."[84] The experience which came to Paul through the Gospel remains at the center throughout his letters.

The thought recurs many times in the New Testament that witness or testimony is a true source of knowledge. The thought of personally communicating the Gospel as a witness of the faith was ever present. This bears upon the life and work of Paul for he came into contact with some of the early followers of Jesus who testified they had been with Jesus. In speaking of this matter of communication generally, Jonathan Edwards said:

> To depend upon the word of another person, imports two things: First, to be sensible how greatly it concerns us, and how much our interest and happiness really depends upon the truth of it; and, secondly, to depend upon the word of another, is so to believe it, as to date to act upon it, as if it were really true.[85]

This is the description of what could well have happened to Paul. He relied upon others who had borne witness to the Gospel before him. He believed that his happiness depended on the truth of what was said. He dared to act by the grace of God. In time some of his original ideas changed with the changing circumstances, but the core of his faith contained a unity of the Gospel, its relevancy and urgency. This was his primary concern.

The next subject to be considered will deal with the relationship of Jesus and Paul. While the treatment will not be exhaustive it may help to clarify certain points.

C. *Jesus and Paul*

1. *Differences in Outlook.* At the beginning of this chapter it was said that personality and social attitudes are developed along the lines of certain impressions that are made especially in the days of youth. The reader of the New Testament soon detects some differences in the environmental background of Jesus and Paul. Jesus, for instance, draws more upon the illustrative material of the open country and the surrounding hills of Galilee. He frequently refers to items produced by the soil under the protection of the heavenly Father. Paul was apparently influenced more by the mercantile side of life. Many of his metaphors and legal analogies were drawn from organized society.

But beyond such fundamental matters as these Jesus and Paul both rely upon some of the same sources and influences.

In the past and even today there is the question whether Paul really understood and represented Jesus and the teaching of Jesus correctly. Wilhelm Bousset affirmed that the so-called moral and religious personality of Jesus had no influence upon Paul, and held no significance for his religion.[86] William Wrede makes the teaching of Paul differ radically from that of Jesus and discards Paul as a competent witness in the apprehension of the historical Jesus.[87] Wrede thinks there is value in Paul's mystical teaching for inspirational living, but he regards this as something other than the religion of Jesus. The resemblances between the ethical and spiritual teaching of Paul and Jesus are to be explained by a common Judaism.[88] Rudolf Bultmann boldly asserts that scarcely anything is known about the historical life of Jesus.[89] Paul supposedly was interested only in the fact that Jesus became a man and lived on earth, but paid no attention to the way Jesus lived, his ministry or message.[90] Karl Barth agrees with this view that Jesus as a historical person is hardly worth serious study.[91] Such an extreme attitude does not do justice to the New Testament, and can only be held by the most drastic selective process. Such a view seems to come close to the docetic tendency in the New Testament with certain modifications along the lines of existential philosophy. Commenting on the views of Barth and Bultmann in respect to Jesus and their own faith L. Harold De-Wolf writes:

> It is ironical that such men as Bultmann and Barth should especially identify their own faith with the faith of the ancient church and yet believe that the central historical figure of that historical faith is hardly worth serious study.[92]

Some scholars have maintained that Paul knew the historical Jesus. Johannes Weiss[93] and William Ramsay[94] both claim that they did meet, as does also Charles A. A. Scott.[95] The argument centers on Paul's Corinthian letters in which he mentions seeing Jesus.[96] Others, and by far a greater number deny, the probability of this ever happening. Still Paul likely knew a great deal more about Jesus than his letters indicate. The assumption made by Albert Schweitzer is that the gospel tradition was generally known thus helping to explain Paul's silence about Jesus' life.[97] Johannes Weiss has claimed that during the time Paul was actively engaged in persecuting the Church, he could have acquired clear and definite knowledge of the life and preaching of Jesus, of the beliefs, purposes, and hopes of those who continued to follow him.[98] Gustaf Adolf Deissmann maintained that the total impression of Paul's view of Christ is "dominated by the Gospel tradition."[99] Frank C. Porter has stated that the dilemma of "Jesus or Paul" is unwarranted. Paul in a unique way had the mind of Christ.[100] He had conferred with those best able to recount the gospel story.[101] In summarizing this portion of the discussion it will be useful to cite Paul Wernle as follows:

> Paul never knew Jesus during his lifetime, but nevertheless it was he who best understood him.[102]

A similar evaluation is made by Adolf Harnack in this statement:

> In the opinion of the great majority of those who have studied Paul he was the one who understood the Master and continued his work.[103]

The part that is usually overlooked in a discussion of this nature is that Jesus and Paul did not have identical missions. The problems they faced were not the same in many instances. Paul was confronted with the key problem of the relation of Christianity to Judaism. Some wanted to make the new faith a sect of Judaism. This, if accepted, would have meant a denial

95

of the universality of Christianity and would have imposed Jewish Law and ceremonial rites upon an adherent of the Christian faith. Paul defended the opposing view that Christians were not required to follow Judaism in that respect, and his appeal was to the universal nature of Christianity. He defended universalism in the terms of Jewish thought and tradition. His own background amply provided him with materials to do this. The question of whether Paul truly represented Jesus' teaching can be answered by examining some New Testament evidence along with scholarly statements on the matter.

2. *Dependence of Paul's Teaching on Jesus.* It is assumed that Paul knew about different aspects of the historic Jesus. On the human side Paul knew the following things about Jesus. He was a man; sprung from the Israelites, and of the seed of David; born of a woman, made under the law. He had brothers, one of them was called James; carried on a ministry among the Jews; had a group of disciples; instituted the Last Supper; was betrayed, crucified upon a cross, buried, and rose again.[104]

Even if the Gospels in the New Testament had been lost, much of the character of Jesus could be delineated from the letters of Paul. He tells of the meekness and gentleness of Jesus; his obedience and endurance; his grace and love; his holiness and goodness. These and other virtues are listed by Paul in speaking of the kind of person Jesus.[105]

More than this the words of Jesus are echoed in the teaching of Paul.[106] The Fatherhood of God and brotherhood of man finds a prominent place in the mind of Paul whenever he speaks of God as "Father"[107] and of his fellow man above cultural and ceremonial matters.[108] Has anyone ever given an exposition of the Sermon on the Mount so lucid, compact, and comprehensive as found in Paul's ode of I Corinthians, chapter thirteen? Who saw as clearly the meaning of Jesus' teaching that it is not one's diet but one's moral nature that is the source of evil, as did Paul in chapter seven of Romans? Who understood the filial and redemptive consciousness of Jesus so sympathetically as Paul in Romans and Galatians and Philippians? Back of these Pauline expositions there is a close affinity with the teaching of Jesus.[109] On many occasions Paul appealed directly to the behavior of the Master as the chief norm for the disciples.[110] At times when this appeal is not so obvious it is still undeniably present. Behind the words of Paul looms the clear figure of one in whom Paul found the main source of inspiration for living.

The ethical standards of Jesus and Paul show a striking similarity. Benjamin W. Bacon has made the keen observation that Paul was under necessity to delineate the character of Jesus in order to maintain the moral standard of the church from within, and to vindicate it against its detractors from without, and that this stress upon the implications of the Christian faith led him inevitably back to the historic Jesus.[111] The implication is made by Paul of a direct knowledge of the ethical teaching of Jesus.[112] In at least four passages he alludes to "words of the Lord,"[113] and in various other reminiscences in his letters which are even more important or instructive than the references to tradition, Paul clearly indicates that his mind is subject to the mind of Christ. Charles Harold Dodd strongly supports this view in saying:

> It is evident that Paul had not only yielded to the inspiration of Jesus, but had given careful study to the tradition of His teaching, and based his own ethics on a profound understanding of it.[114]

The opposite point of view is expressed by Rudolf Bultmann who claims that Jesus taught no ethics.[115] Whether one chooses to use the word "ethics" or not it remains a fact that Jesus taught moral and spiritual lessons which people have used as guides for daily living and therefore might properly be called ethical.

In both Jesus and Paul ethics is grounded, not in social well-being, or in virtue for the sake of virtue, but in the will of a just, holy, and righteous God. Both of them stress the inner springs of action, made the moving power of love central, emphasized the distinction between the moral and ceremonial, pointed out the inner meaning of the law as against external conformity, and made religion vital by a direct expression of it in all human relationships.[116] In his discussion of the place of Jesus Christ in modern Christianity, John Baillie has stated:

> I believe that every essential root of the religion of Paul and the Apostolic Age is to be found in the mind of Jesus of Nazareth.[117]

There are numerous texts in the New Testament to support this contention. Paul shows that his mind is controlled by the mind of Christ.[118] He tried his best to approximate the life and teaching of Jesus and is in fundamental agreement with the teaching of Jesus and the implications of that teaching for the Christian faith. It is when the teaching of Paul is viewed in its entirety and its inward non-legalistic character understood, that his affinity with the religion of Jesus is clearly seen. Doubtless there were times when Paul was not happy with his own formulation of the Christian teaching. He probably knew that words often fail to convey deeper meanings. But taking all this into consideration, along with the fact that some of his letters have been lost, Paul was sincerely a true representative of Jesus in all fundamental issues.

One other concern which bears upon the relationship of the teaching of Jesus and the teaching of Paul must be considered. Right from the start Jesus called men to follow Him. A number of men in the New Testament gave up their former occupations in answer to this challenge and followed Him. This relationship of Master and disciple was firmly fixed in the Apostolic Church. John Knox discusses the situation in this early day and says that the Church was composed of those who remembered Jesus and the more important emphases of his teaching, but also many of his actual words.[119] However, Knox goes on to say that the Christians remembered Jesus more vividly as a person than any fact about him or his words.[120] It would hardly seem proper after what has been reiterated several times about the teaching of Jesus, to accept the opinion of Knox that it was in the first instance the memory of Jesus himself which formed the basis of life and faith in the Christian community.[121] To be sure the disciples remembered Jesus, but they were likely found themselves saying at times, "Remember what Jesus said when. . . ." This would have been a very natural part of their acquaintance.

Paul was dependent upon Jesus for the universal outreach of the Christian faith. Like his Master, he sought out the company of publicans and sinners, the sick and sinful, the ostracized and forlorn. Joseph Klausner has strongly opposed this universal aspect of Jesus' teaching on the ground that if it were followed it would mean the end of exclusive Judaism.[122] This was, of course, part of the reason Paul encountered opposition in his attempt to preach to the Gentiles. His Jewish friends were no more kindly disposed to him than they had been to Jesus on this point. The prophets had stressed universalism here and there as well as the psalmists, but Jesus put the idea to work as it had not been done before. Paul appropriated and extended the idea.

In summary, these points have been made in this chapter on the historical background of Paul. First, it was shown that Paul must be understood in the light of several national characteristics including the Jewish, Hellenic, and Roman. But the creative religious experience of Paul holds the key in explaining his life and work. Secondly, it has been reasonably established that Paul was a letter writer and not a theologian with a system of doctrine. His primary aim was to preach and teach the Gospel as it had been told to him and as he interpreted it. Thirdly, there are notable differences between Jesus and Paul which are related to their environment and mission, but in fundamental issues Paul is dependent on Jesus' teaching and reveals many striking similarities. It may be affirmed with Deissmann that there is no need of choosing between two religions, that of Jesus or Paul. "What Paul is, he is in Christ."[123] Yet it would be incorrect to assume that Paul was not really concerned about the life and work of Jesus simply because he does not dwell as much on these matters as he does the meaning of Christian faith. It was previously pointed out that Paul sought out those who had been eyewitnesses of Jesus' ministry in order to understand him better. Fourthly, the section on Jesus and Paul is intended also to provide a point of reference for the paradoxical themes of the next chapter. It may well turn out that Paul is much indebted to Jesus in his own use of paradox.

CHAPTER IV

PARADOXICAL THEMES OF PAUL

The Third Chapter of this book has shown that the background elements presumed to have contributed to the life and thought of Paul are included in the Jewish, Hellenic, and Roman heritage and environment. Yet the single factor which seems to have influenced him most was his own creative religious experience. He is dependent upon Jesus for some of his religious and ethical teaching and appears to share an interest in paradox which Jesus had. When viewed as a person subject to influences both from within and from without, influences which relate him as a person to the peculiar circumstance of time and place in which his lot is cast, Paul's paradoxical themes may be seen in a better perspective.

The aim of the present chapter is to analyze some of his themes to learn if possible their relationship and the quality of truth they represent. The examination will be limited to the following themes: sovereignty and freedom, law and grace, living through dying, strength through weakness, foolishness and wisdom.

A. *Sovereignty and Freedom*

In all generations men have been confronted by the problem of the relationship of sovereignty and freedom. Some of the earliest accounts of religious development show that the nature of Deity was inferred from the manifestations of energy in the universe. Whatever produced instant and most intense terror was personified and was considered to be the mightiest of beings.

Hence the first idea of the supreme power was derived from winds, storms, earthquakes or from the sun, moon, and stars. Since this represented many manifestations of power, belief in many gods was a natural consequence. The gods were interpreted by the effects which were produced on the observers by natural phenomena. The belief in many gods, some friendly some hostile, became the accepted procedure. But these gods were themselves dependent on some greater power, called Fate or by some other name. In time this kind of reasoning gave place to another.

As life became socially more complex men began to think of Deity in terms of the institutions to which they were most directly responsible. Sovereignty was thus associated with government and the universe was regarded as a huge kingdom or empire, of which God was the ruler, a king as became the monarch of such a realm. The case of Israel provides such a governmental analogy. At first there was no earthly sovereign. God was considered a supreme being as shown by several Bible passages.[1] His supremacy, for instance, is spoken of in such words as these, "In thy hand are power and might; and in thy hand it is to make great and to give strength to all."[2] Under the pressure of the surrounding kingdoms, the Israelites insisted on having an earthly king. Thereupon rested a division of power with God the King having supreme sovereignty. This idea appears to have continued its influence in the concepts of the New Testament where the kingdom of God is often mentioned. Slowly but surely there was a transition away from this interpretation based on government with a king at its head to the concept of a family with God as Father. Perhaps the thought originated with the consideration of the first human relation of the family involving dependence, authority, responsibility, and action. Millar Burrows suggests that, "The idea of the Fatherhood of God is very ancient, older even than the idea of God as King."[3] The exact time line may be difficult to fix here, but it is certain that the word "Father" appears in several Old Testament texts.[4] The thing to note is Jesus' new and distinctive way of using the term. The new meaning that he put into the word "Father" was that God is the Father as well as the Creator of the individual. Jesus did not limit God by calling Him Father, for he distinctly states that human fathers, evil as they may be, respond with kindness to their children's requests, and that much more will God give His children what is good.[5] In such stories as the Prodigal Son and the Lost Sheep Jesus further illustrated the meaning he attached to God as Father. Andrew Martin Fairbairn made this observation about Jesus:

> In a moment, at His touch, as it were, a new system of the universe arose, founded on Him. God was changed, invested with a richer nature, a more manifold unity, a fatherliness that made His sovereignty as gracious as it was supreme. . . . Man was changed . . . by this contact of Jesus with the thought and the spirit of man.[6]

The sovereignty and Fatherhood of God are not alternatives, and should be considered as complementary affirmations about the nature of God. Speaking of the new conception of Fatherhood in the New Testament which was spoken of earlier, Albert C. Knudson adds this thought.

> Both Jesus and Paul did not break with prophetic teaching but they did transform it into something higher and nobler. For them God remained a God of righteousness and mercy, but these traditional attributes were lifted to an overshadowing sense of the divine sacrificial love.[7]

Paul evidently learned from Jesus, in ways not always made clear, to use the idea of Father as central to the conception of God, and to apply it in many directions in trying to solve problems in human experience and human conduct. In passing it may be noted that Paul used the Aramaic word for Father[8] in the Greek-speaking church which treasured the word most characteristic of Jesus' teaching.

This discussion leads to a closer look at Paul's ideas of sovereignty in connection with his most central and creative contribution to the concept of God as Father.

In the earliest extant letter, namely, First Thessalonians, Paul speaks of the supremacy of "Our God and Father"[9] to whom prayers are offered. As his correspondence develops with the churches Paul becomes intrigued with the concept of sonship.

In his interpretation of the history of revelation and religion in Galatians he thinks of an ordered process from tutelage to sonship, crowned "when the time had fully come" when God made it possible by sending forth his Son that "we might receive adoption as sons."[10] Real sonship thus precedes conscious sonship. This thought is elaborated by William Newton Clarke in this way:

> The divine Fatherhood is the tenderer name for the creatorship. Human beings are held to God's heart as His own, because they are His own, since He gave them their existence. . . . But as in the human race, the Father is aware of the relation long before the children suspect that it exists, and knows why men are His own, long before they begin to understand it.[11]

As Paul reflects upon the matter of sonship he says to the Galatians, "For in Christ Jesus you are all sons of God."[12] In this and other similar texts the thought of God is overshadowed by Paul's immense enthusiasm for Christ. Perhaps it was the purpose of his letters which had something to do with this emphasis. In any case Paul is aware that the provision of his apostolic mission came from God[13] and that the revelation of God through Jesus cannot be considered apart from the truth and life in Jesus. Paul indicates the change of status which takes place in the Christian life. He says, "As long as" the heir "is a child" he is "no better than a slave, though he is owner of all the estate," but "through God you are no longer a slave but a son, and if a son then an heir."[14] Since the main thought in this reference will be taken upon in connection with the letter to the Romans it will be passed by here.

It was part of Paul's own experience which brought about a new concept and changed attitude toward God. It was not that he had accepted an intellectual doctrine of the Fatherhood of God; it was rather that through his faith in Christ he exchanged the consciousness of being a servant for that of being a son of a Divine Father, and in that spirit he says, "For all who are led by the Spirit of God are sons of God. . . . When we cry, 'Abba, Father!' it is the Spirit himself bearing witness with our spirit that we are children of God."[15] Commenting on this statement of Paul, Gustaf Adolf Deissmann has remarked: "As though it were by instinct he cried 'Abba' in his prayers, and 'the Abba' of the praying Jesus resounded as far as Galatia and Rome."[16]

Creation in the Divine image makes it possible for man to rise to a new relationship with God. There is a new spirit of inspiration and motivation which is expressed in a purposive life. Gerald R. Cragg deals with the words "sons" and "heirs" as used by Paul in Romans and states that the meaning goes beyond that of descent.

> The background of Jewish patriarchical society made Paul and his readers familiar with the kind of contrast which Isaac and Ishmael presented — the one was a son, the other only a child of the household. Those who are led by the Spirit (vs. 1-11) have gone beyond the formal membership in an ecclesiastical body to claim the standing — they can appropriate only if they possess insight and understanding and devotion which kinship presupposes.[17]

Although Paul is dealing with the words "son" and "slave" in his letter to the Galatians mentioned earlier, the contrast helps to clarify his general position. God is the Father of all, but not all are His children in the same sense. Some are sons, some are slaves. Jesus appears to have made a similar distinction. He said to certain Pharisees who had just claimed their sonship to God, "You are of your father, the devil."[18] They were sons by creation and by right, but they had not claimed their birthright. In the Gospel of John there is a comparable thought, "But to all who received him, who believed in his name, he gave power to become children of God."[19]

At the beginning of the letter to the Colossians Paul states that grace and peace are manifestations of God's Fatherhood.[20] He proceeds to discuss the relationship of Christ to believers, leaving the relationship to the Father in the background, but the latter soon becomes apparent. "Your life is hid with Christ in God."[21] This is a reference not to proximity and inclusion in space, but to fellowship with Christ in communion with God. The believers are "hid in" God by reason of His fatherly love and filial nature. The mediator through whom the believers come to realize the Fatherhood of God is the "beloved Son."[22] Creation and redemption are the terms in Colossians which manifest the idea of Fatherhood.

In the extant Corinthian letters the idea of the Fatherhood of God is overshadowed by practical interests, but it can be shown that Paul's thoughts in these letters are not only compatible with, but can be explained by, the thoughts put forth elsewhere. Take, for example, the quotation from Hosea, "and I will be father to you, and you shall be my sons and daughters, says the Lord Almighty."[23] Again in his attempt to break down group rivalry Paul states, "whether Paul or Apollos or Cephas or the world or life or death or the present or the future, all are yours; and you are Christ's; and Christ is God's."[24] In the last analysis God has power to give the increase and hereby His sovereignty is recognized.

The preceding survey of Paul's letters has shown that a distinctive and creative use was made of the concepts of Fatherhood and Sonship. J. Scott Lidgett once remarked that this relationship was supreme for Paul. Writing with this thought in mind he said:

> The sovereignty of God is transfigured by but is present in His Fatherhood, and His righteousness sets forth the nature of His love, and is the grandest manifestation of it.[25]

This love manifested itself in the grace of God which met Paul while he was yet a sinner. It was a love which was able to sustain and constrain him in his missionary endeavor.

Keeping in mind the filial aspects of the discussion to this point, attention is now directed to a different but related aspect of the subject of sovereignty.

There are four chapters in Romans which merit this consideration. Chapter eight, it should be pointed out, was written from the standpoint of Christian experience. Paul addresses himself to faith and experience. He believes that salvation springs from the unceasing activity of God. In this connection he uses the word ΠΡΟΘΕΟΙΣ to signify the general intention of God to provide a plan of salvation without a direct reference to individuals comprised in the plan. The word foreknowledge ΠΡΟΥΝΩΟΙΣ implies the distinct recognition of the individuals who should believe. Those whom God foreknew he foreordained to become conformed to the image of His Son.[26] In all of his teaching Paul has but one condition of being conformed to the image of Christ and that is faith. Hence the meaning of his expression, "Those he foreknew," would be, those whom he foreknew as persons who would accept his grace in Christ. Not every one responds to God's call so that there is no necessity of salvation simply on the basis of a call. Charles Harold Dodd has put forth this interpretation:

> Paul maintains that God always and in every age is free to deal personally with men. And that our destiny, therefore is not decided by some mechanical force or by Fate but

we are free, responsible beings, able if we will, to hear the call of God and respond to it . . . a real fresh start is possible at any time, where God comes into fresh touch with man.[27]

The response of love is a foreseen acceptance of God's grace. Taken in its context where Paul is encouraging the believers not to be dismayed over the things which befall them, the thought of God's call was a re-assuring reality.[28] In a similar vein Paul wrote to the Philippians, "I am sure that he who began a good work in you will bring it to completion at the day of Jesus Christ."[29]

As Paul moves into chapters nine through eleven in Romans he gives the fullest statement of God's sovereignty. It first appears as though God is so great and powerful that none dare question by a whisper His will. He refuses whom He refuses, and saves whom He saves. Such an interpretation of Paul's thought must be further examined. Paul was confronted with a particular problem regarding the "chosen people" of Israel, the keepers of the Law, who refused the New Covenant, and were therefore rejected. In presenting his argument Paul offers a clue to rabbinical method and teaching. In the Old Testament God is represented as hardening Pharaoh's heart,[30] but the writer goes on to describe Pharaoh as hardening his own heart also.[31] Everything seems to depend on God, "For he says to Moses, 'I will have mercy on whom I have mercy, and I will have compassion on whom I have compassion.'"[32]

Paul perceives that there is a problem involved in this idea of sovereignty and freedom. If it is true that God chooses and rejects a nation, without any regard to its own action, this puts upon God the stigma of being grossly unjust. Paul tried hard to answer this criticism which he apparently knew would be directed against his position. He suggests several answers, none of which really satisfy him.

God had long since planned that the Jews as a nation should

be pushed aside so that some of them, the faithful remnant of whom the prophets spoke, should be saved along with the believing Gentiles.[33] Having said that God so planned the matter, and that He must therefore be right, Paul sees a weakness in his argument. He knows that actually God did not reject the Jews for no other reason than that He so willed it. The Jewish people had only themselves to blame.[34] They were shown God's plan of righteousness through the New Covenant but they refused to accept it in preference to a way of righteousness which had been superseded. It was on this account, and not of any arbitrary will of God, that the Jews were dismissed.

And yet Paul was not satisfied with this reasoning. He states that behind the actions of God if man were able to discern them, he would see a wise and just purpose. In their rejection of God the Jews are responsible for their actions. But this is all temporary, and by their act of rejection, they served a blessing for the whole world. Paul firmly believes that at some future time the Jews will again share in God's favor, they will become in a far larger sense His people. He lets it be known in his letter to the Romans that his work with the Gentiles involves the ultimate welfare of the Jews.

In the final analysis, God rejects nobody but His grace is rejected by both Jews and Gentiles. Paul allows for real human freedom, and even his interpretation of the significance of the rejection of Israel is more in keeping with the conception of an overruling than with a determining providence.

Speaking from the vantage point of Christian faith, Paul strikes a paradox. On the one hand, man is free. On the other hand, he is bound. When Christ captivates a man, paradox as it seems, that man is free. This is the key to Paul's conception of freedom. The "slave of Christ" is the free man, for Christ is the Lord of life "and where the spirit of the Lord is, there is freedom."[35] There are at least two meanings in the word freedom. He speaks of freedom as it has to do with fulfilling the purpose of life which involves a choice, but also freedom as a way of life. Both of these meanings are included in Paul's thought, but the latter is predominant.

Freedom for Paul, as Johannes Weiss put it is "the ability to do what we really wish, and yet also the gift 'to desire that which is pleasing to God.' "[36] In other words, to be free is to be bound by the character of God, to know life as directed by freedom, and to have found the conditions of fulfillment. One of Paul's mightiest expressions of freedom was given in these words: "For he who was called in the Lord as a slave is a freedman of the Lord. Likewise he who was free when called is a slave of Christ."[37] This is to say a slave in relation to Christ is a freedman. Paul is not dealing with the question of human slavery as such, but he recognizes that in his spiritual condition a slave can be set free from the slavery of sin.[38] Likewise the man who was called being free is Christ's slave in that he can no longer do as he likes because he is bound to his spiritual Master and Lord.

By freedom Paul means basically the privilege of being governed by the Spirit of God. Invariably Paul gives limitations within which freedom must be exercised. The freedom he commended was superior to Pharisaic legalism and meant the opposite of antinomianism inasmuch as it was freedom for which "Christ has set us free."[39] This kind of freedom is not to give an opportunity for the flesh, "but through love be servants of one another."[40] The limitation in this instance is the claim of love. This is Paul's antidote for the harmful restrictions of the letter of the law and dangers of freedom from law: love, expressed in mutual service. This thought is amplified in the following quotation:

> Having urgently dissuaded the Gentiles who were formerly enslaved to gods that are not really gods from being enslaved to law . . . he now, perhaps with intentional paradox, bids them serve one another, yet clearly not in the sense of subjection to the will, but of voluntary devotion to the welfare, of one another.[41]

110

This is to be a continuous attitude and activity for the Christian. In I Corinthians Paul states his own commitment: "For though I am free from all men, I have made myself a slave to all, that I might win the more."[42] He voluntarily submits himself to great curtailments in order to win men for Christ. He tries to find something in men with which to identify himself thereby hoping to make gains for his Master. Thus he becomes in a sense a free slave. To be truly free therefore, is not to be emancipated from all authority, to be one's own master: it is rather to be subject to God through Christ.[43] The ancient error is sometimes repeated by those who think of freedom as consisting in emancipation from all ties. Walter Lippmann once presented a devastating word-picture of those "free" people who insist on throwing off all restraints and should therefore be extremely happy, if their position is correct.[44] Yet life has shown that they are not happy, serene, and composed. Externally they may appear to be free, yet internally they are slaves. The illustration Jesus gave of the prodigal son clearly demonstrates how real freedom comes through complete surrender to the will of God in servant form. Jesus himself has shown the meaning of freedom in his life and work in the servant form of expression. It may well be that Paul understood this kind of ministry and thus appealed to his hearers to be servants of one another. He states, "We who are strong ought to bear with the failings of the weak, and not to please ourselves."[45] Social responsibility is an essential part of Christian living. John W. Oman has made note of two possible choices regarding the use of life in this world.

Either God so directs the world that it serves only material ends, and then the way to use it is efficient direction of our energies to self-interest; or He has made it to serve spiritual ends, and then the way to use it is by utter devotion to His purpose. . . . If one is right, the other is wrong; and there is no middle way.[46]

111

It goes without saying which of these choices was accepted by Paul.

In a crucial matter which involved the exercise of freedom in religion, Paul gives these emphatic words in the Galatian letter. "For in Christ Jesus neither circumcision nor uncircumcision is of any avail, but faith working through love."[47] Commenting on this text, Ernest DeWitt Burton has remarked that for "the disclosure of the apostle's fundamental idea of the nature of religion, there is no more important sentence in the whole epistle, if, indeed, in any of Paul's epistles."[48] The words $O\dot{v}\tau\epsilon\pi\epsilon\rho\iota\tau o\mu\eta$ . . . $o\dot{v}\tau\epsilon$ $\dot{\alpha}\kappa\rho o\beta v\sigma\tau\dot{\iota}a$ imply that Paul is not only opposed to the Jewish requirement that everyone who would obey the Law must be circumcised, but that he also repudiates every conception of religion which makes physical condition of any kind essential to it. Paul recognizes the fact that if the Galatians accept the Jewish rite as religiously necessary they are bound to keep the whole law. He states, "You are severed from Christ, you who would be justified by the law; you have fallen away from grace."[49] Paul could easily have made the same statement about uncircumcision if he had been addressing men who were inclined to adopt this as essential to religion. As a matter of fact Paul does say to the Corinthians:

> Was any one at the time of his call already circumcised? Let him not seek to remove the mark of circumcision. Was any one at the time of his call uncircumcised? Let him not seek circumcision. For neither circumcision counts for anything nor uncircumcision, but keeping the commandments of God.[50]

The point which Paul is making here is that a physical rite or some other physical condition is not essential to the salvation he has in mind. "Faith is for Paul, in its distinctively Christian expression, a committal of one's self to Christ, issuing in a vital fellowship with him, by which Christ becomes the controlling force in the moral life of the believer."[51] This is Paul's answer to those who would try to claim that freedom from the Law leaves life without moral guidance. Moreover, freedom in the Christian faith lies in keeping the commandments. The commandments can be summed up, as both Jesus and Paul did, in terms of love to God and one's neighbor.

William Adams Brown has shown how Paul resolved the paradox of law and freedom. The solution lies in Paul's own experience. "He faced the problem of adjusting his new insight to the accepted standards of society, that is, the offer of free salvation to anyone who would accept God's free gift through faith in the living Christ."[52] Some of Paul's expressions may reveal how he arrived at this position. In the Galatian letter, for instance, he interprets his new found faith in freedom as sonship, as release, as endowment, and as achievement. He is called to be "no longer a slave but a son."[53] Raymond T. Stamm has called this phrase "Paul's proclamation of emancipation."[54] In his experience with the law Paul had come to know the meaning of having the shackles of slavery released.[55] It meant moving from that which the Law could not satisfy to a new understanding of righteousness in Christ. Paul's slavery consisted of several different kinds. He was mentally enslaved as a Pharisee believing that tradition and law was the only true way of salvation. He was morally enslaved as a persecutor of the Christians. Socially he was enslaved by the customs and beliefs of his own and other ages. Spiritually he was a slave to law as obtaining righteousness until he became a slave to God by enlightened choice. Freedom, as already noted, also had the meaning of an endowment for Paul. "God sent forth his Son . . . so that we might receive adoption as sons. . . . So through God you are no longer a slave but a son, and if a son then an heir."[56] Freedom is a gift to be used. It is in such fashion that Paul is able to say, "I can do all things in him who strengthens me."[57] In yet another sense freedom is an achievement for those, including Paul, who will not give up their freedom also meant for Paul to be released from the slavery of son

113

to "have become slaves of righteousness," or "slaves of God."[59] Those who are in a right relation to God through His forgiveness find that "there is freedom."[60] In these several ways Paul presents his thoughts of freedom under the sovereignty of the heavenly Father.

The freedom of man has great possibilities, but it has also proved to be a liability. Man has been in active rebellion against God's will as sovereign over his life. In the language of the Bible this is sin. Sin involves a strange paradoxical combination — it attracts and repels. Man, although a sinner, remains God's creature. Paul sees sin as disobedience to God.[61] He constantly reminds his hearers not to continue in sin, not to sin against the weak.[62] He speaks of Christ dying "for our sins."[63] Sin is also an inner attitude of mind and spirit.[64] Sin often conquers the best efforts of those who try to overcome it. Sin unless it is overcome results in decay and ruin of the nobler nature of man which Paul calls death. In Romans he states that "sin reigned in death "[65] and again "the wages of sin is death."[66] There is a law of sin in the flesh which prevents man from doing the right. The law can only show what sin is, and in so doing it gives further incitement to sin.[67] In addition to these concepts Paul seems to regard sin as an influence or power external to man. What is the nature of this power? Charles A. Anderson Scott gives this summary answer, saying that some scholars have insisted that sin for Paul is "something external and objective," a "personified external Force." "And conversely," it is claimed, "we do not find any indication of sin (in the singular) being conceived of as individual and personal."[68]

In keeping with Jewish monotheism, Paul does not deny the possible existence of superhuman beings, but he insists on the supremacy of God. He tells of all sorts of angels and demons and spiritual powers but it is not clear whether he ascribed to them a personal nature. [69] Whether or not he ascribed real existence to the gods of other lands is not clear. In one passage he refers to them as nothing at all[70] while in another he identifies

114

them with demons.[71] In either case, whether they had real existence or not, they were subject to God as all demons were, including Satan, "the god of this world."[72] God is supreme over angels, demons, and spiritual powers.

One other aspect of this discussion on freedom and sin is lifted up by Reinhold Niebuhr in the assertion that the Christian doctrine of sin presents the seemingly absurd position that man sins inevitably and by a fateful necessity, but that man is nevertheless held responsible for actions which are prompted by an ineluctable fate. He contends as follows:

> The explicit scriptural foundation for the doctrine is given in Pauline teaching. On the one hand Paul insists that man's sinful glorification of himself is without excuse. 'So that they are without excuse because that, when they knew God, they glorified Him not as God.' And on the other hand he regards sin as an inevitable defeat, involved in, or derived from, the sin of the first man. 'Wherefore as by one man sin entered into the world and death by sin and so death passed upon all men for that all have sinned.'[73]

The two texts which are cited by Niebuhr lend a different meaning when they are seen in their separate contexts. In the first instance Paul is making the point that God has given man sufficient knowledge to know his Creator. God did not design that man should sin but He did design that if man sinned he should be without excuse. Man has sinned by suppressing the truth and by the futility of his own thinking claiming to be wise where he is actually foolish.

In regard to the sin of the first man it may be shown by comparison that Paul might have reflected upon the usual rabbinical doctrine. Henry St. John Thackeray has explained the view of the Rabbis in these words:

> Though death since Adam reigns generally throughout the

the world, yet it only gains power over the individual on account of his own sin.[74]

Whatever may have been in the mind of Paul concerning Adam the text does not actually say that sin was transmitted through the first man to other men.[75] Paul may simply be applying an idea which was current among the Jews, namely, that Adam had an evil heart and sinned, so do all his descendants.[76] William David Davies has called attention to the double assertion of the inevitability and responsibility of sin as an accentuation of Rabbinic doctrine.[77] Sin is inevitable to the extent that man in his freedom chooses to rebel against the will of God.

At best the nature of man's freedom is complicated. Man is free to choose the form of his obedience, but he never is completely free to exercise his freedom. Sin has a tendency to weaken the good man seeks to do. Sin delights in the good man leaves undone. Man is not in complete control over all the influences that effect his life. He is limited by physical laws in the realm of Nature. In his social life he is limited by parentage, native talent, social advantages, education or lack of it. Psychologically there are limitations in such things as inner pulls, complexes, inhibitions, prejudices, fears, phobias, superego, past choices, lack of purpose. Spiritually man is limited by his neglect of communion with God, the cultivation of his soul, and all things which hinder his relation to God. Yet in spite of his limitations man can and does exercise his freedom under the sovereignty of God.

Paul significantly points out that the Divine sovereignty is directed toward the salvation of men. He thinks of God as a moral being. Having made things as they are in creation, He assumes the responsibility for what He has made. His sovereignty will be victorious in the end. It cannot be admitted that the view of Paul is that of determinism. Such a view would make nonsense of his general moral and religious position. He allows for human freedom to accept or reject the grace of God.

In their interpretation of Romans with special reference to

chapter eight, William Sanday and Arthur C. Headlam have made this observation.

> There can be no question that St. Paul fully recognizes the freedom of the human will. The large part which exhortation plays in his letters is conclusive proof of this. But whatever the extent of human freedom there must be behind it the Divine Sovereignty. It is the practice of St. Paul to state alternately the one and the other without attempting an exact delimitation between them. And what he has not done we are not likely to succeed in doing.[78]

Writing some years later Arthur C. Headlam made this further observation that free will and sovereignty do not present an insoluble antinomy. He states his view in this manner:

> The two great truths of universal law and of free will are in fact not antagonistic but are two different aspects of the same problem. If you look at my actions from the point of view of science, you are able to describe the manner in which I must inevitably do things, but if you look at my actions from the side of my own experience you find that I am an originating cause.[79]

There is always a great temptation to draw speculative inferences from what Paul says. It cannot be stressed too often that questions of a philosophical nature which are raised today about such matters as son and sovereignty, predestination and freedom requiring distinctions between what God does without human effort or agency and those actions conditioned by the choice and character of man, were not raised in a philosophical manner by Paul. Yet in some manner perhaps impossible for man to formulate adequately the sovereignty of God must not only be compatible with, but must ever imply the freedom of man.

Life finds its basic meaning in relationship to God. This relationship in its most creative aspect is a relationship of love. Jesus has demonstrated through his life and teaching that loyal and loving sonship to God is a human possibility. It is not enough to recognize the intellectual aspects of this matter of relationship. According to the Scriptures it was not God's intention at Creation to leave men to themselves. If the relationship of love is to have personal meaning men must learn to make an obedient response to the help and grace of God. This was Jesus' secret. He lived by the help and grace of God. He became aware of new dimensions of love and obedience. There were human capacities for goodness which he was certain could be developed in the interrelatedness of love between God and man, and between men as "neighbors."

Paul had a deep knowledge and internalized experience of this cardinal point, namely, the sovereignty in love. He recognized that contact with God meant the possibility that all human experience might be lifted to new levels of peace and power. God is the key to a new world of significance and purposeful living. If man does not love God and his neighbors, and work to increase that love and enable it to prevail on earth, it matters little how much he knows about God.

Although the relationship of sovereignty and freedom is not worked out by Paul in a philosophical manner, there are several levels of contact between God and man which Paul recognized such as the natural and spiritual. The most outstanding of these contacts is, of course, the life relationship which is expressed by God's sovereignty in love and in man's freedom by choice.

In the remaining paradoxical themes of Paul to be covered in this chapter further light will be cast on the meaning and significance of the preceding discussion on the first theme. Attention will now be directed to the second theme.

B. *Law and Grace*

In reading Paul's New Testament letters it soon becomes

evident that his meaning and use of the word "law" is not the same at all times and at all places. This fact should be borne in mind along with another, namely, that his subject matter in respect to "law" is not the same in each case.

Many things have been said and written concerning Paul's treatment of the Law. Albert Schweitzer speaks of "The peculiarly inconsistent attitude of the Apostle to the law."[80] James W. Parkes has charged Paul with inconsistency bordering on dishonesty in his use of the Law.[81] D. William Wrede in a section of his book on "Gesetz und Glaube" has used the term "rätselfhaft" in connection with Paul's ideas of the Law.[82] That is to say in translation Paul's view of the Law is enigmatical, problematic, unintelligible or mysterious. At first sight Paul seems to be strangely inconsistent in his attitude toward the Law. For instance, he ascribes Divine authority to the Law and himself observes the Law in its external ritual.[83] At one point he states, "The law is holy, and the commandment is holy and just and good."[84] Paul recognizes the value of the Law. The Legislations are among the privileges of Israel.[85] The Hebrews are favored because they "are instructed in the law."[86] The Law has acted as custodian to bring men to Christ.[87] At this level of his religious development Paul saw a unity in the Law, one could not choose part, and reject part, obey some and ignore the rest.[88] However this conception of the Law did not keep him from stressing certain elements of the Law as for example, "the whole law is fulfilled in one word, 'You shall love your neighbor as yourself.' "[89] On another level Paul is opposed to the Law. He speaks of it as "a yoke of slavery," something from which he needed to be delivered.[90] The Law came "to increase the trespass."[91] He does not say that the Law came to increase "sin" but to increase trespass. Yet in another place it is "the Law that leads to sin and death."[92] Again he says, "that no man is justified before God by the law, men are under "the curse of the law."[93]

On the basis of such alternate words of praise and blame it is not difficult to see how Paul may be charged with inconsistency.

Nor would it be surprising to hear the charge of self-contradiction if these two texts were brought together. "Christ is the end of the law"[94] and "Do we then overthrow the law by this faith? By no means! on the contrary, we uphold the law".[95] It is obvious that two such statements could mean that either there is an outright contradiction or that there is a difference in Paul's meaning of the word "Law".

It will be useful at this juncture to examine such letters as Corinthians, Galatians, and Romans to see what usage Paul makes of the term "Law". In I Corinthians he makes his defense for preaching the gospel and among other things makes this significant statement:

> To the Jews I became as a Jew, in order to win Jews; to those under the law I became as one under the law — though not being myself under the law — that I might win those under the law. To those outside the law I became as one outside the law — not being without law toward God but under the law of Christ — that I might win those outside the law.[96]

Hans Lietzmann has remarked that Paul followed the example of Jesus in pressing from the letter to the spirit. Understanding Paul in this way can lead to an understanding of his meaning when he occasionally speaks of the "fulfilling of the Law" by those who are followers of the Christian Way.[97] Lietzmann offers this word of explanation:

> It was no contradiction of his general position that, on occasion, he undertook a vow according to Jewish rites . . . subjected himself to the prescriptions of the ceremonial law . . . prepared . . . to carry out a ceremonial vow in order to supply mistrustful brethren with a proof of his faithfulness to the Law . . . in accordance with his fundamental missionary principle.[98]

120

It was not an uncommon thing in Judaism to accommodate one-self to some other form of religion in order to make a proselyte. Paul may have employed this missionary method which was known to him.

In regard to the passage cited before the above quotation, Kaufmann Kohler gives this interpretation of Paul's view of the Law:

> The original attitude of Paul to the Law was accordingly not that of opposition as represented in Romans and especially in Galatians, (later interpolations do so) but that of a claimed transcendency.[99]

The point in the present discussion is not whether Paul's letters were subjected to "interpolations" or whether he originally held a transcendent view of the Law. It is obvious even in the statement by Kohler that Paul underwent a change in his point of view on the Law. The issues which are dealt with respecting the Law in Romans and Galatians leave no doubt that Paul placed faith first in religion.

The Law was profoundly venerated by the Jews who subscribed to it. It was believed that the Law served as "an antiseptic" for the "evil impulse"; its words "are compared to a medicine that preserves life"; one may overcome evil by "immersing himself in the study of the Law".[100] Yet in spite of serious attempts to believe in the Law, Paul came to the conviction that it presented an obstacle to faith in Jesus Christ. Paul was no Marcionite, rejecting the Old Testament. In his mind the Law served several useful purposes. He speaks of it as a custodian, a tutor, having charge of the world in its childhood. Unless the attempt is made to understand Paul's own experience with the Law there is little chance to understand such a reference. It must be viewed through his controversy with the Judaizing Christians.[101] This was a creative conflict through which Paul gained some new perspectives. These perspectives

121

included a view of God as a God of grace, a fresh understanding of divine revelation in personal terms, a positive sense of moral power.

In Galatians the Judaizers insisted that Christians must become Jews according to certain customs and practices. They wanted the Law restored[102] and regarded as God's chief revelation and as the way of obtaining righteousness. This argument filled Paul with indignation. In his defense he describes the condition of the Jewish Christians before their conversion as a state of "slaves to the elemental spirits of the universe," and their present disposition to return to the observance of the Law as returning to "the weak and beggarly elemental spirits, whose slaves you want to be once more."[103]

In speaking of the importance of this particular controversy, William Morgan has stated that Paul "more clearly than any of his contemporaries . . . understood how far-reaching were the principles involved and how big the issues at stake."[104] Johannes Weiss observed that the situation was of "far more significance than merely a literary event."[105] Without Paul's defense, writes James Moffatt, "Christianity may not have reached us at all."[106]

In urging the contrast between the Law and the Gospel, Paul maintains, both have a respected position. "Is the law then against the promise of God? Certainly not; for if a law had been given which could make alive, then righteousness would indeed be by the law."[107] The true relation of the Law to the Gospel is that of a subordinate position and preparatory responsibility. The Gospel exists because Christ lived and died for all men. Paul may well have said in Greek, ἐγὼ γὰρ διὰ νόμου νόμῳ ἀπέθανον ἵνα θεῷ ζήσω. "For I through the law died to the law, that I might live to God."[108] The Law in Judaism had proved itself powerless to do this very thing, to "make alive" that is to create within men the life which is akin to the life of God. It was not that Judaism had nothing to say on the inwardness of religion. The teaching of the prophets and Jesus amply illustrate this point. The problem lies elsewhere. In Judaism as elsewhere the inwardness of religion was recognized in theory, but in practice it was largely ignored. The proper motivation was lacking.

Some of Paul's expressions have been interpreted to mean that Christ delivered all men from Mosaic Law, as for example these words, "Christ redeemed us from the curse of the Law."[109] Now it would hardly seem natural for Paul to mean that Christ delivered from the curse of the Mosaic Law those who had never lived under that Law. It is therefore a mistake to interpret his language here as though it were universal when it applies to the specific situation at hand. That the Gentiles, or the great mass of mankind, were never bound by the Mosaic Law, is one of Paul's chief contentions. Yet in Romans it is noted that while the Gentiles did not literally know the Mosaic Law, they did have what the law requires. It "is written on their hearts."[110] Paul aimed to go behind the Law to a new kind of understanding of life. Christ had redeemed men "That upon the Gentiles might come the blessing of Abraham in Christ Jesus, that we might receive the promise of the Spirit through faith."[111] Long before Moses and the Law, God had accepted Abraham on the grounds of simple faith. The Law was a subsequent matter, coming in four hundred thirty years after the convenant with Abraham which he accepted in faith. The Law by no means annuls "a covenant previously ratified by God, so as to make the promise void. For if the inheritance is by law, it is no longer by promise; but God gave it to Abraham by a promise."[112] This is a way of saying that the Law is in a subordinate position to the promise.

In the letter to the Romans the basic issue was not that of the Judaisers as it was in Galatians. Rather it was a concern about the relation of the law to the gospel and Paul discusses this subject for the purpose of edification and instruction. Again as in Galatians he offers alternating contrasts of praise and blame in dealing with the "Law." He speaks of the Law as having come to an end, yet the Law continues to be useful.[113] He objected strenuously to the Law as a system of external requirements or legislation by which "righteousness" was to be secured by merit, but he upheld the content of the Law in terms of Divine requirement bearing on the characters and conduct of men. He clearly took exception to religion as a system of rules which often become a substitute for the higher inward spiritual life. He once said on this point, "He is not a real Jew who is one outwardly. . . . He is a Jew who is one inwardly."[114]

From this line of reasoning Paul was led to an examination of the history of the Law. He came to the idea that the Law had been interpolated between the time of Abraham and the time of Christ. The Law had served a useful purpose but it had failed to do what it was intended to accomplish. The codified rules instead of symbolizing a deeper level of meaning had been accepted generally as an end in themselves. Paul knew by experience what a dead weight tradition can be and like Jesus and Jeremiah he saw that the law was never really fulfilled until it was graven on the tables of the heart.

It puzzled Paul how the Law which was inspired of God actually had become detrimental or sinful. In his argument to show that the Law quickens the consciousness of sin, he guards against saying that this fact is due to any real moral defect in the law itself. "What then shall we say? That the law is sin? By no means! . . . . Did that which is good, then, bring death to me? By no means! It was sin, working death in me through what is good. . . ."[115] The law had brought the knowledge of sin and death,[116] "the very commandment which promised life proved to be death"[117] to Paul. This was Paul's way of saying that the Law had in fact mocked men by setting itself up as the way of attaining the righteousness which God required. Paul found that the prohibitions of the Law were actually awakening in him sinful suggestions and thus enticed him to do evil.[118] The Law stirred up impulses and aroused desires but it could not provide the moral and spiritual power to keep one from sinning. But Christ does for men "what the law could not do."[119]

124

When the constraint in the commandment is consciously recognized sin is "provoked to opposition . . . when sin thus becomes conscious defiance, it incurs guilt and deserves punishment."[120] The Law brings wrath[121] and the judgment of sin. L. Harold DeWolf has cited one of Paul's illustrations, having to do with one particular prohibition which has a bearing on the present discussion. He makes the following statement:

> Before a man knows that it is immoral to covet, he may lustily seek to gain his neighbor's property for the sake of the property only. But after he has learned that God forbids covetousness his coveting partakes also of an angry, willful animus. Instead of a formally innocent, though materially evil, desire for a good thing — the property — it is now a formally sinful desire for an evil thing — success in getting what he knows he has no right to take from his neighbor and self-assertive defiance of God's law. Knowledge of the law has thus made possible willful sin and become the means by which the former material sin brought the unhappy man into open rebellion against God.[122]

In this situation Paul saw the world of law which provoked disobedience and ended in punishment, but he also saw the world of grace to be confirmed in man's response of faith.

Paul is sometimes severely criticized for his so-called negative interpretation of the Law by those who claim that his treatment, especially in regard to sin, does not do justice to the positive function of the Law as a guide to good conduct. Otto Pfleiderer, for instance, has argued that Paul's view of law in its relation to sin stands in contradiction to the historic purpose of the system which Jews universally recognized, namely, to restrain transgressions and entice to righteous conduct. Pfleiderer affirms that the law itself never recognized sin in Paul's terms of multiplying transgressions, and that there is no basis in the Old Testament for such a negative idea.[123] Perhaps some of the difficulty here lies in understanding what Paul meant when he said that the Law came "to increase the trespass"[124] with no mention of sin. As previously pointed out the Law was not in itself sinful, but its prohibitions resulted in sinful acts on the part of man. Actually Paul had many positive things to say concerning the Law and ascribed certain advantages to the Jew for having obtained it to be used in worship and the embodiment of truth.[125] John Knox and W. M. Macgregor have shown convincingly the service which Paul regarded the Law as having performed.[126] It was the things which the Law did not accomplish which brought Paul to realize a "new" righteousness in Christ. Hence he concludes that the chief purpose of the Law was to reveal the sin of men in terms of willful opposition to God and this in turn was to drive them to Christ. In this regard the Law is seen in its negative and preparatory function. What the Law could not do, or better still was not intended to do, God accomplished by sending His Son that "the just requirement of the law might be fulfilled in men who walk not after the flesh, but after the spirit."[127]

A new plane of righteousness had been established with the coming of Jesus. In the Sermon on the Mount he made a clear distinction between a new kind of righteousness and the "righteousness of the scribes and the Pharisees."[128] The difference between what Jesus taught and what the established Jewish doctrine maintained was not the heretical claims against Jesus but rather his ability to arrive at the true meaning and purpose of the Law.[129] He did not come to destroy the Law but to give it its full meaning. Paul, as a faithful Pharisee tried to obtain righteousness through minute observance of the Law. He speaks of this in terms of "a righteousness of my own".[130] It was this motive and application regarding the Law which finally enabled Paul to realize that his effort was hopelessly wrong. He became convinced that God had revealed a higher righteousness through Jesus Christ.[131] Paul probably had some of the doubts or misgivings about the Law which were in the mind of the rich young ruler who came to Jesus knowing that he lacked something. Perhaps Paul knew and endorsed the Pharisees' criticism of Jesus as the friend of sinners and tax gatherers. He may have known Jesus' answer to his critics that he came "not to call the righteous, but sinners."[132] The question which troubled Paul was not so much about his ability to keep the Law as it was about the value of such righteousness through the Law. Jesus, as stated in the beginning of this paragraph, established a new plane of righteousness. The Sermon on the Mount serves as an illustration of this fact. Wilfred Lawrence Knox has made the observation that "Paul would have seen no incompatibility between his own teaching and the thoughts of the Sermon on the Mount as a new Law."[133] According to Paul the gospel is "the law of the Spirit of life in Christ Jesus."[134] Men must "become the righteousness of God" be "conformed to the image of his Son."[135] It is here that Joseph Klausner[136] misses the key point of Paul's Christian experience, namely, that of seeking righteousness in relation to Christ. Auguste Sabatier has pointed out that God bestows upon man His righteousness in the very act of redeeming him. The following quotation gives a clear picture of Sabatier's position:

> The δικαιοσύνη θεοῦ is righteousness of which God is the author, and which He gives freely, in contrast to the righteousness which man seeks by his own efforts ἰδία δικαιοσύνη. This righteousness exists already in God as an attribute and active force; it is transferred to man, and realized in him by action of Divine grace. . . . While the word χάρις indicates the act of love by which God saves man, the phrase δικαιοσύνη θεοῦ simply defines the nature and moral quality of this Divine act.[137]

In the light of what has been said thus far it becomes necessary to take a closer look at Paul's most favorite word "grace." It has been said by Sabatier after a careful study of this term that

No other word occurs oftener in Paul's writing. It designates the love of God in action, as it intervenes definitely and directly in the destinies of humanity in order to raise it.[138]

Charles A. Anderson Scott has amplified and illuminated this idea. He states that "Grace is love in motion; love making its arrival in the experience of men."[139] Paul refers "to the grace given us,"[140] and to "grace in which we stand"[141] in regard to God's forgiving goodness penetrating the human heart and taking possession of the will.

There are different significations of the word "grace" in the experience of man in respect to particular needs and circumstances, but it is highly improbable that Paul had in mind different kinds of grace. William Manson, after making a study of grace in the New Testament, found that Paul gave the word a new connotation. Religion rests on God's self-giving. It is His will to free man from sin and to endow man with a higher life. Paul uses the word grace for the Divine influence in the heart of man whether raising him to a new status, conferring special gifts, or inspiring to new activity. It is a dynamic and not a material entity which Paul has in mind. He was asked to discuss grace-gifts, but he chose to stress the Spirit that gave and faith whereby man could accept what was offered.[142]

This analysis may be useful in trying to make a further study of the relationship of law and grace as Paul comprehends it in his letters.

It is clear that Paul the Pharisee believed that the supreme and exclusive indication of God's favor to Israel was through the gifts of the Law which revealed the knowledge and the will of God. Seen in this light it is not hard to understand the problem the early Christians had respecting the Law. The situation is well stated by Otto Pfleiderer:

The offense caused to the Jewish Christians by the actual course of events was based on the impression which had

long been deeply rooted in the Jewish mind, that the Chosen
People, in virtue of their legal covenant, could make good
a documentary claim to hold the prerogative in the kingdom
of Christ. In view of this self-righteous claim, Paul reminds
them of the truth which was fundamental in his own as
in every true religious life — of the unconditional dependence
of man on the free grace of God, with whom none may
litigate and bargain, since He owes no man anything.[143]

Paul the Christian made the shattering discovery that the good
toward which he was moving already included God's *ἔλεος*
mercy which accepts man while he is yet a sinner. In other
words Paul experienced God's *χάρις* grace as the energy
or action of love reaching out to the undeserving. The motive
of salvation as Paul sees it is love. "God shows his love to us."[144]

In order to understand clearly the meaning Paul attached
to the word grace, several passages in his letters must now be
examined. In I Corinthians he writes, "I worked harder than
any of them, though it was not I, but the grace of God which
is with me."[145] The reader of such a text needs only to recall
the miles Paul traveled, the letters he sent, the opposition he
faced, in order to realize that Paul met life with utmost energy
and determination. Yet no sooner does the thought cross his
mind that he has done it all than he adds God was doing it all.
In some way these two things go together in the Christian life.
The paradox involved in the above text has been given this
interpretation by Donald M. Baillie who states:

> Its essence lies in the conviction which a Christian man
> possesses, that every good thing in him, every good thing he
> does, is somehow not wrought by himself but by God. This
> is a highly paradoxical conviction, for in ascribing all to
> God it does not abrogate human personality nor disclaim
> personal responsibility. Never is human action more truly
> and fully personal, never does the agent feel more per-

fectly free, than in those moments of which he can say as
a Christian that whatever good was in them was not his
but God's.[146]

Although Paul makes no attempt to delineate God's action from
his own, he may well have realized that he could not enter into
any mutually personal relationship with God unless God was
at one and the same time entering into relations with him which
were both one-sidedly and mutually personal. Elsewhere Paul
makes the remark, "By the grace of God I am what I am,
and his grace toward me was not in vain.[147] Again he states
with reference to the ministry of reconciliation through Christ,
"Working together with him, then, we beseech you not to accept the grace of God in vain."[148]

A related but different paradox of grace than the one cited
from I Corinthians may be seen in Paul's great statement of
fact in II Corinthians given in these words:

> All this is from God, who through Christ reconciled us
> to himself and gave us the ministry of reconciliation; that
> is, God was in Christ reconciling the world to himself, not
> counting their trespass against them, and entrusting to us
> the message of reconciliation.[149]

The message here concerns the "new creation" which was instituted with the coming of Christ. Donald M. Baillie has chosen
to call the paradox of the incarnation the supreme paradox.
"The mistake," he believes is not to assert it in respect to "God
in Christ" but rather "to miss the paradox everywhere else."[150]
An elaboration of this thought appears in an interpretation of the
incarnation by William Ralph Inge. He suggests that the incarnation be thought of in this manner:

> God is love, and so He gives Himself entirely to us, primarily
> in order to perfect the work in us which He began when

He created us in His image, but also, since we have sinned, to redeem us from sin and its consequences. There is thus a potential, inchoate incarnation in ourselves, made possible by the objective incarnation in Christ, who willed to be the first-born among many brethren.[151]

Paul sees in the paradox of the incarnation a reconciliation indirectly evoked by giving a clear demonstration for the faith that God is love. Through faith Paul speaks words such as these, "the love of Christ controls us, because we are convinced that one has died for all; therefore all died. And he died for all, that those who live might live no longer for themselves but for him who for their sake died and was raised.[152] Paul believed in the inexhaustible love of God who spared not His Son that He might reconcile the world to Himself. He thus found a new concept of God, a new attitude toward God. James Moffatt expresses the sentiment of Paul in this general conclusion:

> The New Testament begins and ends with the conviction that those who experience the love of God possess something which is for themselves far more than food and raiment, and which therefore, as experience and belief, must be passed on to others. This is the supreme service, no matter what other charities may be bestowed.[153]

Paul could not long look at Jesus without seeing the Cross nor could he talk long without mention of the Cross. One of his paradoxical statements contains these words, "We preach Christ crucified, a stumbling-block to Jews and folly to Gentiles, but to those who are called, both Jews and Greeks, Christ the power of God and the wisdom of God."[154] This is a doctrinal paradox according to Ernest F. Scott, "the greatest paradox of Christianity."[155] L. Harold DeWolf remarks, "The paradox is to Paul not only doctrinal. It is also of common experience in the Christian community."[156] Evidence of this appears in Paul's own words:

> We are treated as impostors, and yet are true; as unknown, and yet well known; as dying, and behold we live; as punished, and yet not killed; as sorrowful, yet always rejoicing; as poor, yet making many rich; as having nothing, and yet possessing everything.[157]

The "stumbling-block" to which Paul refers may well have brought to his mind that the Cross once caused him great difficulty. He had to undergo a change of mind and heart before the crucified Christ became the burden of the Gospel message. God's grace is made manifest through the Cross in wisdom and power. That which seemed to stand as a great obstacle became the corner-stone of the edifice of faith.

Another of Paul's striking paradoxical remarks is found in his Philippian letter. He seems to reproduce in new terms what Jesus said about the kingdom of God in such statements as these, "it is your Father's good pleasure to give you the kingdom"[158] and "But seek first his kingdom and his righteousness, and all these things shall be yours as well."[159] Paul is concerned about the grace of God in relation to man's response. He gives his thoughts to the Philippians in this fashion:

> Therefore, my beloved, as you have always obeyed, so now, not only as in my presence but much more in my absence, work out your own salvation with fear and trembling; for God is at work in you, both to will and to work for his good pleasure.[160]

These words have been interpreted in several ways. Joseph Barber Lightfoot offers this view with Paul saying: "It is God working in you from first to last: God that inspires the earliest impulse, and God that directs the final achievement: for such is His good pleasure."[161] Krister Stendahl cites P. Ewald's interpretation which indicates incisively that the contrast Paul intends to make here is between his own supervising activity and God's work. The context shows Paul paying tribute to those who were zealous in faith and obedience while he was present with them. Now that he is about ready to depart he assures his readers that God will be with them in his stead, and that is the important matter.[162] Their obedience was not to Paul, but to God as exemplified in Christ.[163] Paul was anxious that "every one be fully convinced in his own mind."[164] He believed that "every sound tree bears good fruit."[165] Each person is responsible to the Lord.[166] Such was the personal faith of Paul and such was his own experience. John Burnaby has put forth the interesting thought that "Wherever we find this combination of faith, complete reliance upon the grace of God, with eager unwearying activity in His presence, we have the authentic note of New Testament Christianity."[167]

In his teaching Paul found it necessary to reconcile the assurance of Divine grace with the demand that Christians must develop moral courage and maintain moral vigor. He had taught that "where sin abounded, grace abounded all the more."[168] Some apparently took this to mean that they were at liberty to do evil, and let God's grace provide the way out. Paul met his hearers by asking some pointed questions. "What shall we say then? Are we to continue in sin that grace may abound? By no means! How can we who died to sin still live in it?"[169] In fact, one of the most valuable and permanent aspects of Paul's letters is his insistence that the followers of Christ must not tolerate moral laxity and that the Spirit must yield worthy fruits.[170] In the letter to the Galatians he offers these words of encouragement, "let us not grow weary in well-doing, for in due season we shall reap, if we do not lose heart."[171] Again he urges his hearers to live and walk in "newness of life."[172] Paul denies that anyone is compelled to sin, and warns of the need of constant vigilance, "let anyone who thinks that he stands take heed lest he fall."[173] Such passages as the foregoing are unmistakable evidence of Paul's sense of moral responsibility even though he makes frequent reference to the grace of God. Peter A. Bertocci makes note of the fact that God's grace "does not annul the human will as agency."[174]

Paul makes the positive assertion in his letter to the Romans, "We know that in everything God works for good with those who love him, who are called according to his purpose."[175] He is not saying that everything in life is good, for instance, famine and war, but rather that God does not work in opposition to those who love him. The higher the aim is in life the more difficult it may be to attain the goal yet there is encouragement for God works "with those who love him". No finer words could express this idea than Paul's own: "I press on toward the goal for the prize of the upward call of God in Christ Jesus."[176] Speaking of Paul's previous text above, John W. Oman has remarked:

> He knows that he is making the most unlikely affirmation, about the most unlikely people, and for the most unlikely reasons. But he also knows that what he calls reconciliation turns it from an incredible paradox into the most triumphant certainty.[177]

God's intention and His purpose was revealed in Jesus' life and work. Out of his own life and thought Paul had come to know that those who were publicans and sinners, were yet included in grace, in God's forgiving love.

Both Jesus and Paul were much concerned over God's purpose of grace. Was it universal in scope? In Paul's day the major portion of the Jewish population did not listen to the glad tidings.[178] Although Paul labored among them at intervals for many years, he had hope of saving some only.[179] Yet he looked for a better day. Israel would be saved.[180] Not, of course, the Jews of all ages, but, as the context requires, the Jews of some unknown future period, after the fullness of the Gentiles should have come in. So far as the Gentiles were concerned only a part accepted the invitation of the gospel. Some who heard the preaching of Paul were perishing.[181] The minds of some were blinded by the god of this world, so the light of the gospel could not dawn upon them.[182]

Yet at some time Paul believed that the gospel would have a wide triumph. The Gentile world would come into the fellowship of Christ.[183] The language here is rhetorical, but Paul anticipates an extension of the gospel which would surpass anything he had seen or known. He thought that the purpose of God's grace was destined to have a wide fulfillment.

In contrast with the narrow Pharisaic teaching of his own day, Paul taught that God is supreme over all the world, and hence his salvation is universal. "Is God the God of Jews only? Is he not also the God of Gentiles also? Yes, of Gentiles also, since God is one. . . ."[184] Paul held that a precedence had been set in God's promise to Abraham.[185] Universal salvation was promised through grace which man may accept by faith. This was the twofold thought which Paul expounded in his letter to the Romans, and this constitutes what he calls his gospel.[186]

Paul not only appealed to the Old Testament but also to his own commission to preach to the Gentiles[187] as evidence of God's purpose of grace as universal. In addition to this Paul's ideas of the character of God, the deepest thought regarding Christ, in terms of love and concern, involves the same universality.[188]

In his comparison of Christ as the last Adam in relation to the entire human race corresponding to the first Adam, Paul stresses the universal note.[189] When Christ died he died for all,[190] and when he rose it was the first born into a spiritual kingdom designed to include all men so far as they believed.[191] Whether Paul believed that all souls would at last enter Christ's kingdom is not altogether clear. In Romans he speaks first only of those who believe in Jesus Christ,[192] but a few verses later the context is not so limited to Christ's relationship to believers.[193] The context seems to have widened from church history to world

135

history including all men. Perhaps Paul intends to say that while salvation through God's grace is made available to all men it is not accepted by all. Paul is certain, however, that God has revealed himself so that men are without ignorance concerning his action.[194]

There is a glimpse of a still greater realization of God's grace. Paul thought of nature as sometime to be delivered from the bondage of decay into the liberty of the glory of children of God.[195] Perhaps he thought of a new earth which should be adapted to spirit as the present one is adapted to the body. He does not elaborate upon his idea in this connection.

Paul holds that when all things are brought into harmony with Christ, then there will have to be a removal of the elements of disorder which infinite grace could not win.[196] All enemies shall have been put down and given over to their fate, far from the face and glory of the Lord.[197] When this is accomplished, all things will be reconciled to God through Christ.[198] In Philippians, Paul represents Christ as receiving honor and acknowledgment from all created beings, and as receiving this because of his death on a cross.[199] At some future age, all things will be summed up in Christ when through the conquering power of his self-sacrifice there shall be realized a cosmic and eternal harmony. This outlook of Paul gives his most comprehensive thought of Christ along with his interpretation of grace. Reinhold Niebuhr arrived at the following conclusion after a study of Paul's position:

A survey of Pauline thought must lead to the conclusion that there is no contradiction in his elaboration of the doctrine of grace. There is, at least, no final contradiction. There is, on the contrary, a profound understanding of the complexities of genuine newness of life in 'love, joy, and peace' for those who have broken with self-love in principle and yet of the possibility of sin even on this new level of righteousness.[200]

136

The last clause above recalls a point of view shared by Jesus and Paul regarding the possibilities of sin. But it is also to be remembered that Jesus preached of forgiveness and love by which sin may be overcome in victorious living. God's help is assured to those who seek His counsel and purpose.

The concern of this section has been an analysis of law and grace. It is now possible to state that the relationship between them is not one of logical contradiction. The evidence points toward different levels of meaning between these two words "law" and "grace" which seem to be opposites. Paul admits that the Law has made its education, moral, and religious contribution to the life of Judaism. But he came to understand another kind of law, namely, a law of faith not based on a system for securing righteousness. He learned by experience that the Law was either inadequate or was never intended to surplant the promise made to Abraham through faith. Paul's purpose was to show that salvation must be accepted through faith in what God has done in Christ. That which the Law was unable to accomplish was made possible on a new level of righteousness revealed in the life and teaching of Jesus Christ. In the Incarnation Paul saw that God was in Christ. Here divine activity and human activity were united in one divine-human life. Here also was a potential incarnation for believers who accepted God's grace and entrusted their lives to Him.

When Paul declares that he will "not be enslaved by anything,"[201] he is giving a real insight into a new dimension of faith. His own experience taught him that slavery to things can be conquered only by slavery to God. He was captured into slavery to Jesus Christ. He calls himself both the "prisoner" and "slave" of Christ. That is to say Paul does not consider himself a slave to anything, but to some One. Here is the *hauptpunkt*, the main point of his faith. On the basis of this relationship he moves into another level which has religious and social significance. He says, "I have made myself a slave to all."[202]

In the Cross of Christ grace is manifested in holy forgiveness which is the greatest moral paradox. Undeserving sinners may come to acknowledge that Christ died for them. The Law awakens the consciousness of sin according to Paul. He found through psychological insight that which the Law was able to disclose but could do nothing to relieve. Paradoxical as it may appear, this is a common experience. Paul found that the command gave an impulse to sin. He also found through faith that the power of deliverance from the sinful impulse was given through Jesus Christ.[203] Whatever the approach man may take Paul held that no man can deliver himself by his own efforts. Man needs the grace of God. The two laws in man's nature operate on different levels. Paul writes, "For the law of the Spirit of life in Christ Jesus has set me free from the law of sin and death."[204]

It may appear at times that Paul ascribes all to the grace of God, yet upon closer examination he does not abrogate human personality nor disdain personal responsibility. This is a paradoxical conviction which is reflected in his moral and social admonitions. God takes the initiative, man makes the response.

The most significant dramatization of the relationship of law and grace may be seen in the Incarnation. Here one finds not two opposites, but two different ways of imparting truth. The Law contains enduring moral content for Paul, but it is through Grace that he enters into new life with Christ. The way of righteousness through the Law is now superseded by faith in a new righteousness revealed in Christ and in the new life of believers.

C. *Living Through Dying*

The subject of physical death is no more popular today than it probably was in the days of Paul. Yet man is mortal and death is inevitable. All efforts to disguise this part of creaturehood are of no avail in altering the fact of death. The late Sigmund Freud, the founder of modern psychoanalysis, wrote a little monogram entitled "War and Death" during the first World War. According to Willard L. Sperry's summary, in this book Freud said that

Modern man is essentially dishonest in the presence of death. He keeps the idea at arm's length during his lifetime and concedes it only with perplexity and resentment as it finally forces itself upon him in the circle of his home or in his own person. He does not know what to think of it, because for so long he has studiously avoided thinking about it at all. Therefore, all that may lie beyond the inevitable mediatorial fact of death, is even further removed from his mind.[205]

This analysis by Freud points out a number of weaknesses in the contemporary evaluation of life and death. Further evidence of this is given by Charles R. Salit who states:

Man accepts a paradox that offers him life and rejects a logic whose conclusion is death. When a person dies, his friends, his relatives, as a rule, will offer all sorts of excuses. No matter how old or how sick the deceased might have been, his death could have been prevented. . . . No high-pressure salesman as yet has sold to us the fatal slogan that man was born only to die.[206]

Douglas Van Steere made the following observation about life and death:

We live in an aspirin age, where any discussion of death is regarded as morbid, as defeatist, as a betrayal of, or a treason against life.[207]

Undoubtedly this represents a view which is widely held today, but there are also those who see and share the sentiments of Walter Chalmers Smith in these paradoxical lines of poetry:

All through life I see a cross —
    Where sons of God yield up their breath;
There is no gain except by loss;

There is no life except by death;
There is no vision but by faith.[208]

This, then, is the paradox — living through dying! This is the part of human experience which is the primary concern in this section of this book.

When it is said that a man is dead the usual meaning is that his bodily organs have ceased to function. But in the New Testament the words "death" and "life" have more than a physical meaning. "We know that we have passed out of death into life."[209] The transition did not take place when breathing ceased, but during the span of mortal life. This is a strange use of plain words, but Jesus approved it. "This my son was dead,"[210] he said in one of his great parables; "was dead," but no funeral procession made its way to an open burial place. In giving the challenge of his mission in life before those who were to perpetuate it Jesus said: "He who finds his life will lose it, and he who loses his life for my sake will find it."[211] The key which will unlock this paradox is located in the phrase "for my sake." Jesus was speaking to men who were alive physically, but who were not necessarily alive spiritually.

With this brief background it may be easier to visualize the significance of life and death in the mind of Paul. Starting with his use of the word $\zeta\acute{\alpha}\omega$, live, it is necessary to observe that he had one or several meanings in mind. This characteristic is, however, not peculiarly his own for words today carry several different shades of meaning. There are at least four main levels of life which are indicated in Paul's letters: (1) Physical life, to be living, in contrast with dying or with the dead.[212] The living God in contrast with lifeless idols.[213] In the metaphorical sense men "get their living,"[214] or "stand fast in the Lord."[215] (2) Psychological and ethical life, in a qualitative sense indicating the way one is to live.[216] (3) Life in terms of soteriology, ways of salvation.[217] (4) Life beyond, to live after death, possess eternal life.[218] These connotations of living and dying are perhaps the

140

main ones and it needs to be said that Paul does not always sharply distinguish his thought between them.

From the standpoint of his Christian faith Paul believed that Jesus had "died for all; therefore all have died. And he died for all, that those who live might live no longer for themselves but for him who for their sake died and was raised."[219] The meaning Paul seems to attach to these words is that Christ took upon himself the sins of all so that when the crucifixion took place the power of sin and death was destroyed, "therefore all have died".

In the midst of several paradoxes in II Corinthians, Paul remarks, "as dying, and behold we live."[220] It is very unlikely that what follows in the first part of each of the remaining five clauses expresses the viewpoint of Paul's opponents and what stands second expresses actual fact. The New Testament leaves no doubt that Paul faced strong opposition and that some rejoiced over him as a dying man whom they had stoned. But the point Paul apparently intended to make is similarly expressed in words such as these, "always carrying in the body the death of Jesus, so that the life of Jesus may also be manifested in our bodies."[221] The *νέκρωσιν*, literally "the putting to death" of Jesus is being re-enacted in a series of sufferings in Paul's life. Alfred Plummer has made this observation which throws light on this situation. "The missionaries were perpetually being delivered unto death for Christ's sake. They were never free from peril. Enemies were always seeking their lives, as they sought His life."[222] The triumph which Paul experienced was put into the words cited earlier, "and behold we live."

In yet another context Paul says, "So we do not lose heart. Though our outer nature is wasting away, our inner nature is being renewed every day."[223] Here Paul is simply stating the difference between the physical nature which is subject to deterioration and the spiritual nature which each day shows some advancement.

The life that comes to Paul through such experiences as those alluded to in this discussion is the resurrection life. Through the living Christ, Paul knows both that his suffering and hardship was a kind of death. But death is more than physical decay, a metaphor he uses in writing to the Romans.[224] The twofold outlook of Jesus helps to see what Paul may have meant. Before Calvary Jesus had said, "unless a grain of wheat falls into the earth and dies, it remains alone; but if it dies, it bears much fruit."[225] By death his Spirit was released into a full and fruitful life. As a grain of wheat must lose its life to be fruitful, so must man die to self that he may live to God. Paul was aware of a continual laying down of the life of the body through which the life he had in Christ might be manifested and released. It was in this vein of thought that he appealed to his friends to present their "bodies as a living sacrifice, holy and acceptable to God,"[226] as their "reasonable" service. This outlook shaped Paul's attitude in handling adversity and provided the spirit in which he was able to bear hardships. Gustaf Adolf Deissmann has written of this aspect of Paul's attitude as follows:

> The peculiarity of the Pauline attitude is this, that he dared the paradox of regarding suffering in communion with Christ as something quite normal and necessary.[227]

Adversity and suffering might turn some men against God, but these things made Paul maturely religious. He used suffering when it came creatively and consecrated it to the purpose of God. Thus he is able to say, "we rejoice in our hope of sharing the glory of God. More than that, we rejoice in our sufferings . . . because God's love has been poured into our hearts through the Holy Spirit which has been given to us."[228]

In dealing with the Pauline paradoxical theme of living through dying something more needs to be said concerning his thoughts of human suffering. Neither Jesus nor Paul has a theoretical solution to the problem of suffering which prematurely destroys the body. But Jesus by his own attitude and outlook reveals and communicates the spirit by which "death is swallowed up

142

in victory."[229] Paul sees the redemption of suffering as a part of the redemption Christ brings through the Cross and the Resurrection. Moreover, Paul recognizes that suffering takes place on different levels. Jesus made it plain that God suffers with suffering humanity, but that in the suffering of love, life is reborn to better things. Even the suffering which men bring on themselves through sin and selfishness can be transformed and made to serve God's redeeming purpose. Paul's sufferings were not all free from the bitterness of self-reproach or some defect of character. Yet he found the way of using suffering in a creative sense and as a purifying power. His experience allows him to say, "suffering produces endurance, and endurance produces hope, and hope does not disappoint us."[230] He believes "that the sufferings of the present time" are not worthy of comparison with that which shall be revealed.[231]

The evidence thus far presented makes it clear that Paul conceived of life and death on several levels. He knew of death on the physical plane of existence. In this sense man dies a little every day from the moment of his birth. He also knew of the eternal significance of living through dying in a spiritual and moral sense. At one point he finds assurance in the words of the Psalmist who speaks to God in these words, " 'For thy sake we are being killed all the day long; we are regarded as sheep to be slaughtered.' "[232] In spite of everything external which could and did happen to Paul, including the possibility of physical death, he held firmly that nothing "will be able to separate us from the love of God in Christ Jesus our Lord."[233] In reference to things which obstruct his pilgrimage he says, "in all these things we are more than conquerors through him who loved us."[234]

The paradoxical theme of living through dying has an essential bearing on the spiritual and moral life. It is on this level that men need to "practice in dying the little deaths," as Steere has so well expressed the thought.[235] They need to discover something come alive for God. This line of thought is to be found in Paul's letters. He speaks of the old self as being crucified with Christ, and of the new self as being raised with Christ. It is on this account, he says to the Romans, that "you must also consider yourselves dead to sin and alive to God in Christ Jesus."[236] The words which follow immediately are an emphatic declaration of what is expected of Christians who are not under the rule of Mosaic Law. He writes:

> Let not sin therefore reign in your mortal bodies, to make you obey their passions. Do not yield your members to sin as instruments of wickedness, but yield yourselves to God as men who have been brought from death to life, and your members to God as instruments of righteousness.[237]

That is to say men are to yield themselves, give God the "right of way" in order to become instruments of a new righteousness.

Paul has something further to say on this subject in his letter to the Galatians. He takes glory in the Cross of Christ, "by which the world has been crucified to me, and I to the world."[238] Sometimes these words are taken to mean that a man who has been brought into new life through Christ is to set out with fierce aggression to fight the old life. The picture is given of such a one nailing his old interests and pleasures on the cross in order to crucify them. Actually the meaning here is something very different. When a person becomes alive in Christ he obtains a new set of interests, attention is directed elsewhere, imagination awakened, love won. And having gotten this far, a certain law of life is given charge which will enable a man to do certain things without having trouble. It is a law of life that when interest is enticed in one direction it is withdrawn from another. In other words as the Christian life develops certain things are no longer wanted. There is no need to crucify them. They are crucified in Christ who died once for all, but men must die "little deaths" in order to live for God through

Christ. By employing the double contrast of dying and living, law and God, Paul declares in Galatians:

> For I through the law died to the law, that I might live to God. I have been crucified with Christ; it is no longer I who live, but Christ who lives in me; and the life I now live in the flesh I live by faith in the Son of God, who loved me and gave himself for me.[239]

The meaning of the words Χριστῷ συνεσταύρωμαι "I have been crucified with Christ" seem to indicate that Paul was thinking of his own death "I" to the Law as crucified and that a new "I" lives. He recognized in the death of Christ on the Cross that sin and selfishness had been crucified and that through the acceptance of what God had done in love new life came to him. The text under consideration does not permit a literal interpretation. Ernest DeWitt Burton has noted three elements, which with varying degrees of emphasis are present in Paul's expressions related to the words "I have been crucified with Christ" cited above.[240] The first element is associated with certain benefits which come to the believer through Christ's experience.[241] The second element has to do with a spiritual fellowship with Christ in respect to these experiences.[242] The third element may be seen in the experience of the believer who passes through a similar or analogous experience.[243] There are many different strands which enter this thought of being crucified with Christ, and these may be explained in terms of Paul's faith that both the death of the old life and the birth of the new are determined by God through Christ.

As Paul is approaching the trial mentioned in his letter to the Philippians, he realizes that he may not be acquitted. He nevertheless wants his readers to know that he will bring honor to Christ to the best of his ability and with the help of God, "whether by life or by death."[244] He says: "For me to live is Christ, and to die is gain."[245] These words have been taken by some as

145

a paradox and by others as an epigram. The kernel of truth in Paul's statement seems to favor the latter. He means that his life, even while he possesses it, is not his own but solely devoted to service for Christ. It is not likely that he wished the words to be read as though he were contrasting life and death in this instance. They are both the same, except that death will bring him in a large measure all that he has been seeking throughout life. He sees that even as an historical fact the life of Jesus is not ended. Jesus lives in and through those who suffer with him and who give their lives in his service. This is Paul's comfort and the ground of his hope. He recognized not only the social nature of man, but even more man's dependence on God. His teaching on this is especially made clear in these words: "None of us lives to himself, and none of us dies to himself."[246] He reminds his hearers that whether they live or die they belong to God.

Turning now to Paul's thoughts on baptism these two points stand out in relation to the present discussion of living through dying. Baptism, for Paul, signified passing through death to life, as if the individual had not lived before. It also signified that those who "die" to their old selves will be "raised" to newness of life by Christ. As the believer was submerged beneath the water, he "died," that is, he re-enacted in his own person the death by which Christ redeemed him. And then, as he was raised up from the water. This signified that a new life had now begun, for now he shared in the risen life of Christ. As Paul put it, the believer had died and risen with Christ. The intent and effect of baptism was to enable men to "walk in newness of life."[247] It will be helpful to keep in mind Paul's point of view. He is describing not what Christians should do, but what they should become, in consequence of the grace of God in Christ.

Yet another phase of the theme of living through dying appears in Paul's contrast between the first man, Adam, who gave humanity its mortality and the second man, Christ, who gave the hope of eternal life. Quoting from what was probably Genesis, Paul says that "The first man Adam became a living being."[248]

146

This may be his way of saying that all subsequent human life stems from Adam, but from Adam also comes the fact and necessity of physical death. "For as in Adam all die, so also in Christ shall all be made alive."[249] As a matter of teaching and witness Paul believed that a new order of being commenced with Christ. One of the most plausible explanations of the thought of Paul in this connection has been given by Archibald Robertson and Alfred Plummer who state: "In different ways, Adam and Christ were each of them Head of the human race and could represent it. . . . The meaning may be, 'As it is in Adam that all who die die, so it is in Christ that all who are made alive are made alive.' "[250] Basically what Paul is trying to indicate here is that Christ altered the course of human history.

A further clarification of his position is given in his letter to the Romans. There Adam becomes a type for Christ who was to come. Paul states, "as sin came into the world through one man and death through sin," "so death spread to all men because all men sinned."[251] Commenting on these words of Paul, Emil Brunner remarks that the verse,

> does not refer to the transgression of Adam in which all his descendants share; but states the fact that 'Adam's' descendants are involved in death because they themselves commit sin.[252]

It is naturally expected that Paul would have gone on to say, "Even so by one righteous man has entered into the world, the life of righteousness," but instead there is a digression extending for five verses before the comparison is resumed in these words,

> Then as one man's trespass led to condemnation for all men, so one man's act of righteousness leads to acquittal and life for all men. For by one man's disobedience many were made sinners, so by one man's obedience many will be made righteous.[253]

Whatever may have been Paul's understanding of the origin of sin he was certain in his own mind that Christ brought an end to the power of sin and death. The victory was in the new life after the manner of Christ's righteousness.

William Ernest Hocking once stated that, "Man is the only animal that contemplates death, and also the only animal that shows any sign of doubt of its finality."[254] When Paul treats the subject of life he is aware that the consummation of life will include life beyond the grave. His conception of the life thus contemplated reveals certain distinctions which he apparently made in the light of other views which were held and taught in his day. Among the Jews there were those who believed in a resurrection involving the return of the body and soul or spirit of man. Paul challenged this notion by saying that "flesh and blood cannot inherit the kingdom of God."[255] Among the Greeks there were those who believed in the "immortality of the soul" which meant the final release from a body thus leaving a disembodied soul.[256] In his teaching Paul insisted on some kind of body in his interpretation of the resurrection. Some skeptics inquired, "With what kind of body do they come?"[257] To which Paul answered that it is a "spiritual" body.[258] He went on to speculate concerning this spiritual body which he believed would take the place of a body of flesh. He conceives of the body as the organ of personality by which an individual is recognized. He illustrates his meaning by the use of seed grain which is sown into the ground, seemingly, it dies, but later it comes to life again. "What you sow," he says, "is not the body which is to be. . . . But God gives it a body as he has chosen."[259]

In another place, thinking of the life which has begun but which is to continue hereafter, Paul says, "For now we see in a mirror dimly, but then face to face."[260] And again he states, "we all, with unveiled face," seeing the glory of the Lord "are being changed into his likeness from one degree of glory to another; for this comes from the Lord who is the Spirit."[261] Thus Paul sees the present in the framework of what is to be. He believes that man's true citizenship is in heaven.[262] His hope in life beyond the grave is an indispensable part of the gospel, for without it "we are of all men to be pitied."[263] It cannot be said that Paul is unaware of the general doubts of men respecting the finality of "death" in Hocking's words, but it can be stated firmly that Paul contemplates different levels of being. His faith is anchored in God who created him and who brought about "the new being" in Christ Jesus.

It will serve a useful purpose now to gather up the main thoughts of this section on living through dying. The first matter of importance is the fact that Paul speaks of life and death in different connotations and contexts. He knows about physical death. Man is born with the death sentence in him. He dies every hour he lives. But Paul also came to know that man may live and die spiritually in a situation of sovereignty and freedom, law and grace, object and subject. Jesus had stated the need of dying to the "old" and being born to the "new" in a nocturnal interview with Nicodemus. This seems to have been Jesus' way of saying that man must die to self and become alive to God. Such words as "new life" and "new creation" are common ones with Paul for they seem to express the nature of his own creative religious experience. It is at this level, namely, living through dying in a spiritual sense that Paul's paradoxical theme unfolds. His own acquaintance with the power of regenerating faith has opened to him a dynamic resource of life's inner meaning. It is the things men die to and whom they live for that give higher quality to their lives. Paul frequently refers to such matters as "dying to the Law" and "dying to sin" that he may live for Christ. It is within this context that his paradoxical theme of living through dying can best be understood.

The movement of Paul's thought is from a sense of inner relationship to God toward ethical application and overt action. It is on this level that his paradoxical theme under consideration reveals its relationship "in newness of life" not only for the individual but in the Christian community.

149

The tremendous passion for life may be God's paradoxical way of expressing the intense significance of death as life's consummation. The death of Jesus was not the doom of His abounding life. His death not only embodies life's intensity but interprets it. It is the whole passion and power of life eternal. Paul laid claim to eternal life which commences here but continues into the hereafter. He looked beyond physical death to a new level of being.

D. *Strength Through Weakness*

Anyone who has taken the time to examine Paul's letters has been impressed by his strength rather than by his weakness. He lived a hazardous life! As the Psalmist of old, Paul waits for the Lord to renew his strength yet seeks that he may find. His own weakness gives him a chance to draw on the deeper reservoirs of strength. Sometimes he is scared, despondent, discouraged, but what is more important he also knows from whence his help comes. In his letters Paul confesses his weaknesses. Blaise Pascal once made the interesting observation expressed in these words:

> La faiblesse de l'homme parait bien davantage en ceux qui ne la connaissent pas qu' en ceux qui la connaissent.[264]

That is to say, "The weakness of man is far more evident in those who know it not than in those who know it." As already stated this would not apply to Paul in so far as he admits the need of strength beyond his own. He found strength through weakness in paradoxical situations.

In order to see this more clearly certain aspects of his life and thought need to be considered bearing in mind the physical, mental, moral, social, and spiritual levels on which Paul moves.

Paul had some natural abilities which may be seen in what he says or sometimes in what he implies in his letters. He sincerely believed that God had called or set him apart for the gospel ministry before he was born.[265] He was studious and capable of persuasive argument. He was a pioneer in spirit. Adversity presented him with an opportunity to risk his faith. Spiritually Paul had an intense struggle with himself, a world to be conquered.

Archibald Joseph Cronin in his autobiography tells of his experience with nominal Christianity. He confesses he knew well enough what he ought to do. But it was a very bitter step for a person who had met with the success he enjoyed. The weeks grew into months . . . he continued with his pride and self-complacency. Then he surrendered his life to God and made the immense discovery of why he was alive.[266] To a degree Paul had a similar experience leading to the Damascus road. He learned that repentance was not weakness but the highest creative activity of human personality. He made the amazing discovery of asking for God's help in his weakness only to find that this is the way to true strength. He saw that faith must go deeper than intellectual understanding. God's grace is wider than the reaches of man's mind and includes those whom some would seek to exclude.

It is, indeed, a strange part of life that out of weakness strength may be born. In a German village a certain profligate drunkard wooed and won the heart of a village maid who was tubercular. The village saw no chance for such a home, yet one day out of that Nazareth Beethoven walked to write his "Moonlight Sonata." Human weakness may become a doorway to strength. Nowhere is this more evident than on the level at which God enters life and becomes "twisted together" with the life of man. Here is the highest relationship of strength through weakness known to man.

In I Corinthians Paul boasts of his weakness in order that the strength of God in Christ may be manifest. He continues his thought by saying, "when I am weak, then I am strong."[267] At first this remark seems very ambiguous if not contradictory, but further examination reveals that when Paul is weak in realizing his own limitations then he is strong in knowing the adequacy of God. This paradoxical assertion sums up Paul's estimate of what he achieved, and the words which follow illustrate different kinds of weakness. The admission of weakness was an achievement for him. The physical handicap which he terms "thorn" was unable to defeat him. He makes a catalogue of things that concern weakness.[268] The conclusion Paul draws is that in such hours or moments of weakness he knows, and others can see, that he is weak, and he knows, and they know what he has accomplished in his weakness. Paul had learned that God's grace was sufficient for him, for God's "power is made perfect in weakness."[269] This knowledge he gained by experience, he taught those who witnessed his work, how much can be accomplished in spite of hardships and afflictions. *ἀρκεῖ σοι ἡ χάρις μου*. The point of Paul's own weakness could become the place of God's power. In another chapter of I Corinthians he speaks of weakness,[270] but not necessarily in terms of a "thorn",[271] but simply by way of contrast with God's power.

Again and again the handicapped people of the world have demonstrated greatness in spite of physical limitations. Their struggles for advancement and health have developed latent capacities. Physical weakness can and often does bring people into a position where they are open to the Spirit of God. They learn to lower a draw bridge which permits God to cross over to walk and talk with them. Paul admonishes the Thessalonians: "Rejoice, always, pray constantly, give thanks in all circumstances. . . ."[272] He confesses his own weakness in asking them to pray for him, "Brethren, pray for us."[273] There is a sense of need which turns into prayer and confidence in God. In Romans he says, "the Spirit helps us in our weakness; for we do not know to pray as we ought, but the Spirit himself intercedes for us with sighs too deep for words."[274] Words may be and frequently are inadequate in prayer, yet Paul states, "I will pray with the spirit and I will pray with the mind also; I will sing with the spirit and I will sing with the mind also."[275] There is strength that comes from prayer.

In writing to the people at Corinth Paul makes the statement that "God chose what is weak in the world to shame the strong . . . so that no human being might boast in the presence of God."[276] Here as elsewhere the reader must try to understand that Paul draws a contrast having in mind the things of the physical world and the things of the spiritual. Human weakness as such may be the servant of God while human strength without God may be His rival.

This relates to Paul's view of the Cross of Christ. Outwardly the crucifixion might seem to be an exhibition of weakness. Those who sought to destroy Jesus believed they had gained a victory at Calvary. But with superb daring Paul calls this a Divine weakness for only in this manner could Divine power really be manifested.[277] Jesus "was crucified in weakness, but lives by the power of God."[278] In order to illustrate the surpassing quality of God's love, Paul points to the fact that Christ died for all men without regard of their worthiness.[279] This is the measure of the love of God. His strength is revealed in acts and conditions which humanly speaking may be signs of weakness.

On occasion Paul has been accused of over-emphasizing the so-called weakness of man. At first sight this criticism seems to be justified. However, a closer look at his purpose in writing may reveal this. What Paul was unable to do for himself, God was able to do for him in Jesus Christ. The general admonitions and instructions make it clear that Paul presupposed human freedom and responsibility. The tone of the following text more nearly expresses his attitude than any claim of human weakness or helplessness. He says:

Not that we are sufficient of ourselves to claim anything as coming from us; our sufficiency is from God, who has qualified us to be ministers of a new convenant, not in a written code but in the Spirit; for the written code kills, but the Spirit gives life.[280]

In the letter to the Philippians he states, "I can do all things

in him who strengthens me."[281] That is not to say that Paul
expects to do what is really impossible, rather he wants to acknowledge the source of his strength in the Christian life. And
in Romans he stands with undaunted spirit claiming that he is
not ashamed of the gospel for "it is the power of God for salvation to every one who has faith."[282] In this event hearing or
reading the gospel becomes the channel for belief and trust in
God through the life and work of Christ. From this action comes
strength. The Colossian letter contains this inspiring benediction,
"May you be strengthened with all power, according to his glor-
ious might, for all endurance and patience with joy, giving thanks
to the Father, who has qualified us to share in the inheritance of
the saints of light."[283] There is strength for meeting trying and
difficult aspects of life which comes as a heritage from those
who have borne "light" in the past.

Paul was not unaware of the danger which lurked behind the
human boast of strength. He recognized the fact that a person's
character may be weakest at the point where he thinks himself
strongest. The strong points may be left unguarded or they may
be exaggerated out of all true proportion to their real nature.
The opposite danger might well be leaving the weak points without sufficient care or protection. Paul frequently reminds his
readers to be "on guard" in matters of faith and daily living.

In writing to the Corinthians, Paul describes the glory of his
ministry. Suddenly there rises in his mind the contrast between
the divine treasure and his own personality in which the treasure is to be borne. He speaks of himself as an "earthen vessel"
in order to illustrate how fragile the body really is. Then he
proceeds to enumerate some of the adversity and hardship he
and his friends have encountered.

> We are afflicted in every way, but not crushed; perplexed,
> but not driven to despair; persecuted; but not forsaken;
> struck down, but not destroyed; always carrying in the body

the death of Jesus, so that the life of Jesus may also be manifested in our bodies.[284]

In each of the four situations thus described Paul comes to the secret of his strength which is his dedication and his renewal of faith. Floyd V. Filson suggests that the words "struck down" may imply more than physical attack, for Paul also suffered through the disloyalty of the church at Corinth.[285] Perplexities often drive a man to find strength beyond his own resources. James Dillet Freeman has written a poem entitled "Strength" which portrays this thought particularly in the last four lines.

> Who was not threatened, never quailed;
> Who was not tempted, never fell;
> Who was not tested, never failed.
> Go ask not of the quick and well,
> But of the ones who agonize,
> What wholeness is; the fallen only
> Can tell you what it means to rise.
> To learn of friendship, ask the lonely.
> Go ask the ones who broke and ran
> What courage is, not those who stood;
> None may know less of virtue than
> The saint who has been only good.
> For those who went beyond their strength
> Alone can tell the measure of
> The heart's capacities, the length
> To which despair may go, or love.[286]

There is every reason to suppose that Paul shared in the sentiments of which Freeman speaks.

In times of social and religious upheaval and transition a man reveals his strength or lack of it. Paul, in the midst of the controversy over the relation of the Christian Way to Judaism, demonstrated remarkable strength. Different viewpoints were strongly urged and outbreaks of violence were not uncommon. The issue was finally taken before the Jerusalem Council. There Paul defended to the utmost this point, "For freedom Christ has set us free; stand fast therefore, and do not submit again to a yoke of slavery."[287] This was his banner and fortunately for the Christian Church he never surrendered it to the opponents. Then, there were those at Antioch known as Judaizers who provoked trouble and disrupted his work by sowing seeds of dissension. Even Peter at Antioch fell prey and according to Paul's comments did not live up to his convictions.[288] Paul insisted that a man is a Christian in becoming a new creation in Christ, and as such he is free. Besides these examples, Paul also mentions that his work was thwarted by perverse and evil men.[289] Yet in spite of all these things Paul was certain of God's providential care and power in the message with which he had been entrusted.[290]

There are many who take great pride in whatever displays energy, mastery, valor. But there is no strength comparable with what is required of the hero of the spirit, the man called to set his conscience in opposition to the standards and conventional beliefs of his day. He will need physical fortitude and indomitable courage, but that is not all he needs. The part that makes Jeremiah's courage stand out is that at the time of his call he believed it was against his temperament to engage in God's work.[291] Yet God made him "a fortified city, an iron pillar, and bronze walls, against the whole land."[292] The mood expressed in the case of Jeremiah is similar to that in which Paul speaks of his weakness in contrast to the kind of strength which seemed to be the ideal of many of his hearers. He exults in the very characteristics which some most deprecated. "If I must boast, I will boast of the things that show my weakness."[293] Things which appeared to some men as being without strength enabled Paul to move in the direction of increased likeness to Christ.[294] The things Paul is weak enough to suffer and to endure show the excellency of the power of God as revealed in Christ. "I will all the more gladly boast of my weaknesses, that the power of Christ may rest upon me."[295] The point Paul apparently wants to put across has to do with human inadequacy on the one hand and renunciation of self-sufficiency on the other hand. God "is the source of your life in Christ Jesus,"[296] he reminds the Corinthians.

It is a favorite device of evil to suggest that the service of God is for the weak. John W. Oman has wisely cautioned people against seeking trials of their own making. Men can be strong only by what teaches them their own weaknesses.[297] There is no gain in trying to rationalize or minimize human mistakes, but there is great gain in knowing how to free them, how to learn from them, and how to find strength to go on. Paul assures his readers that by the power of the living Christ who dwells in them, the believers shall become true disciples as they proximate to the knowing and the doing of the will of God.[298] Christ in them is "the hope of glory."[299] The basic concern of Paul was to stress a proper relationship with God through Christ and to encourage men to ally themselves with the will of God in line with the teaching of Jesus.

Mention was made earlier of Paul's bodily weakness or affliction. Perhaps some elaboration on this and the manner in which it was regarded will be instructive. He called it a "thorn in the flesh" which baffled him.[300] It may have been a disfigurement due to disease, epilepsy, eye trouble, or none of these. No one has finally determined the nature of this bodily condition. Whatever it was Paul's work was interrupted by it. In writing to the Galatians he calls attention to a violent attack of illness.[301] He had to turn aside from the appointed route to visit them. In this situation his ties with the Galatians were definitely strengthened for they gave their sympathetic understanding. Almost the opposite reaction took place in Corinth where some charged without pity or understanding that "his bodily presence is weak,"[302] and thereby tried to discredit his work. At one point Paul called his bodily affliction a "messenger of Satan."[303] Three times he prayed that God might take it away. The thorn was not removed, but in his extremity he made a great discovery. The answer came back from God, "My grace is sufficient for you, for my power is made perfect in weakness."[304] Paul was assured that his help and happiness came from God. This opened his eyes to the truth that human weakness can minister to spiritual power. Elsewhere he sees strength through weakness in a contrast having to do with two kinds of dwelling places. He states "that if the earthly tent we live in is destroyed, we have a building from God, a house not made with hands, eternal in the heavens."[305]

Paul was a man of many moods. He reveals so much of himself that some have drawn the conclusion that he had a very complex nature. It is not hard to find sharp contrasts of mildness[306] and severity,[307] but these in varying degrees may also be found in other men. He has great humility, and yet again utters words of majestic self-confidence. In First Corinthians he remarks:

> For I am the least of the apostles, unfit to be called an apostle, because I persecuted the church of God. But by the grace of God I am what I am. . . . I worked harder than any of them, though it was not I, but the grace of God which is with me.[308]

In a sense Paul expresses himself here in a mood which the prophet Isaiah experienced when he said, "I have laboured in vain, I have spent my strength for naught; yet surely my judgment is with the Lord, and my work with my God."[309] This is finally the real test whether or not God is included in the work which is being done. Paul tells how he was able to overcome one of his weak moments at a time when it might have been simpler and easier not to preach. Yet he preached Christ crucified at Corinth knowing that this would awaken resentment both from the Jews and from the Gentiles.[310] He found strength in doing that which he believed he was called to do.

Paul told the people at Corinth that he fought against his own lower nature. "I pommel my body and subdue it, lest after preaching to others I myself should be disqualified."[311] He feared that he might not win acceptance with God.[312] Looking at this problem from another angle he confesses in his letter to the Romans that different forces are at work in his inner life. He puts the matter in this fashion:

> For I delight in the law of God, in my inmost self, but I see in my members another law at war with the law of my mind and making me captive to the law of sin which dwells in my members. Wretched man that I am! Who will deliver me from this body of death? Thanks be to God through Jesus Christ our Lord![313]

In spite of his weakness toward sin Paul claims the strength of victory through God. He admits, "I can will what is right, but I cannot do it."[314] But "the law of the Spirit of life in Christ Jesus" has set him free "from the law of sin and death."[315] The Romans are called upon to "walk not according to the flesh but according to the Spirit."[316] In other words, Paul appeals to them as moral responsible beings.

James Arthur Hadfield touched upon the problem of moral incompetence as related to the will of man. He claims that those who look to the will alone for their source of strength run the risk of disaster. He believes that for practical action the will is dependent on instinctive emotions. His argument runs as follows:

> The freedom of the will may be a doctrine which holds true of the healthy, and indeed the exercise of the will and determination is the normal way in which to summon the resources of power; but the doctrine that the will alone is the way to power is a most woebegone theory for the relief of the morally sick — and who of us is whole? Freedom to choose? Yes! But what if, when we choose, we have no power to perform? We open the sluice-gates, but the chan-

nels are dry; we pull the lever, but nothing happens; we try by our will to summon up our strength, but no strength comes.[317]

Whether this analysis is accepted or not members of Alcoholics Anonymous groups as well as professional gamblers who want to begin a new life know the need of strength beyond their own. Habits and attitudes play a large part in conditioning the way men live.

In the Old Testament story of Samson it is pointed out that he used his strength for unworthy ends.[318] He knew his strength came from God, yet insisted upon using it for destruction and revenge. In the case of Paul the situation is very much different. He knows that his strength comes from God and coupled with this knowledge is a strong sense of social responsibility. In the eyes of the world the "brethren" may appear as social nothingness but "God chose what is weak to shame the strong."[319] The contrast here is between those who acknowledge their human weakness and those who boast of human strength. God chooses to help those who are humble and contrite in spirit.

"We who are strong ought to bear with the failings of the weak, and not to please ourselves; let each of us please his neighbor for his good, to edify him," Paul says to the Romans.[320] Similarly he wrote in I Corinthians: "Let no one seek his own good, but the good of his neighbor."[321] Again in II Corinthians he expresses genuine concern for all the churches as he writes, "Who is weak, and I am not weak? Who is made to fall, and I am not indignant?"[322] In dealing with the question respecting the custom of eating certain foods Paul avoids abstractions as if either the use or the abstinence was right. He does not urge the Church to secure a rule enforcing its wishes. Instead Paul agrees with the "strong" and yet counsels them to regard the scruples of the "weak" and to limit their liberty in love to keep a brother from stumbling.[323] It hardly needs to be said that Paul is driving home that point that self-interest and service are

160

rivals in the common mind. But he also knows that moral and social weakness can be elevated to the level of edifying strength. He reminds the Galatians, "if a man is overtaken in any trespass, you who are spiritual should restore him in a spirit of gentleness."[324] His sense of social responsibility is seen again in this statement, "Bear one another's burdens, and so fulfil the law of Christ."[325] Without doubt Paul knew there is a limit how far a man can bear the personal tragedy, sin, and suffering of another. Yet shared burdens become lighter, minds are relieved when the strong help the weak. In another connection Paul wrote, "each man shall have to bear his own load."[326] There are two different meanings which must be considered here. In respect to the word "load" or burden which each must bear for himself, Jesus employed the same term φορτίον when he invited the entire world to himself saying,

> Come to me, all who labor and are heavy-laden, and I will give you rest. Take my yoke upon you, and learn from me; for I am gentle and lowly in heart, and you will find rest for your souls. For my yoke is easy, and my burden is light.[327]

To bear one's burden in this manner is Christian experience. To assist another with his burden is to apply Christian experience. It is to fulfill the law of Christ as servants of God or better still as sons in whom the Father is well pleased. There are sentiments in this poem by Richard Burton which one might imagine as having run through the mind of Paul.

> Not, in the morning vigor, Lord, am I
> Most sure of Thee, but when the day goes by
> To evening and, all spent with work, my head
> Is bowed, my limbs are laid upon my bed.
> Lo! in my weariness is faith at length,
> Even so children's weakness is their strength.[328]

161

Paul was under a great amount of pressure in carrying out his ministry. He knew of inner accomplishments and outward failures. Yet the remarkable fact remains that he found strength through weakness.

The preceding section has dealt with the relationship of Paul's paradoxical theme of strength through weakness on different levels of his nature. It has been pointed out that when Paul speaks of being weak at the same time strong, he must mean that the weakness and the strength are not on the same level. The specific situation in question had to do with some infirmity which threatened his vitality and usefulness, yet empowered him. When he acknowledged the weakness of his own efforts he became strong in the strength of God. He learned how inadequate his own resources were in times of stress and strain. Here indeed is a paradox. The weak often turn out to be the strong; and the strong, the weak.

It is a curious fact that out of strength comes weakness. Here is the reason for man's undying need of God. In many instances man is insufficient at the very point he thinks he is sufficient. He is weak just where he thinks he is strong. It is impossible for a proud man, by his own efforts, to overcome his pride, since he would be proud of his own accomplishment, and would thus fall victim to spiritual pride. This involves a psychological paradox. The more man tries to extricate himself from sin the deeper he becomes involved. Those who know they are weak and seek Divine aid, in their weakness are made strong.

The Cross reveals this paradox and points the way to the redemption of power. At the Cross the love of power gives way to the power of love. Here the weak are given strength, and the strong are redeemed from pride. Christ came to redeem people from their sins; He was intent upon putting an end to their real weakness and filling them with a new power for creative activity.

Paul learned the secret and source of true strength in relation to God. From this perspective came new confidence and deeper understanding of the application of the gospel message in personal and social situations.

E. *Foolishness and Wisdom*

The preceding pages of this volume have shown Paul's keen interest in teaching and learning. He was a man who exercised faith and reason. In this section the attempt will be made to understand his paradoxical theme of foolishness and wisdom. Some background material from the Old Testament may throw light on this theme or at least show how some of Paul's predecessors thought of wisdom.

One of the better known expressions on this subject is that of the Psalmist who says, "The fear of the Lord is the beginning of wisdom; a good understanding have all those who practice it."[329] The meaning here has to do with a reverent conviction of God's reality and a believing faith and acknowledgment of man's obligation to worship and to serve Him. It is not awestruck terror as the word "fear" might tend to imply. The Lord in whose fear lies wisdom is the living God who has revealed Himself to patriarchs, prophets, priests. As the balancing clause of a similar text, recorded in Proverbs has it, "and the knowledge of the Holy One is insight."[330] The prophet Jeremiah has the Lord say:

> Let not the wise man glory in his wisdom, let not the mighty man glory in his might, let not the rich man glory in his riches; but let him who glories glory in this, that he understands and knows me, that I am the Lord who practices kindness, justice, and righteousness in the earth; for in these things I delight.[331]

The writer of Ecclesiastes learned from experience that happiness does not come upon the search for happiness. He tells how he gave his heart to seek out concerning all things that are under the heaven and that this was vexation of spirit.[332] The inference from this may well be drawn that knowledge of things in this world alone is not enough for man to live by. Man needs the kind of understanding that goes behind and beneath "worldly" things and live insight into the great issues of his origin and destiny. At this level God must be taken into account.

Invariably human knowledge pretends to be more than it is. The mind is always in danger of being stunned by intellectual pride. This is not, however, to say that the mind should be discounted in determining the difference between one thing and another. Paul Elmer Moore has a relevant word on this subject. He writes:

> We must admit, in sober sadness, that the intellect too brings its temptations, that the man who reasons is prone to deceive himself, that science has a tendency to close the mind in a narrow circle of self-complacency, and that the professed agnostic is pecularily liable to a callous conceit. Such, we know, was the discovery of Socrates, when he set out on his search for the wise man, and found everywhere, the most prominently there where reputation for wisdom was greatest, that men thought they knew what they did not know at all.[333]

A more recent statement was made by Edwin McNeill Poteat showing a further application of man's tendency toward intellectual deception. Poteat remarks:

> The paradox of intellectual progress is that the more one knows the more one senses the limitations of knowing. Not only are there limits within man's intellectual endowment, they are in the nature of the knowable. The illusion of scientism lies just here. When the formula that can integrate the twin facts of gravitation and electromagnetism is finally established — Einstein said he had it but could

not prove it experimentally or explain it fully with the mathematical vocabulary he had — the phenomena of the universe will not be packaged and the universe secure within a tight equation closed to further inquiry.[334]

The sum of this quotation is that those who are truly wise know how little they actually know in relation and in proportion to what may be known.

Strange though it may seem Paul dealt with this same problem in his letters. In I Corinthians he draws a comparison between different kinds of knowledge as follows:

We know that 'all of us possess knowledge.' 'Knowledge' puffs up, but love builds up. If one imagines that he knows something, he does not yet know as he ought to know. But if one loves God, one is known by him.[335]

Paul is applying his thought in a special sense to knowledge which "puffs up" when without "love." Apparently there were those who claimed with pride to have "knowledge" that idols are nonentities and who, therefore, see no reason to avoid the alleged sanctity or contamination which the "weaker" members fear. Paul points out abstinence from eating meat offered to idols does not separate man from God, nor does eating bring man nearer. The important thing is not to trip up the man who is not well established in faith. The first step to knowledge is to know what ignorance is. Without love there is only the appearance of knowledge. Such "knowledge" breeds conceit in the attempt to seem learned or in trying to gain the recognition of men.[336] Further evidence of Paul's position is given in a hypothetical case in which he confesses that if he were able to "understand all mysteries and all knowledge . . . but have not love, I am nothing."[337] In another connection he makes the distinction between present attainment of knowledge on one level and future expectation on another level. He states, "Now I know in part, then I shall understand fully, even as I have been fully understood."[338]

In chapters two and three of I Corinthians, Paul gives considerable thought to the so-called "worldly" wisdom which has crept into the church. He must have known of the conditions which prevailed in many instances. He knew that in spite of subtle systems and brilliant rhetoric, society was going to pieces. Men were living and dying without hope.[339] He was aware of a degrading idolatry.[340] His critics claimed at Corinth that his preaching lacked "wisdom" in the sense of a gnostic, speculative, philosophical exposition of faith. This gave him the opportunity to reaffirm that the gospel he preached is the one wisdom of God. He proceeded to the paradox that the gospel possesses a "wisdom" of its own, an inherent range of deeper truth. In these words Paul restates his purpose in visiting the Corinthians:

> I did not come proclaiming to you the testimony of God
> in lofty words or wisdom. For I decided to know nothing
> among you except Jesus Christ and him crucified.[341]

In other words Paul did not attempt to preach with eloquent Greek rhetoric or with Hellenistic *gnosis* lest the cross of Christ should lose its power. He decided not to claim any other knowledge than that of God's revealed purpose in the startling paradox of Christ crucified.[342] He is pointing to the center of his message and not to the circumference. "We preach Christ crucified,"[343] Paul said, as if he meant to say there is some relationship between man's sin and the Cross. And, indeed, there is. The sins which crucified Jesus are the sins of men everywhere.

There is also a deeper relationship between man's sin and the Cross in the profound truth that God's suffering love is revealed there "reconciling the world" and us "to himself."[344] That is to say the Cross manifests the greatest power there is to redeem man and change his life and lift him above the sins that claim him. It is the power of suffering love. As Paul put it elsewhere, "God shows his love for us in that while we were yet sinners Christ died for us."[345] This does not mean that everyone who takes Christian love seriously will die a martyr's death. It does mean that if men try to love as God loves them and show such love to their fellowmen they would better be prepared for suffering.

This leads to further exploration into Paul's position in regard to the Cross. The Jewish hopes in his day were based on the expectation that someone would restore the glories of the kingdom of Solomon and David. Part of their deep disappointment in Jesus can be traced to his refusal to become a military leader, after the pattern of Judas Maccabees, to throw off the Roman yoke. The sign of "Christ crucified" was to them sufficient and decisive evidence that Jesus was not the one who would do this.[346] The Greeks were looking for a philosopher who would be a skillful and original disputant eloquent in worldly wisdom. Jesus was just the reverse of what many Jews and Greeks expected. He made no pretensions of such kingly rule or earthly wisdom. His was the way of compassion and reconciliation.

Paul knew that he faced a wall of opposition when he announced the challenging paradox of the crucified Christ which was σκάνδαλον (scandal, an unspeakable offense) for the Jews[347] and μωρία (folly, foolishness) for the Gentiles. The preaching of the Cross was utterly repellent to the Jews since many believed the Torah was being undermined. There was strong opposition to the Greeks and others who were invited indiscriminately into open fellowship. The folly of the Cross in the Greek mind seems to imply a perverse confusion of values, the foolish choice of lesser goods. But Paul insists that this so-called folly is in reality a higher wisdom. "For the foolishness of God is wiser then men."[348] This is a general statement which includes all men. It is a statement which can be distorted when men try to identify their own foolishness as "the foolishness of God." Paul was thinking and speaking of God's method of salvation involving two points, namely, the spiritual power of the gospel and its unlikeness of what men were inclined to demand. How well Paul knew the truth involved here.[349] At first he had himself objected strongly to the gospel of the early church and sought to destroy the followers of Jesus. The time came, however, when he surrendered his life to God and made the affirmation that what seemed like foolishness was wiser than his wisdom. He realized all that Jesus Christ was and all that He achieved by word and deed and spirit, is a revelation of God. "He who has seen me has seen the Father."[350] That, too, is axiomatic with Paul. It is a foundation stone of his faith.

The contrast which Paul makes between the word $\sigma o \phi \acute{\omega} \tau \epsilon \rho o \nu$, the wisdom of men in general and $\mu \omega \rho \acute{o} \nu$, a foolish thing on God's part[351] may well be his formulation of paradox of Jesus that a man must lose his life in order to find it.[352] This Christian paradox points to the fact that Christ's power in man's life is not in the first place what He promises, but in what He asks of man. The setting of this particular paradox makes it clear that Christ puts demands upon man. He warns his disciples not to think of a life of ease. All this precedes the introduction of the paradox.

Paul's conception of knowledge is derived from the prophetic idea of knowing God in the Old Testament. God has made Himself known. In speaking of their knowledge of God the prophets mean that God is known in His inner being and through His activity. Paul shows how God's act of redemption in Jesus Christ has a bearing on what he preaches. On the one hand, his message is a simple proclamation[353] of what God has done. On the other hand, in his own estimate, he himself has been in instance of the weak and foolish things of the world confounding the mighty and wise.[354] His preaching was "in demonstration of the Spirit and power."[355] He was convinced that faith should not "rest in the wisdom of men but in the power of God."[356] James Moffatt has noted that Paul lay stress on the content, rather than on the method, of the message.[357] The emphasis was

168

on proclamation of the gospel. Paul admits that his oratorical skill was not the best,[358] but he saw evidence of God's grace in the changed lives of those who received and acted upon the gospel message. It is when we come to know the power of God at work that they doubt no longer. "One thing I know, that though I was blind, now I see."[359] Paul did not forbid the best use of natural gifts in proclaiming the gospel. His own natural defects were involuntary, and he tried to be rid of them.[360] But the primary duty was to deliver the message of the gospel, and as a witness to make the facts stand out.

Attempts have been made to interpret Paul as a man who belittled learning. Actually Paul does not advocate obscurantism which denies mundane knowledge of culture. He draws attention to the inadequacy of such knowledge. Clarence Tucker Craig has made this observation of Paul's position:

> He was a man of real though restricted scholarship. He does not disparage knowledge as such. But he is very certain that it does not bring men to God. That depends upon God's own act of redemption in the cross of Christ.[361]

The Cross signified for Paul not only a revelation of the wisdom of God but also the power of God. In making contact with Jesus' followers it was evident to Paul that they knew the power of the spiritual life and its source in God. He came to see that "it pleased God through the folly of what we preach to save those who believe."[362] In offering some explanatory comments Paul might have begun with this text, "For the word of the cross is folly to those who are perishing, but to us who are being saved it is the power of God."[363] Then he could have added, "The Jews demand signs and the Greeks seek wisdom."[364] But instead he inserts a free combination of a text from Isaiah[365] and a text from a Psalm.[366] The former passage deals with the emergency situation at the time the prophet faced the worldly-wise politicians in the Assyrian crisis. In order to reinforce and emphasize his argument Paul resorts to a paradox. "Has not made foolish the wisdom of the world?"[367] Paul concedes to the side of opposition that the cross seems to have the aspect of folly and stumbling-block, but seeing that when it is submitted to the test of experience and application it proves itself "the power of God, and the wisdom of God," it must be concluded that "the foolishness of God is wiser than men."[368] So with cogent reasoning and solemn irony Paul convicts the scorners of impotence and folly, for all know that there is neither in God. Then as if this were not sufficient evidence to support this paradox he adds these words of a general nature.

> For consider your call, brethren; not many of you were wise according to worldly standards, not many were powerful, not many were of noble birth; but God chose what is foolish in the world to shame the wise.[369]

This passage sweeps together three special classes of people as Jeremiah[370] had done, though Paul singles out those who are wise according to "worldly standards". He adds a term for non-entities, things that are not,[371] to describe those in the Church as they appear to men in the outside world. The wise in this world's wisdom receive considerable attention in Paul's Corinthian letters. This may be for the reason that he saw this as a particular fault in the Church there. In another general statement he remarks:

> Let no one deceive himself. If any one among you thinks that he is wise in this age, let him become a fool that he may become wise. For the wisdom of this world is folly with God.[372]

Again Paul finds it convenient to use the Old Testament to fortify his argument. He employs passages from Job[373] and from a Psalm[347] having to do in both cases with the oppression of the poor. The latter passage actually uses the term "man" instead of "wise" which would indicate either a slip in quoting or a deliberate change of words. The essential thing, however, is that Paul cautions the entire community which includes any self-styled σο φός among them against being deceived about the way to attain real wisdom. He is saying that whoever thinks that he is wise with "worldly wisdom," let him be born foolishly wise, that is, drop his silliness in order to become wise generally with heavenly wisdom. It is not the wisdom shown to be fool-ishness, to which Paul asks men to turn as a Savior, but the folly of Christ.

Several times in this discussion reference has been made to "the wisdom of this world." What does Paul mean by this phrase? What may be learned from his use of the word "wisdom"?

A few comments on these questions may be useful at this point. Paul fought just as hard against "the wisdom of this world" as against the attempt to obtain righteousness before God through the Law. The wisdom of this world and righteous-ness based on Law were to his mind both characteristic of the man who is seeking to assert himself before God. Just as Christ is the end of the attempt to gain righteousness by means of the Law, it must apply in the same sense that He is the end of the wisdom of this world. Henceforth, says Paul, "Let him who boasts, boast of the Lord,"[375] and this applies equally to Jews and Gentiles. "For it is not the man who commends himself that is accepted, but the man whom the Lord commends."[376]

The "wisdom of the world"[377] to which Paul refers is a de-finite way of thinking consisting of certain contents. Without going into the study of the wisdom of God (σοφία, sophia) as pictured in the Old Testament, it can be stated that the Wisdom Literature appears in the teaching of Jesus.[378] But there is this distinction. Jesus took much of the old wisdom of the sages and used it to impart new and tremendous truths about the Kingdom of God which gave men new light in which to examine the realities of life and death. True wisdom is to be rooted in a right relationship or attitude toward God, according to Jesus.

The insights and interpretation given by Jesus in regard to the meaning of wisdom and its relation to God are further developed by Paul in at least two passages where he is endeavoring to bring out the significance of Christ. Paul exalts Christ to the point of conceiving wisdom incarnate in Him; Christ was "the wisdom of God," "our wisdom".[379] Paul was sure that the reality of God was revealed in Christ. In Christ are "hid all the treasures of wisdom and knowledge."[380] The wisdom of God is manifestly operative in what Christ was and did.[381] Elsewhere Paul speaks of imparting "a secret and hidden wisdom of God, which God decreed before the ages for our glorification."[382] It is a fair assumption that Paul's thought may have been influenced here by several Old Testament passages which move on similar lines.[383] The question is sometimes raised whether Paul claimed esoteric knowledge or wisdom claimed by the mystery cults. This issue may be clarified by showing that Paul actually rebuked the Corinthians who attempted such claims or imagined themselves to be equipped to unravel the deepest secrets of God. Paul charges that with all their "wisdom" and their Hellenistic learning and mystery cults, none had really understood God's method of revealing Himself in Christ through wisdom and power. The point is that they did not appreciate this higher wisdom and have thereby proved their incapacity. If they had understood "they would not have crucified the Lord of glory."[384] To Paul the wisdom of God was one of the "gifts of the Spirit of God."[385] God in his love has prepared wisdom for men from the beginning and is now revealing it to them according to their spiritual capacity and their willingness to put it to honest trial. Love is the key which unlocks this treasure chest of wisdom. The wisdom of God, born of love, can be revealed only to those who love. The gospel is not on trial before the natural, unspiritual man. Michelangelo is not on trial before the clay modeling class of the kindergarten. Even so must men understand that the Cross foiled its perpetrators.

Before going on to another matter it should be stated that Paul also speaks of the wisdom of this world in other terms. One reference may suffice to show this difference. He says in II Corinthians, "We destroy arguments and every proud obstacle to the knowledge of God, and take every thought captive to obey Christ."[386] It is clear in this passage that Paul means to use all the available knowledge and wisdom at his command to advance the truth of the gospel in order to win the obedience of men to Christ. It would be a mistake to think that Paul was discounting the knowledge and experience he actually had in general when he deals with specific objections to the use of "wisdom" as he so well outlines them. For instance, he relies firmly on the monotheistic base of Christian faith.[387] As a man who had been confronted by the revelation of God in Christ, Paul could not pretend that he did not bring the experience of this fact with him to any discussion of God. It is precisely this knowledge and experience which formed his view of what is ultimately significant in life.

In a large measure the recurrent contrast between foolishness and wisdom represents a great paradoxical theme for Paul. He throws a different light on this theme by his own testimony when he says to the Corinthians, "We are fools for Christ's sake, but you are wise in Christ."[388] This may be the counterpart of Paul's statement which he made earlier when he said to them, "let him become a fool that he may become wise."[389] Paul is issuing a warning to the builders who use different materials in constructing life. If they would build for eternity they must become as fools, for the wisdom of God is folly in the sight of worldly men.

In a different context Paul warned the Corinthians that in praising himself he would be acting like a fool.[390] Nevertheless not many verses later he confesses, "I have been a fool!"[391] He is not quoting the Corinthians, but is making a criticism of himself. He implies that he was not guided by any sound principle, but states "you forced me to it."[392] Instead of commendation and appreciation for his work among them, they gave heed to the insinuations of the Judaizers and others who sought to discredit him. Paul was thereby compelled, greatly against his will, to commend himself in order to free the Corinthians from the destructive influences of such individuals. But for this reason, he would never have committed such a folly.

Again it was at Corinth that Paul met the vexing problem of several factions revolving around prominent leaders.[393] Reference has already been made to these party divisions in the section of this work dealing with strength and weakness. The point of interest here is that instead of attempting a solution on the basis of argument or outward compulsion, Paul turned to their party strife with an ethical application. As long as they engage in such strife they are men of the flesh and do not possess the Spirit through which alone true wisdom comes. He reminds them that in God's Church it is He who gives the increase. They are not to be rivals, but fellow-workers for God. This situation had some of the familiar aspects of controversy which Paul encountered elsewhere.[394]

Paul recognized that mental ability may develop into a conceit of self-esteem on the one hand, and an over-bearing treatment of those who are less intelligent on the other hand. Either attitude blinds men to the realities of life. In a solemn warning Paul says, "Do not be deceived; God is not mocked, for whatever a man sows, that he will also reap."[395] And again, "Do not be deceived: 'Bad company ruins good morals.' "[396] Such expressions as these may have been intended for the worldly-wise, but their application need not be so limited. There is a word of warning here indicating a real risk involved in associating with those who lack sound judgment. Moreover there is a warning against unwise choices in view of the assured harvest.

The only wisdom the Corinthians can rightly point to, says Paul, has its source and nature in Christ "whom God made our wisdom, our righteousness and sanctification and redemption."[397] This wisdom imparts love and spiritual truth to men of the Spirit[398] to whom are revealed "What no eye has seen, nor ear heard."[399] There is an inner transformation which changes men who accept what the Spirit gives as an endowment. Paul draws this contrast, "The unspiritual man does not receive the gifts of the Spirit of God, for they are folly to him, and he is not able to understand them because they are spiritually discerned."[400] Does Paul mean to say, "worldly people, devoid of the Spirit,"[401] as Jude calls them? Not very likely for he was not himself incapable of movement toward the spiritual on the Damascus road. Paul is stating that God reveals Himself through His Spirit and that this revelation is imparted to and through men who have received the Spirit in ways which must be spiritually discerned. The point he makes is that man may be so occupied with his own material and intellectual interests that he has no mind to decipher what the Spirit of God has to impart.[402] Archibald Robertson and Alfred Plummer have made this revealing observation:

> Man as man is a spiritual being, but only some men are actually spiritual; just as man is a rational being, but only some men are actually rational. Natural capacity and actual realization are not the same thing.[403]

This statement tells of the significant difference in human levels of understanding in man's nature. It helps to see an important distinction in the kind of life man chooses to live. In a paradox of obvious meaning, Paul said to the Colossians: "Set your minds on things that are above, not on things that are on earth."[404] And to the spiritually minded in his Philippian letter he gave the assurance that the upward call of God in Christ Jesus would guide them, but if they were otherwise minded, "God will reveal that also to you."[405] They are to be guided and led by the grace of God which they have already received.

Paul's paradoxical theme of foolishness and wisdom is given further study in the letter to the Romans. The setting is different, and the people are different. But the gospel is needed there as much as anywhere else. Paul addresses himself to the two-fold theme: (1) Salvation is by faith "to every one who has faith"; and (2) Salvation is for all mankind "to the Jew first and also to the Greek."[406] Having said this much Paul proceeds to speak of the revelation of God. He says: "Ever since the creation of the world his invisible nature, namely, his eternal power and deity, has been clearly perceived in the things that have been made."[407] But men have thought more of the creature than the Creator, and by their impiety and iniquity suppress the truth of God in its disclosure and practice. They hinder the truth of God concerning their true nature. As a consequence of such action

> they became futile in their thinking and their senseless minds were darkened. Claiming to be wise, they became fools, and exchanged the glory of the immortal God for images resembling mortal man or birds or animals or reptiles.[408]

That is to say men who esteem their own thoughts and desires as the supreme standard of judgment have in effect given up the quest to discover God's righteousness and thus find themselves surrounded by mental impotence and confusion. The phrase "they became fools" coined in the Greek word $\dot{\varepsilon}\mu\omega\rho\acute{a}\nu\theta\eta\sigma\alpha\nu$ has the meaning to make dull or foolish. Since people of this description do not give God His rightful place their actions make them dull to His way for life. They subject themselves to idolatry. This does not mean that they cease to be God's creation. Some light of God's truth reaches them through human reason and consciousness for they have a conscience and are responsible for their choice.[409] God may also be known through His visible works of creation. Men are without excuse. As Paul's purpose unfolds he reaches the point of saying, "But now the righteousness of God has been manifested . . . through faith in Jesus Christ for all who believe."[410] Paul issues a general warning on the dangers of disobedience to God having in mind the human tendency toward idolatry.[411] His insight has been illustrated time and time again.

Elsewhere Paul takes up another aspect of this problem in connection with food offered to idols.[412] Here is truly one of the great landmarks in the history of human liberty. The question of food, while important for Paul, does not hold his attention for long. He soon raises the discussion to a higher level, and arrives at a solution for a transitional problem which can never lose its significance. Rather than cause a "brother" to stumble, Paul shows the strength of wisdom by not eating such food.[413] He urges others to avoid using their Christian liberty as a "stumbling-block" to the weak.[414] There must be mutual forbearance as well as personal conviction. The important thing is whether the work of God is built up or hindered. Christ did not please himself but sought His Father's will.

The theme of foolishness and weakness has a bearing on human pain and suffering. It was noted in discussing the paradoxical theme of law and grace that God's suffering is manifested in the Cross of Christ through love. By this demonstration of suffering-love mankind has been able to endure hardship as well as to gain the wisdom of knowing how to deal with suffering when it comes. Men are not to seek or impose self-inflicted harm to themselves or to others. This kind of suffering is neither wise nor necessary in the Christian faith. There is a higher wisdom which arches over the foolishness of men and this wisdom finds its most rewarding expression in love. In the closing lines of his verse play called "Good Friday," John Masefield has one of his actors say these significant lines concerning wisdom:

> I cannot see what others see;
> Wisdom alone is kind to me,

Wisdom that comes from agony.

. . . .

Wisdom that lives in the pure skies,
The untouched star, the spirit's eyes;
O Beauty, touch me, make me wise.[415]

There is wisdom that human blindness can reveal and understand even as this act has done. Then there is wisdom for those who see wisdom in the lilies of the field and in trustful and dedicated lives.

Paul, in his letter to the church at Colossae takes note of the good work being done there and prays that the people might

be filled with knowledge in all spiritual wisdom and understanding, to lead a life worthy of the Lord, fully pleasing to him, bearing fruit in every good work and increasing in the knowedge of the Lord.[416]

It was Paul's great desire to "present every man mature in Christ. For this I toil, striving with all the energy which he mightily inspires within me."[417] Jesus has spoken of making men "whole." Paul pursued his vocation with a disciplined mind and enriched in Christian experience. His faith was oriented toward God in the service of Christ Jesus.

To what then does this section come? The first impression of Paul's paradoxical words is that he seems to deny to reason its proper rights, to glorify at the expense of thought the acceptance of another's assertions, and to regard intellectual depth as something alien to the gospel. In reality, however, he does no one of these things. The first thing to remember is that "the wisdom of the world" which Paul has in mind was the so-called wisdom of the mystery cults, Hellenistic speculation, and the Rabbinical hair-splitting of the Jews. What Paul contrasts is not faith and reason, but faith and the demand for signs or for an intellectual display. The second thing to recall is that faith in no wise discounts reason, though, the appeal to faith is not an appeal to reason alone. Faith is an act of the whole man, and it is to the whole man that the gospel appeals. Man's nature is rational as a whole. Heart, and mind, and conscience are meant to work together, and illuminate one another. And faith is the response of the whole man to a message and to a person, that appeal to his nature as a whole. Thus it is that, rational as the gospel is, it is not always the most "wise" people who accept it. It is rather the people in whom heart, mind, and conscience have full play. Much depends on the receptiveness of the individual. Spiritual wisdom is spiritually discerned. The strange thing is that when one lives in and through his Christian faith, it is precisely then that faith, by its own nature, brings new resources and understanding, insights and demands into his life.

Paul knows of divine wisdom which may appear to men as foolishness. Yet the foolishness of the Cross proved that the power of love was more powerful than the shrewdest wisdom of men. This is to say there is a kind of foolishness which actually turns out to be wisdom. Paul came to know wisdom in knowing what is foolishness. The testing ground for man is faith and reason in relation to God and fellowmen. There are different levels of understanding and experience which must be taken into account in any realistic appraisal of life. It is not wisdom to be wise only in the things of earth which can be measured or possessed as so much property. The spirit of man is restless until it finds a dwelling place, a house not made with hands but made of things eternal.

CHAPTER V

THE NATURE AND PURPOSE
OF THE PAULINE PARADOX

In Chapter Four the attempt was made to study some specific paradoxical themes of Paul such as sovereignty and freedom, law and grace, living through dying, strength through weakness, foolishness and wisdom with the view of determining their relationship and the quality of truth they represent.

This chapter will be devoted to a general study of the nature and purpose of the Pauline paradox. The first thing to remember is that Paul's paradoxes reveal a remarkable knowledge of Jesus' spirit and teaching. William Kilbourne Stewart expressed his view on this point as follows:

> The Pauline paradoxes harmonize admirably with the Gospel mood, and furnish a partial refutation of the charge that Paul was a stranger to the mind of Jesus.[1]

Paul no doubt also learned through his Pharisaic training how to make effective use of paradox. He seems to delight in using this literary and religious form of expression.

A. *Paul's Reasons for Using Paradox*

1. *Effective Way to Present Ideas.* One of the reasons Paul used paradox probably was that he found it to be an effective way of getting and riveting attention on some hidden or ne-

glected truth. He may have realized as Jesus did that by introducing something strange or surprising in the form of paradox the curiosity of the hearer might be aroused by some memorable phrase which would linger in the memory.[2] Speaking of the use Jesus and Paul made of paradox as a rhetorical device DeWolf remarks:

> It seems often to have been an intentional means of stimulating more earnest and penetrating thought. 'For whoever would save his life will lose it' implies no logical contradiction, since the saving and losing have obviously to do with different levels of being. But the utterance of such a paradox does tend to set the hearer to thinking about his experience, and by the rational contemplation of such experience as Jesus' words recall to mind, he may well come to a profounder understanding of his duty, which is to say, of God's will for him.[3]

Mandell Creighton gave these reasons for the use of paradox which indirectly bear upon this discussion. He said: "The two chief means of teaching are exaggeration and paradox. One or other is necessary to attract attention and show reason for independent thought."[4] And again, "Paradoxes are useful to attract attention to ideas."[5] A new thought often requires a change of preliminary concepts.

2. *Presence of Seeming Logical Contradictions.* Did Paul use paradox in such a manner as to involve himself in real logical contradiction? This question is often posed by scholars and the answers vary considerably. G. G. Findlay has this to say about Paul, "He seems to some a man of contradictions."[6] It may be added that others take the opposite point of view. James S. Stewart claims:

> Paul can contradict himself, can land himself at times in hopeless antinomy, can leap without warning from one point of

182

view to another totally different, can say in the same breath 'Work out your own salvation,' and 'It is God which worketh in you,' but through it all and beneath it all there is a living unity and a supreme consistency — the unity, not of logic, but of downright spiritual conviction, the consistency of a life utterly and at every point filled and flooded with the redeeming love of God.[7]

The passage cited by Stewart can be interpreted otherwise as was shown in Chapter Four. The context makes it clear that Paul was using sound logic and persuasion. Arthur Darby Nock had this to say of Paul:

He makes no attempt to harmonize concepts which may seem logically inconsistent. He never says 'probably' or 'possibly' the only shading of language which he employs is his occasional distinction between the instruction and teaching which he gives as coming from Jesus and which he gives as of his own authority — and he clearly expects his disciples, in fact, to follow both equally.[8]

This statement points up the fact that Paul did not seek to work out a close system of thought. Some of his remarks may seem on the surface to be logically inconsistent, yet upon closer study reveal an inherent relationship on a different level of meaning. In regard to the thought that Paul expected his followers to receive both his and Jesus' teaching equally, may it not be said that Paul endeavored to express the spirit and meaning of Jesus' life and work so that he did not conceive of his own teaching as being essentially different from the teaching of Jesus in that respect.

Paul threw the light of the gospel in many different directions depending largely on the issues and the practical necessities which called forth his letters. It is well said by Amos N. Wilder that:

Our chief handicap in regard to Paul is not, however, the special categories in which his thought necessarily moves; but rather the level at which it moves. . . . Paul like Jesus is dealing with ultimates, and it is only as we crave an answer with regard to ultimates that we can enter at all sympathetically into his thought world, his issues and his convictions.[9]

There are various levels of meaning and being which such words as physical, mental, spiritual, moral, and social imply. The subject matter involved in Paul's paradoxical themes must be analyzed in the light of this fact.

3. *Experience Affords Truth in Paradox.* One of the most enlightening comments made by Paul about his own experience appears in Philippians in the phrase, "For I have learned."[10] (Ἐγὼ γὰρ ἔμαθαν). This is to say study and observation contributed to this knowledge. Intellectually he learned from others. But he also gained truth through his creative religious experience in contact with God. His paradoxical themes are related to life and reflect spiritual-ethical connotations.

Marcus Tullius Cicero once determined to make a study of the ethical doctrines of the Stoics because he wanted to test and see if the paradoxes which they put forth were true to experience. He states his findings as follows:

These doctrines are surprising, and they run counter to universal opinion — the Stoics themselves actually term them paradoxa; so I wanted to try whether it is possible for them to be brought out into the light of common daily life and expounded in a form to win acceptance, or whether learning has one style of discourse and ordinary life another; and I wrote with the greater pleasure because the doctrines styled paradoxa by the Stoics appear to me to be in the highest degree Socratic, and far and away the truest.[11]

One example of such a Stoic paradox will have to suffice here, namely, "That only the wise man is free, and that every foolish man is a slave."[12] While it would not be proper to draw conclusions from the statement by Cicero in respect to the Pauline paradoxes, it is nevertheless true that experience plays an important part in both cases. Paul solved many of his problems in religious experience and moral action. He knew that it was a part of probability to expect that many improbable things can happen in life.

A brief resumé of Paul's reasons behind the use of paradox would include his literary appreciation of many forms of expression, but especially of paradox. His cultivation of paradoxical themes indicates the knowledge, for example, that divine grace in relation to human moral force or power cannot be reduced to statement without making the form of the statement double. Henry J. Cadbury has made the observation that the relation of man's effort and God's effort has been a baffling problem, but that the rabbis discussed it centuries ago and tried to safeguard both answers. He goes on to say, "psychology characteristically recognizes how more than one emphasis can be in an individual mind."[13] The alleged logical contradictions may be attributed to the failure of understanding the "plane" on which Paul moves as well as the different relations to truth and experience.

B. *Paul's Sense of Obligation to Resolve Every Paradox*

1. *The Moral Necessity of Choice.* Paul believed that morals and religion are indissolubly united. He knew that there is no middle ground on moral issues, for even indecision is decision which often permits evil to operate more effectively. A statement by John Oman reveals how significant the matter of choice is in a paradoxical religious and moral situation. Here in his own words he says:

No truly religious and moral person is ever tempted to

compromise between his own will and God's or to consider them alien and opposite. The heart of all right living is to find ourselves by denying ourselves, to direct ourselves by renouncing our own preference, and to possess our world by losing it. We are persons, and not merely individuals, precisely because we unite in one these seeming opposites, and attain our independence as we find ourselves in God's world and among His children.[14]

The new spiritual life was for Paul a moral life. It meant that important choices had to be made. He believed it was incumbent upon him to think and act in line with what God expected of Him. His religious and intellectual training fitted him to weigh the evidence,[15] and to choose the practical and moral aim[16] in settling church problems as his letters testify. His exhortations to live the moral life follow in most instances the acknowledgment that he is speaking to believers. Robert Newton Flew has characterized the Pauline exhortations in these words, "Be what you are."[17] That is to say Paul was urging people to live a moral life because they had chosen to be Christian. The phrase "in Christ" which Paul uses frequently in connection with the Christian life could be taken to mean "in dependence upon Christ."[18] Paul's entire life was a moral and mental "growing up in Christ."[19] He had a moral sense of obligation to resolve his paradoxes in daily life.

2. *The Ethical Obligation of Daily Life.* Paul was confronted with the problem of the pneumatikoi at Corinth and the results that came because there were those who tried to detach the Christian teaching from moral and ethical requirements. He warned about the judgment to come.[20] Even in his Thessalonian letters where the apocalyptic mood seems to be dominant, he does not omit the ethical aspects of living.[21] Paul stands solidly on the ground that the new moral and ethical life is based on spiritual transformation.[22] He seems to employ the thought of Jesus on a fruit-bearing life, for in Galatians these words appear

after a review of the works of the flesh: "But the fruit of the Spirit is love, joy, peace, patience, kindness, goodness, faithfulness, gentleness, self-control."[23] Other passages of his strike the same or similar ethical notes.[24] Among them is this one in Philippians in these memorable lines: "Finally, brethren, whatever is true, whatever is honorable, whatever is just, whatever is pure, whatever is lovely, whatever is gracious . . . think about these things."[25] The underlying motivation of the ethical obligation in daily life is to be found in Paul's phrase, "the love of Christ controls us."[26]

Paul did not attempt to form a system of ethics. He considers himself a letter writer[27] and preacher of the gospel, but his letters are full of moral and ethical ideas. Percy Gardner points to Romans and says:

> In that Epistle he is mainly bent as in the Corinthian Epistles he is almost entirely bent upon what is ethical, what has relation to conduct, and to human love and hope.[28]

The Christian faith is not guided by a set of rules to be rigidly followed, but finds its direction in a way of life dedicated to God. Its teaching centers in personal relationship to God through Christ and consequently in embodied truth.

In his study of the Church, Ernst Troeltsch found two forms of social influence, the conservative and revolutionary. He analyzes these influences in the following manner:

> May it be that the two forms of social influence which have just been indicated, which are apparently diametrically opposed to each other, are not after all two equally possible applications existing side by side, but that perhaps they really belong to each other and are united in the fundamental idea from which they sprang? . . . Although both these tendencies may at times diverge very widely, they might perhaps still be united in an inner relationship, and form a

united stream of development for the sake of the great ends to be realized.[29]

Troeltsch discerns a personal reflection of these two tendencies at work in Paul's teachings. The conservative social attitude calls into question the existing institutions, while the revolutionary tendency recognizes the orders of society as orders of creation. He goes on to say:

> It is my belief that, without danger of a forced construction, we are right in saying that the Pauline turn of thought in relation to social matters corresponds to the spirit and meaning of the Gospel.[30]

The study of eschatology and social responsibility which was made by Ray C. Petry led him to conclude that the eternal and temporal concerns have consistently been interlaced. In speaking of Paul he made this observation:

> Every letter that Paul writes to his Christian friends is full of his preoccupation with the new world that is yet to be. Because of this fact — by no means in spite of it — he enjoins upon them a type of conduct in the existing society that shall prove their allegiance to their future city.[31]

Paul was not a spectator sitting on a bleacher seat watching the "game" of life. His letters are proof positive that he was an active participant in the affairs of daily life. He was spiritually, ethically, and socially concerned about the application of the gospel. He did not stand apart and simply observe the preoccupations and needs of men. Emile Durkheim laid it down as a sociological requirement that a student of religion must not take account of his own religious experience, and it is repeatedly stressed that the observer must not become involved in the subject's attitudes.[32] This point of view is untenable for any conscious act must be

188

interpreted in the light of the total situation, and this includes the person's attitudes at the moment of reaction, thus such detachment as Durkheim desires is an arbitrary exclusion of important data. Paul offers a view which includes an outgrowth of his personal convictions and ethical understanding based on the spirit and teaching of Jesus. In his letter to the Philippians he makes the appeal: "Have this mind among yourselves, which you have in Christ Jesus."[33] The word "mind" may be taken in a twofold sense. It means obviously Jesus' manner of thinking and living, but likewise the "new creation" of life in Christ for the believer.[34] Both aspects must be kept in mind when one interprets the gospel or translates it into life.

3. *The Mystical Element in Testimony.* It has at times been argued that mysticism was not in keeping with the Jewish religion. William Ralph Inge once stated, "The Jewish mind and character in spite of its deeply religious bent, was alien to mysticism."[35] This view is challenged by Jewish scholars in publications which deal with the mystical element of religion.[36] The evidence they present points in the direction that Paul very likely knew of this aspect in Judaism before he came into contact with the Christian Way. If this is correct, and there is good reason to suppose it is, then the statement by Albert Schweitzer that Paul "is the only one who knows only 'Christ-mysticism' "[37] cannot be taken as final.

The testimony of Paul guards against taking mysticism as absorption into God in Christ where the individual loses all personal identity. Paul believes that those who know God in terms of inner reality become the sons of God.[38] He clearly states, "It is no longer I who live, but Christ who lives in me," and this is followed immediately by "the life I now live in the flesh I live by faith in the Son of God."[39] The mystical element is thus carried into the new experience of the Christian life where it is developed in terms of social expression. Rufus M. Jones has given this excellent thought or definition of mysticism:

189

Mysticism is the type of religion which puts the emphasis on immediate awareness of relation with God, on direct and immediate consciousness of the Divine presence. It is religion in its most acute, intense, and living stage.[40]

In other words, the true mystic is he who lives religion, and not one who simply thinks or processes it. Jacques Maritain has offered the following evaluation of mystical life:

Thirty years ago in France, the word 'mystic' stirred up all sorts of reactions of mistrust and uneasiness; one could not hear it spoken without immediately being on one's guard against an eventual invasion of fanaticism and hysteria. . . . Now we understand better and better that the more or less pathological counterfeits of the mystical life are doubtless numerous, but that the true mystics are the wisest of men and the best witnesses for the spirit.[41]

By taking such statements as the two preceding ones into account it may be easier to deal with the subject of true mysticism.

Paul believed here were duties which accompany the Christian life.[42] His view of the Church and the general basis of his ethical teaching is convincing testimony of applied mystical faith. His paradoxical themes in many instances cannot be understood without the admission of the mystical element of religion.

4. *The Missionary Requirement of Unambiguous Preaching and Teaching.* It is evident from the nature of Paul's letters that he was endeavoring to clarify issues rather than confuse them. He says in II Corinthians, "For we write you nothing but what you can read and understand."[43] He had a dislike for the ambiguous because it did not edify the other person. In I Corinthians he indicates that he preferred to speak five intelligible words, rather than ten thousand in a tongue which no one understood.[44] When Cephas came to Antioch Paul accused him and certain others of acting insincerely and not straightforward

about the truth of the gospel in respect to the Gentiles.[45] In several passages Paul mentions false teachers who perverted the truth.[46] He admonishes the brethren at Corinth for their jealousy and strife in taking sides as ordinary men. He asks, "What then is Apollos? What is Paul? Servants through whom you believed, as the Lord assigned to each. I planted, Apollos watered, but God gave the growth."[47]

The content of the gospel points to the method of relationship as basic to its effective communication. Paul believed that men are enabled to trust God, to love others, and become mature persons in Christ only because God has taken the initiative in loving them. But God's love as revealed in Jesus Christ is communicated to men through those who love and care as they have been loved. The truth of the gospel must be spoken in words and accents which are understood by those who are addressed if there is to be an intelligible response. Paul's missionary work brought him to many different places and into contact with a great variety of people. He was not content to let remain in the center of his teaching and preaching that for which he could give no reasonable account. Everywhere he went he proclaimed in word and deed that different backgrounds and different thoughts can be reconciled in a common loyalty. On the basis of Christian experience fellowship embraces diversity as both the Gospels and Paul's letters indicate. The Church is not to be set against the world, but those within the Church are called upon to witness according to their Christian experience in the world. Elias Andrews has well stated:

> The Gospel is only adequately and effectively communicated to the world in the measure that the Church identifies itself with the purposes of God for humanity, and seeks to reveal in its witness the life divine as sacrificial love.[48]

In dealing with Paul, John W. Oman makes a statement which has significance here in terms of the missionary requirement of unambiguous preaching and teaching. Oman attempts to show that Paul's usual beginning place was moral sincerity.

> Then he reasoned from men's experience of God's goodness in life and from their groping after Him in worship to His presence in their hearts. Finally, he gave a reasoned presentation of the significance of Jesus Christ for faith, all set in the atmosphere of humble and sincere dealing with one's own soul, in which alone men can see the things in which they ought to believe.[49]

Perhaps it should be stated before closing this discussion that in most instances in Paul's letters he presupposes some concept of Jesus and his teaching otherwise there would not be the expected response. However, the general tone of his missionary endeavors is one of communication through a divine-human relationship manifested in love and response to life.

To recapitulate: This chapter has shown that Paul had a keen sense of moral responsibility in making choices. Although he did not try to establish a system of ethics, his teachings reveal unmistakably the ethical obligations of daily life. Paul's testimony in respect to his faith in Christ as well as to the social application of his faith makes it clear that the mystical element in religion mean inner and outer relationships and not absorption into God in Christ. Finally, Paul believed that the missionary requirement for unambiguous preaching and teaching was based on the clear communication of the gospel through the personal experiences of the followers of Jesus Christ. The truth concerning God and man could, he believed, be demonstrated in the occurrences and happenings of daily living.

C. *Paul's Own Understanding of Paradox*

1. *A Clue to His Own Nature.* In Chapter Four and elsewhere in this work quotations from Paul's letters and state-

ments about Paul reveal important aspects of his own thought or what scholars have offered by way of interpretation. The interest here is to see what clue there may be to his own nature relative to his understanding of paradox. The first thing to take note of is the sheer pressure of experienced facts in religion which finds expression in his paradoxical themes. Walter R. Matthews has made the notation that a paradoxical character is attached to every activity of the mind and emerges with full force in religion. He states:

> We shall be mistaken if we suppose that the paradox and the difficulties to which it gives rise are peculiar to religion, for they exist in every level of spiritual experience. The theory of knowledge, the theory of ethical values and the theory of beauty, all have their fundamental problems which arise from the central situation — that of the self in contact with an object with which it can neither be wholly identical nor from which it can be wholly different. This paradox manifests itself with peculiar intensity in the life of religion, precisely because religion is the most intense form of the spirit's being.[50]

Paul, like the Hebrew prophets before him, believed intensely that God reveals Himself in ways that are accessible and intelligible to the mind and spirit of man. As a man in communion with God, Paul assumed that his experience could be productive of the fruits of the Spirit. He had an unshaken confidence in God and in his own mission. Eric Lane Titus has remarked:

> We should not blame him because the lines were not always clear, that the customs of the day, the petty disputes which, close up, seemed so important, sometimes obscured his vision. The marvel is that amid all the distracting forces he returned consistently to the central affirmation of his new-found faith: For it is the God who said, "Let light shine

193

out of darkness," who has shone in our hearts to give the light of the knowledge of the glory of God in the face of Christ (II Cor. 4:6).[51]

The great features of human attractiveness to Paul's personality are the many contrasts which he contains within himself. It can be affirmed with a statement by William Cleaver Wilkinson that "Paul, like his Lord, was fond of paradoxes, and, like his Lord, he presented in himself a miracle of paradoxes reconciled."[52] For instance, he "died with Christ" to all the evil which draws men away from God, and he rose with Christ to begin living the new life "in Christ." The aim of Paul henceforth was not only to become, but to be, what Christ had made him, namely, a son and heir of God. In being able to reach beyond self and in communion with God Paul released the springs of creative living. He was deeply sensitive to the fact that his own nature was being transformed by the grace of God. He had real convictions about life and destiny and these convictions issued in a sense of vocation.

2. *A Clue to His Calling.* Paul's response to God and to human need constitutes an important part of his call. He had sincere convictions about his calling to preach the gospel. He states that "necessity is laid upon" him through a commission.[53] In his letter to the Galatians he tells of being set apart for his mission even before he was born, and that it was through God's grace that he was called.[54] Here is a striking similarity between the call of Jeremiah and that of Paul.[55] Both men see in retrospect that God has been involved in their lives even before they became conscious of this fact.

Paul not only believes that he has been called, but he also writes to the Corinthians saying "consider your call."[56] He was making a general statement, but the meaning could also apply specifically to individuals. The call to every man is distinct and in ways which can be understood. The gospel is communicated through personal relationship to God in Spirit and in embodied

194

truth. This is a noteworthy revelation of God and a great discovery of man. In the case of Paul it meant, for instance, that through the Son of God's love sinners became sons. It meant that instead of trying to obtain righteousness before God through the Law he could accept the free gift of God's grace and move to a higher level of righteousness. These are but two of the salient points of Paul's faith. It may be remembered that in Galatians he relates that he "advanced in Judaism beyond many of my own age among my people," indicating how extremely zealous he was for the traditions of his fathers.[57] His basic attitude here shows the action as continuing not as simply a statement of fact.[58] Although the nature of this advance is not spelled out, it could have been his intention to convey the thought that he had moved to a new level of being as a Christian. In any case he does state in Philippians, "I press on toward the goal for the prize of the upward call of God in Christ Jesus."[59] This is significant in view of the nature of Paul's own understanding of paradox in relation to his call.

Paul was deeply conscious of his own inadequacy as one responsible to God. But he was willing to do what he could do by the help of God. His preaching of the gospel of the Cross at Corinth will serve as an illustration of this point.[60] He sensed his own limitations, but he was confident that the Spirit of God would verify his message by transforming the lives of those who believed. In this he was not disappointed and took courage. Elsewhere in his thought of the power of the gospel Paul is led to observe that the gospel is hampered by the limitations of "earthen vessels".[61] In this paradox the contrast is between the priceless treasure and its humble, fragile "vehicle" which emphasizes the relation between the divine power and the human messenger. Paul goes on to relate some of the humiliations and sufferings which he has survived by the life of Jesus within him. The physical sufferings in the ministry of Jesus are a living death, but the inner secret which sustains him is a dying life.[62] Closely related to this paradox is another which follows. The ministry which means humiliation and vicarious suffering brings life in those to whom he ministers.[63] Therefore in the same "spirit of faith" as the Psalmist,[64] Paul speaks out, assured that the power which raised Jesus from the dead will enable those who share his death to be presented with them, who are spared the apostolic sufferings of mortal flesh, before the throne of God.[65] "So we do not lose heart," says Paul. "Though our outer nature is wasting away, our inner nature is being renewed every day."[66] This passage is not a paradox, but simply indicates that the physical nature is subject to deterioration while the spiritual nature shows steady advancement.

The clue to Paul's calling lies in his tremendous faith in God and in his own sense of unworthiness to preach the gospel. He was a flaming witness. Truth lived in him. It was to a great extent his fertile ingenuity and fiery enthusiasm which helped to enlarge the borders of the Christian movement.

3. *The Reasonableness of His Position.* Paul is a man who makes different impressions on different people. He reveals so much of himself that often he is misunderstood not only by those to whom his letters were directed but by scholars in contemporary circles. Ernest F. Scott has stated:

> It has been the misfortune of Paul that so many of the words he uses have come to be theological terms, which only a trained thinker can be expected to understand. Paul himself was not aware that his language was of this kind. He detested vague, high-sounding phrases, such as were employed by false teachers at Colossae and elsewhere, and studied to express himself, not in a religious jargon, but in familiar words which would convey a sense of reality.[67]

The part that Paul's picture language plays in his letters is not to be treated lightly. He relies very much on the use of symbolic figures of speech, comparisons, and analogies. In order to understand Paul it is necessary to understand and interpret his word pictures as well as the literary and literal words. Such a procedure, in the study of Paul, serves as a safeguard against the attempts to treat his words as propositions which fit the pattern of a theological system. George B. Findlay recognized the fact that Paul has been charged with confusion and obscurity by some scholars. His reply to this charge is summed up in the following statement:

> His obscurities are those of depth, not of dimness or confusion; the obscurities of a mind profoundly sensible of the complexities of life and thought and sensible to their varying hues, their crossing lights and shadows, — of a man who, with all he knows, is conscious that he only 'knows in part.' If we must speak of defects, they are the defects of a teacher, who is too full of the grandeur of the truth he utters, and too much absorbed in the Divine work of his calling, to make words and style his care.[68]

The really important thing for Paul in the Christian religion is the relationship of God and man as expressed by two great words, namely, grace and faith. The word he uses to indicate the supreme relation between one man and another is love. The meaning of this two-fold relationship has been observed in Chapters Four and Five of this work. Therefore it will not be necessary here to amplify what has been said.

The present section is to show the "reasonableness" of Paul's position. In what sense does the term "reasonable" apply to the meaning of Paul's statements? The first thing to remember is that faith for Paul means the total response to God of mind and heart and soul and strength. This obviously includes the use of reason, for it involves belief, trust, and decision. But it is not an appeal to reason alone. It is the whole man responding to a message and to God. In writing to the Corinthians Paul uses argument and persuasion to present the gospel. He says, "Knowing the fear of the Lord, we persuade men; but what we are is known to God, and I hope is known also to your conscience."[69] Here Paul makes an appeal to reason and conscience. Elsewhere he calls attention to the responses men make in terms of hope, love, sorrow, and forgiveness.[70] In his letter to the Romans he called the brethern "by the mercies of God," as he has unfolded them,[71] to commit their bodies as living sacrifices to God. Then Paul added, "which is your λογικήν, reasonable service."[72] In other words it is a "logical" service they are to render to God for what He has done. It is not what they own, but their own selves that God desires.

In a study of Paul's use of the conjunction ἵνα, Ethelbert Stauffer arrived at the conclusion that " 'Not leading hither, but directing thither' is the key to his thought." (" 'Nicht Herleiten, sondern Hinfuehren' ist das Prinzip dieses Denkens.")[73] The foregoing passage illustrates the point that Paul sought to direct attention to the personal relationship which should exist between God and men. On the basis of this relationship their minds are to be μεταμορφοῦσθε transformed, transfigured[74] and so capable of proving by test, of ascertaining and appreciating in experience what things are "good and acceptable and perfect" according to the will of God.[75] Christian faith has values which can be learned from the incidents which show its presence and from those which reveal its absence. All men have faith, but there is a difference in the kind and the quality of faith they have. Faith oriented toward God is the kind of faith Paul sets forth in his letters. This is more than a matter of disposition, for it involves the inner life of man. The "reasonableness" of Paul's position is taken here to mean that his teaching counts on the use of reason to receive, interpret, and transmit whatever revelation and discovery have to offer.

In brief, Paul's deeply religious nature, his calling and commission, his devotion and determination in the quest of truth which can be embodied and demonstrated are the best possible proof of his own understanding of paradox.

CHAPTER VI

SUMMARY AND CONCLUSION

A. *Summary*

1. *Varied Aspects of This Study.* In summarizing the results of this work it will be useful to recall the main aspects of each chapter. In Chapter One it was made clear that the object of this study was to determine the relation of certain paradoxical themes as set forth by Paul, with the view of finding the quality of truth they have to offer. Nine of his New Testament letters were chosen as primary source materials for this analysis, namely, Roman, I and II Corinthians, Galatians, Philippians, Colossians, I and II Thessalonians, and Philemon. As a working hypothesis it was suggested that Paul's paradoxical themes might reveal and communicate meaning by the method of personal relationship. Several different possibilities were projected in regard to Paul's use of paradox. It was noted that other solutions would probably appear as the study progressed. There are a limited number of resources which deal expressly with the subject under consideration. The contemporary significance of this work is accentuated by an increasing number of books and articles dealing with paradoxical problems which confront man and society.

2. *Nature of Paradox.* In the first section of Chapter Two the discussion revolves around the definition of paradox. It is pointed out that experience and expression of experience often involves any one or several factors such as the rhetorical, semantic, religious, psychological, ethical. The attempt was made to distinguish paradox from a number of literary forms in order to

set it in clearer perspective. In this general treatment of paradox it was noted that men have employed paradox in poetry, in science and that it has more than standing room in the Bible. The section on contemporary theological usage of paradox bears considerable fruit in terms of different levels of comprehension and communication as set forth by scholars. The discussion of the meaning of words reveals a sense of inadequacy which, in the nature of the case, accompanies every attempt to convey experience. There are mysteries which are recognized by both science and religion beyond man's present understanding and knowledge. There are natural and psychological limitations in man's nature which have to do with the world without and the world within. Yet in spite of these recognized limitations religious communication takes place and religious faith is established.

3. *Historical Background.* No man lives on an island or in a vacuum isolated from men and events of history. In Chapter Three the Jewish, Hellenic, and Roman background of Paul is discussed in terms of relative importance. But the salient feature was his own creative religious experience which released the springs of living water to feed his soul. The most valuable part of his original contribution does not rest so much in the formal expressions of faith as in the living dynamic which enables him to demonstrate the power and the spirit of truth. Such truth requires an association with persons. In the case of Paul it meant first of all a personal relationship with God through Christ Jesus, and secondly a right relationship to one's neighbor. The sections dealing with differences and similarities between Jesus and Paul arrive at the conclusion that Paul had a remarkable insight into the convictions and teaching of Jesus. The high evaluation given to Paul by Hans Lietzmann on this point is accepted. "He had never sat at the feet of the Master, but nevertheless was the only one amongst the apostles who really understood him."[1] It was suggested that there may be similarities in their use of paradox and the evidence has supported this contention.

4. *Some Paradoxical Themes of Paul.* The Fourth Chapter consists of the study and exegesis of these five paradoxical themes of Paul: sovereignty and freedom, law and grace, living through dying, strength through weakness, foolishness and wisdom. The aim is to discover the internal and external level of meaning indicated by these themes. The theme of sovereignty and freedom is viewed in its historical development and in terms of personal connotations. God is seen as the manifestation of energy, as a King, and as a loving Father. Paul developed the latter concept and made it central in his thought of sonship. He saw that God through the Son of His love enabled sinners to become sons. Here a new relationship was established which gave meaning to freedom. Paul is free, yet bound. He is free from "slavery," but accepts a new kind of bondage. As a man freed from the crowd's opinions, he is now a man bound by the crowd's needs. The theme of law and grace receives considerable notice in Paul's letters. He pays tribute to the historical, moral and religious contributions which the Law has made to Judaism and as a "custodian" to the Gentiles. But he learned by experience that salvation is received through grace and faith. A new level of righteousness was obtained in Christ which took precedence over the Law. The Incarnation demonstrates the paradox of grace. It remains for men to understand the true nature of incarnate being in themselves. The theme of living through dying has more than physical meaning, for Paul wishes to signify the spiritual and ethical aspects of life. Men are to die to their "old selves" and be born or raised to "newness" of life in Christ. Paul apparently believed that a new order of being commenced with Christ. Physical death was not the final word in Paul's view. He saw in the present life the framework of what was to be in the future life beyond. The theme of strength through weakness points to the fact that human inadequacy can be an opening wedge through which God may enter and strengthen human life. The admission of weakness and need of help in prayer is not to be misconstrued as helplessness, but as a sign of reliance

upon the true source of power. In a particular circumstance Paul spoke of being weak, yet strong. Here he recognizes his own limitations, but also the adequacy of God. The Cross of Christ seemed to come as a sign of weakness, but Paul saw in the Cross the Divine power of God for salvation. But that is not all he saw, for he reminds his hearers that strength is a moral and ethical responsibility. Those who are strong must help bear the burdens of the weak even as Christ has done. The strong are to limit their liberty in love rather than cause the weak to stumble. Mutual forbearance and personal conviction must govern daily life according to Paul. The theme of foolishness and wisdom emphasizes the human tendency toward intellectual pride. Man pretends to have more knowledge than he actually possesses and this often breeds conceit or an over-bearing spirit over the less fortunate. The key issue which Paul lifts up has to do with the Cross. The "wisdom of the world" was incompetent at the point of knowing there was a higher wisdom in Christ crucified. The suffering love of God was revealed there, and consequently the ministry of reconciliation impinges upon the life and action of men everywhere. Paul did not disparage true knowledge, but he saw some dangers and limitations of human wisdom when contrasted with the divine wisdom. He knew the meaning of wisdom as an inner relationship to God which could be expressed in moral and ethical living. It is not wise to have only earthly wisdom as Jesus declared, and to ignore the heavenly wisdom which determines the destiny of the soul. That is to say there are different levels of wisdom which are open to men for their journey through life.

5. *Nature and Purpose of the Pauline Paradox.* The aim of Chapter Five is to present a general picture of the Pauline paradox in respect to its nature and purpose. A number of possible reasons are given for his use of paradox. He may have used it to get attention or to arrest interest by the element of surprise. Some of his remarks may appear to be logically inconsistent, but a closer examination will reveal that he is ac-

tually moving on different levels of experience. His seeming contradictions are truths in fact. He applies truth in different relations. Paul resolves many of his paradoxes within himself, and in their application to daily life. His sense of obligation to resolve every paradox is indicated by the moral, ethical, mystical, and missionary features of his faith and work. He was deeply conscious of his own unworthiness to preach the gospel and accepted the task with a great sense of responsibility to God. Experience taught him to understand what will do in life, by finding out what will not do. His sensitive religious nature plus the constraint of his calling forms the basis for his tremendous enthusiasm and zeal in preaching the gospel. The paradoxical themes he develops are evidence of his attempts to reach men's minds and hearts in order to establish a personal relationship with God as revealed in Christ. His themes can best be understood in the light of different levels of being and in different relations to communicable truth.

B. *Conclusion*

1. *Main Conclusions of This Study.* Such light as has been discovered in regard to the relationship of Paul's five paradoxical themes may be gathered up and emphasized in the following main conclusions:

First, the paradoxical themes which are the basis of this study reveal a relationship between God and man which is both one-sidedly and mutually personal. The gospel is communicated by the method of relationship with God taking the initiative.

Second, Paul conceives of truth as being capable of demonstration in the spiritual and psychological relations of life. He is a thinker in whom reverence and a sense of moral and social responsibility had sobering and compassionate effects.

Third, the study of Paul's paradoxical themes has led to the conclusion that there is no logical contradiction involved. There is rather a seeming contradiction, but a truth in fact. His words which appear to be in opposition to one another are actually ways of imparting truth from different angles.

Fourth, the evidence points to the fact that the position taken at the outset of his work is essentially correct. It may be reiterated that a paradox points the way to an inherent meaning deeper than is directly articulated. This meaning may lie in the difference of subject matter, in different applications of truth, in a deeper level of being.

Fifth, there is no inflexible method which can be applied to Paul's paradoxical themes since they vary in their subject matter and purpose. For instance, he does not arrive at a philosophical solution in dealing with the theme of sovereignty and freedom. He accepts both as being true in some manner, as did some of his contemporaries. His moral and social admonitions and instructions presuppose man's freedom of response. He is certain that God's sovereignty will not be usurped.

Sixth, it has been established that Paul resolves many of his paradoxes within himself through spiritual and psychological and ethical relations of life. It can therefore be safely assumed that since his paradoxical themes are produced in life they can also be resolved in life.

Seventh, Paul is conscious of different shades of meaning in his use of words. Some of his words obviously reflect the inadequacy of language to express the full meaning he desires to convey. Religious experience can never be more than partially communicable.

Eighth, it is Paul's intention to clarify rather than confuse the issues which relate God and man, and man to man. He tries to avoid the ambiguous thoughts and superficial things of this world. He is a flaming witness intensely interested in bringing people into a vital relationship with God as well as with their neighbor.

Ninth, the paradoxical themes of Paul bring forth new dimensions of depth in their relationship to one another. Men are to die to their old "selves," for example, and be raised to "newness" of life in Christ. The point of weakness in their lives may become the place of God's entrance as the true source of strength.

Tenth, Paul proclaims the duty of the followers of Jesus to make known God's truth and to prove it true by their transformed minds and hearts. His paradoxical themes are an indication of different layers of divine-human experience.

2. *Supplementary Conclusions*: In bringing this study to a close a few supplementary conclusions may be added.

Paul is a man of breadth and depth in the religious life. He was educated into greatness by the increasing weight of his responsibilities and the manner in which he met them. His mind was keenly aware of the fact that part of probability consists in admitting that improbable things can and do happen.

The ceiling of men's minds is not the limit of what God can do. The limitations of human knowledge must be humbly acknowledged in every field of human endeavor. The likelihood that men will soon, or perhaps ever, reduce reality to a comprehensive unity from which everything paradoxical has been removed is too fanciful to contemplate.

Paul is a pioneer in matters pertaining to the personal and social aspects of the Christian faith. His genius in dealing with basic ideas rather than conventional forms reflects both the spirit and the insight of Jesus. His paradoxical themes reveal their relationship at the level on which he moves along with the direction to which he points.

Recent books and magazine articles show new trends in the reappraisal of who Paul was and what he accomplished. There are clear indications that the permanent and distinctive contributions of his life and work have not been lost, but rather that they serve as beacon lights to guide the destiny of those who champion the universal gospel of Christ in every age.

BIBLIOGRAPHY

A. *Books*

Andrews, Elias, *The Meaning of Christ for Paul.* New York: Abingdon-Cokesbury Press, 1949.

Andrews, Mary Edith, *The Ethical Teaching of Paul.* Chapel Hill: University of North Carolina Press, 1934.

Apocrypha. Introd. by Robert H. Pfeiffer. New York: Harper and Brothers Publishers, n.d.

Aubrey, Edwin Ewart, *Man's Search for Himself.* Nashville: Cokesbury Press, 1940.

Aulén, Gustaf, *The Faith of the Christian Church.* Translated by Eric H. Wahlstrom and G. Everett Arden. Philadelphia: Muhlenberg Press, 1948.

Bacon, Benjamin W., *Jesus and Paul.* New York: Macmillan Company, 1921.

Baillie, Donald M., *God Was in Christ.* New York: Charles Scribner's Sons, 1948.

Baillie, John, *The Place of Jesus Christ in Modern Christianity.* New York: Charles Scribner's Sons, 1929.

Baldwin, Chauncey Edward, *Types of Literature in the Old Testament.* New York: Thomas Nelson and Sons, 1929.

Barclay, William, *A New Testament Wordbook.* London: SCM Press, 1955.

Barnett, Lincoln, *The Universe and Dr. Einstein.* New York: The New American Library, 1950.

Barth, Karl, *The Doctrine of the Word of God.* Translated by G. T. Thompson. Edinburgh: T. and T. Clark, 1936.

————. *Das Wort Gottes und die Theologie.* Munich: Kaiser, 1924.

————. *The Knowledge of God and the Service of God According to the Teaching of the Reformation.* Translated by J. L. M. Haire and Iran Henderson. New York: Charles Scribner's Sons, 1939.

————. *Der Römerbrief.* Munich: Kaiser, 1922.

Bauer, Walter, *Wörterbuch zum Neuen Testament.* Berlin: Verlag Alfred Topelmann, 1952.

Berdyaev, Nicolas, *Freedom and the Spirit.* Translated by Oliver Fielding Clarke. New York: Charles Scribner's Sons, 1935.

————. *Slavery and Freedom.* Translated by R. M. French. New York: Charles Scribner's Sons, 1944.

————. *Solitude and Society.* Translated by George Reavey. New York: Charles Scribner's Sons, 1938.

————. *The Meaning of the Creative Act.* Translated by Donald A. Lowrie. New York: Harper Brothers, 1955.

Bertocci, Peter Anthony, *Free Will, Responsibility, and Grace.* New York: Abingdon Press, 1957.

Bianchi, Martha Dickinson and Alfred Leete Hampson, *Further Poems by Emily Dickinson.* Boston: Little, Brown and Company, 1929.

Blunt, Alfred W. F., *The Epistle to the Galatians.* Oxford: Clarendon Press, 1925.

Bousett, Wilhelm, *Kyrios Christos.* Göttingen: Vandenhoeck, 1921.

————. *Jesus.* Translated by Janet P. Trevelyan. New York: G. P. Putnam's Sons, 1906.

Browning, Robert, "Rabbi ben Ezra" St. VII, *Masterpieces of Religious Verse.* Edited by James Dalton Morrison. New York: Harper and Brothers Publishers, 1948.

Bruce, Alexander Balmain, *St. Paul's Conception of Christianity.* New York: Charles Scribner's Sons, 1909.

Brunner, Emil Heinrich, *The Christian Doctrine of Creation and Redemption,* Vol. II. Translated by Olive Wyon. London: Lutterworth Press, 1952.

——. *The Christian Doctrine of God,* Vol. I. Translated by Olive Wyon. London: Lutterworth Press, 1949.

——. *Philosophie und Offenbarung.* Tübingen: J. C. B. Mohr, 1925.

——. *Der Mittler.* Tübingen: J. C. B. Mohr, 1927.

——. *The Philosophy of Religion.* Translated by A. J. D. Farrer and Bertram Lee Woolf. New York: Charles Scribner's Sons, 1937.

——. *The Misunderstanding of the Church.* Philadelphia: Westminster Press, 1953.

Bulcock, Harry, *The Passing and the Permanent in St. Paul.* London Macmillan and Company, 1926.

Bultmann, Rudolf Karl, *Jesus and the Word.* Translated by Louise Pettibone Smith. New York: Charles Scribner's Sons, 1934.

Bultmann, Rudolf Karl, *Theology of the New Testament.* Translated by Kendrick Grobel. 2. vols. New York: Charles Scribner's Sons, 1951-55.

——. *Primitive Christianity in its Contemporary Setting.* Translated by Reginald H. Fuller. New York: Thames and Hudson, 1956.

Brown, William Adams, *How to Think of Christ.* New York: Charles Scribner's Sons, 1945.

Burnaby, John, *Christian Words and Christian Meanings.* New York: Harper and Brothers Publishers, 1955.

Burr, Amelia Josephine, "Certainty Enough," *Selected Lyrics.* New York: Doubleday and Company, 1927.

Burrows, Millar, *An Outline of Biblical Theology.* Philadelphia: Westminster Press, 1946.

Burton, Ernest DeWitt, *Galatians,* ICC. New York: Charles Scribner's Sons, 1920.

Burton, Richard, "Strength in Weakness," *Masterpieces of Religious Verse.* Edited by James Dalton Morrison. New York: Harper and Brothers Publishers, 1948.

Cadbury, Henry J., *Jesus: What Manner of Man.* New York: Macmillan Company, 1947.

Carroll, John B., *The Study of Language*. Cambridge: Harvard University Press, 1953.

Chase, Stewart, *The Tyranny of Words*. New York: Harcourt, Brace and Company, 1938.

Chesterton, Gilbert Keith, *Orthodoxy*. New York: Dodd, Mead and Company, 1938.

Chesterton, Gilbert Keith, *Orthodoxy*. New York: Dodd, Mead and Company, 1938.

Cicero, Marcus Tullius, *Paradoxes of the Stoics*. Translated by H. Rackham. Vol. II, Book III. Cambridge: Harvard University Press, 1942.

Clark, Thomas Curtis, (ed.), *1000 Quotable Poems*, "Ulysses." Chicago: Willet, Clark and Company, 1937.

Clarke, James Freeman, *The Ideas of the Apostle Paul*. Boston: James R. Osgood and Company, 1884.

Clarke, William Newton, *The Christian Doctrine of God*. New York: Harper and Brothers, 1914.

Coates, John Rider (ed. and trans.), *Bible Key Words*. New York: Harper and Brothers, 1951.

Conybeare, W. J. and J. S. Howson, *The Life and Epistles of St. Paul*. New York: Charles Scribner's Sons, 1899.

Cotton, Edward Howe (ed.), *Has Science Discovered God?* New York: Thomas Y. Crowell Company, 1931.

Cragg, Gerald R., *Romans*, The Interpreter's Bible. Edited by Nolan B. Harmon and Others. IX, New York: Abingdon-Cokesbury Press, 1954.

Craig, Clarence Tucker, *Corinthians*, The Interpreter's Bible. Edited by Nolan B. Harmon and Others. X, New York: Abingdon-Cokesbury Press, 1953.

Creighton, Mandell, *Life and Letters of Mandell Creighton*. Edited by Louise Creighton. II. New York: Longmans, Green and Company, 1904.

Cronin, Archibald Joseph, *Adventure in Two Worlds*. New York: McGraw-Hill, 1952.

Culler, Arthur J., *Creative Religious Literature*. New York: Macmillan Company, 1930.

Cumont, Franz, *Oriental Religions in Roman Paganism*. Chicago: Open Court Publishing Company, 1911.

Daiches, Raphael David, *The Paradox of Tragedy*. Bloomington: Indiana University Press, 1960.

Davies, William David, *Paul and Rabbinic Judaism*. Cambridge: University Press, 1948.

Deissmann, Gustaf Adolf, *St. Paul: A Study in Social and Religious History*. Translated by Lionel R. M. Strachan. New York: Hodder and Stoughton, 1912.

————. *St. Paul: A Study in Social and Religious History*. Translated by William E. Wilson. New York: George H. Doran and Company, (1923), 1926.

————. *The Religion of Jesus and the Faith of Paul*. Translated by William E. Wilson. New York: George Doran Company, 1923.

DeMorgan, Augustus, *A Budget of Paradoxes*. Edited by David Eugene Smith. 2 vols. Chicago: Open Court Publishing Company, 1915.

————. *A Budget of Paradoxes*. Edited by Sophia DeMorgan. One Vol. London: Longmans, Green and Company, 1872.

DeWolf, L. Harold, *A Theology of the Living Church*. New York: Harper and Brothers Publishers, 1953.

————. *The Religious Revolt Against Reason*. New York: Harper and Brothers Publishers, 1949.

Dibelius, Martin and Werner Georg Kummel, *Paul*. Translated by Frank Clarke. Philadelphia: Westminster Press, 1953.

Dickie, E. P., *Revelation and Response*. New York: Charles Scribner's Sons, 1938.

Dill, Samuel, *Roman Society from Nero to Marcus Aurelius*. London: Macmillan Company, 1920.

Dodd, Charles Harold, *The Meaning of Paul for Today*. London: Swarthmore Press, (1920), 1937.

————. *The Epistle of Paul to the Romans*, Moffatt New Testament Commentary. New York: Roy Long and Richard R. Smith, 1932.

Duncan, George, *The Epistle of Paul to the Galatians,* Moffatt New Testament Commentary. New York: Harper and Brothers Publishers, 1934.

Durkheim, Emile, *The Rules of Sociological Method,* 8th ed. Translated by Sarah A. Solovay and John H. Mueller. Edited by George E. G. Catlin. Chicago: University of Chicago Press, 1930.

Eby, Kermit, and June Greenlief, *The Paradoxes of Democracy.* New York: Association Press, 1956.

Edman, Irwin, *The Mind of Paul.* New York: Henry Holt and Company, 1935.

Edwards, Jonathan, "Observations Concerning Faith," *Works.* II. New York: Robert Carter and Brothers, 1864.

Eisler, Rudolf, *Handwörterbuch der Philosophie.* Berlin: E. S. Mittler und Sohn, 1922.

Enslin, Morton Scott, *The Ethics of Paul.* New York: Harper and Brothers, 1930.

Evans, Ernest, *Corinthians,* Clarendon Bible. Oxford: University Press, 1952.

Fairbairn, Andrew Martin, *Studies in Religion and Theology.* New York: Macmillan Company, 1910.

——. *Philosophy of the Christian Religion.* New York: Macmillan Company, 1902.

Farmer, Herbet H., *Experience of God.* London: Student Christian Movement Press, 1929.

Feifel, Herman (ed.), *The Meaning of Death.* New York: McGraw-Hill Book Company, 1959.

Findlay, George B., *The Epistles of the Apostle Paul.* London: C. H. Kelly, n.d.

Finegan, Jack, *Beginnings in Theology.* New York: Association Press, 1956.

Finney, Charles Grandison, *Lectures in Systematic Theology.* Edited by J. H. Fairchild. Oberlin: E. J. Goodrich, 1878.

Flew, Robert Newton, *The Idea of Perfection*. London: Oxford University Press, 1934.

Friedländer, Ludwig, *Roman Life and Manners Under the Early Empire*. Translated by J. H. Freese and Leonard A. Magnus. 2 vols. New York: E. P. Dutton and Company, n.d.

Fritsch, Charles Theodore, *The Qumran Community: A Study of the Scrolls*. New York: Macmillan Company, 1956.

Fromm, Erich, *The Art of Loving*. New York: Harper and Brothers Publishers, 1956.

Gardner, Percy, *The Religious Experience of St. Paul*. New York: G. P. Putnam's Sons, 1911.

Garvie, Alfred Ernest (ed.), *Romans*, New-Century Bible. New York: Oxford University Press, 1901.

Gassner, John (ed.), *Twenty Best Plays*. New York: Crown Publishers, (1939), 1941.

Gloag, Paton James, *Introduction to the Pauline Epistles*. Edinburgh: T. and T. Clark, 1874.

Goodspeed, Edgar J., *Paul*. Philadelphia: John C. Winston Company, 1947.

————. *The Apocrypha*. Chicago: University of Chicago Press, (1929), 1938.

————. *Problems of New Testament Translation*. Chicago: University of Chicago Press, 1945.

Grant, Frederick C., *An Introduction to New Testament Thought*. New York: Abingdon-Cokesbury Press, 1950.

Hadas, Moses, (ed. and trans.), *The Third and Fourth Books of Maccabees*. New York: Harper and Brothers, 1953.

Hadfield, James Arthur and Others, *The Spirit*. Edited by Burnett Hillman Streeter. New York: Macmillan Company, 1919.

Hamilton, Edith, *The Roman Way*. New York: W. W. Norton, 1932.

————. *Witness to the Truth*. New York: W. W. Norton Company, 1948.

213

Hampson, William, *Paradoxes of Nature and Science.* New York: E. P. Dutton and Company, 1907.

Harnack, Adolf, *What is Christianity?* New York: G. P. Putnam's Sons, 1901.

Headlam, Arthur C., *Christian Theology.* London: Oxford University Press, 1940.

Hepburn, Ronald W., *Christianity and Paradox.* New York: Pegasus, 1966.

Hocking, William Ernest, *The Coming World Civilization.* New York: Harper and Brothers Publishers, 1956.

———. *Types of Philosophy.* New York: Charles Scribner's Sons, 1929.

———. *The Meaning of God in Human Experience.* New Haven: Yale University Press, 1912.

———. *Thoughts on Death and Life.* New York: Harper and Brothers, 1937.

Holtzmann, Heinrich Julius, *Lehrbuch der Neutestamentlichen Theologie.* II. Tübingen: J. C. B. Mohr, 1911.

Horton, Walter Marshall, *Christian Theology: An Ecumenical Approach.* New York: Harper and Brothers Publishers, 1955.

Hook, Sidney, *The Paradoxes of Freedom.* Berkeley: University of California Press, 1962.

———. *Theism and the Modern Mood.* New York: Harper and Brothers, 1930.

Howlett, Duncan, *The Essenes and Christianity.* New York: Harper and Brothers Publishers, 1957.

Howson, John S., *The Metaphors of St. Paul.* London: Strachan and Company, 1869.

Hoyle, R. Birch, *The Holy Spirit in St. Paul.* New York: Doubleday, Doran and Company, 1928.

Hunter, Archibald Macbride, *Interpreting Paul's Gospel.* Philadelphia: Westminster Press, 1954.

———. *The Unity of the New Testament.* London: SMC Press, 1943.

Hutchison, John A., *Language and Faith*. Philadelphia: The Westminster Press, 1963.

Inge, William Ralph, *Christian Ethics and Modern Problem*. New York: G. P. Putnam's Sons, 1930.

———. *The Things That Remain*. New York: Harper and Brothers Publishers, 1958.

———. *Christian Mysticism*. New York: Charles Scribner's Sons, 1899.

Iverach, James, *The Life and Times of St. Paul*. New York: Anson, D. F. Randolph, n.d.

Jackson, J. J. Foakes, *The Life of Saint Paul*. New York: Boni and Liveright, 1926.

Johnson, A. H., *The Wit and Wisdom of Alfred N. Whitehead*. Boston: Beacon Press, 1947.

Jones, Rufus Matthew, *Studies in Mystical Religion*. New York: Macmillan Company, (1909), 1923.

Jones, Rufus Matthew, Harold Anson and Others, "Prayer and the Mystic Vision," *Concerning Prayer. Its Nature, Its Difficulties and Its Value*. London: Macmillan and Company, 1916.

Jowett, B., *The Dialogues of Plato*. I. London: Oxford University Press, 1924.

Kennedy, Gerald, *The Lion and the Lamb*. New York: Abingdon-Cokesbury Press, 1950.

Kennedy, Harry A. A., *St. Paul and the Mystery Religion*. New York: Hodder and Stoughton, 1913.

Kenner, Hugh, *Paradox in Chesterton*. New York: Sheed and Wood, 1947.

Kenyon, Frederic G., *Our Bible and the Ancient Manuscripts*. New York: Harper and Brothers, 1940.

Kepler, Thomas S. (Compiler), *Contemporary Thinking About Paul*. New York: Abingdon-Cokesbury Press, 1950.

———. *A Spiritual Journey with Paul*. New York: Abingdon-Cokesbury Press, 1953.

Kierkegaard, Sφren, *Philosophical Fragments*. Translated by

David Swenson. Princeton: Princeton University Press, 1946.
Publisher, 1927.

————. *Concluding Unscientific Postscript.* Completed by Walter
Lowrie. Translated by David Swenson. Princeton: Princeton
University Press, 1941.

————. *Sickness Unto Death.* Translated by Walter Lowrie. Princeton: Princeton University Press, 1946.

————. *Christian Discourses.* Translated by Walter Lowrie. New
York: Oxford University Press, 1939.

King, Henry Churchill, *Reconstruction in Theology.* New York:
Macmillan Company, 1901.

Kirk, Kenneth E., *Romans,* Clarendon Bible. Oxford: University Press, 1937.

Kittel, Berhard (ed.), *Theologisches Wörterbuch zum Neuen
Testament.* II, III. Stuttgart: W. Kohlammer, (1938, 1935)
1957.

Klausner, Joseph, *From Jesus to Paul.* Translated by William
F. Stinespring. New York: Macmillan Company, 1943.

————. *Jesus of Nazareth.* Translated by Herbert Danby. New
York: Macmillan Company, (1925), 1953.

Knox, John, *Christ the Lord.* New York: Willett, Clark and
Company, 1941.

————. *Romans,* The Interpreter's Bible. Edited by Nolan B.
Harmon and Others. IX. New York: Abingdon-Cokesbury
Press, 1954.

Knox, Ronald Arbuthnott, *Trials of a Translator.* New York:
Sheed and Word, 1949.

Knox, Wilfred Lawrence, *St. Paul and the Church of the Gentiles.*
Cambridge: University Press, 1939.

Knudson, Albert C., *The Principles of Christian Ethics.* New
York: Abingdon-Cokesbury Press, 1943.

————. *Basic Issues in Christian Thought.* New York Abingdon-
Cokesbury Press, 1950.

————. *The Doctrine of God.* New York: Abingdon Press, 1930.

216

Kake, Kirsopp C., *Paul: His Heritage and Legacy*. New York: Oxford University Press, 1943.

Lalande, Andre, *Vocabulaire de la Philosophie*. Paris: Libraire Felix Alcan, 1926.

Lewis, Edwin, *Great Christian Teachings*. New York: Methodist Book Concern, 1933.

Lidgett, J. Scott, *The Fatherhood of God*. Edinburgh: T. and T. Clark, 1902.

Lietzmann, Hans, *The Beginnings of the Christian Church*. Translated by Bertram Lee Woolf. New York: Charles Scribner's Sons, 1937.

Lightfoot, Joseph Barber, *Biblical Essays*. London: Macmillan and Company, 1893.

————. *Saint Paul's Epistle to the Philippians*. New York: Macmillan Company, 1903.

Littel, Colie Rosalia, *Paradoxia Epidemica*. Princeton: Princeton University Press, 1966.

Lippmann, Walter, *A Preface to Morals*. New York: Macmillan Company, 1929.

Lodge, Sir Oliver, *Modern Scientific Ideas*. London: Ernest Benn Publisher, 1827.

Lowell, James Russell, "Stanzas on Freedom," *Masterpieces of Religious Verse*. Edited by James Dalton Morrison. New York: Harper and Brothers Publishers, 1948.

Luccock, Halford E., *Preaching Values in the Epistles of Paul*. I. (Romans and First Corinthians). New York: Harper and Brothers, 1959.

Lynip, Ryllis Goslin, *Great Ideas of the Bible*. New York: Harper and Brothers Publishers, 1954.

Magee, John B., *Religion and Modern Man*. New York: Harper and Row, Publishers, 1967.

Macgregor, W. M., *Christian Freedom*. New York: Harper and Brothers, 1931.

Major, H. D. A., T. W. Manson and C. J. Wright, *The Mission and Message of Jesus.* New York: E. P. Dutton and Company, 1938.

Manson, William M., "Grace in the New Testament," *The Doctrine of Grace.* Edited by W. T. Whitley. London: Student Christian Movement Press, 1932.

Marcel, Gabriel, *Creative Fidelity.* New York: The Noonday Press, 1964.

Maritain, Jacques, *Ransoming the Time.* New York: Charles Scribner's Sons, 1941.

Markham, Edwin, "A Free Nation," *Masterpieces of Religious Verse.* Edited by James Dalton Morrison. New York: Harper and Brothers Publishers, 1948.

Masefield, John, "Good Friday," *Verse Plays.* New York: Macmillan Company, 1925.

Matthews, Walter R., *God in Christian Thought and Experience.* London: Nisbet and Company, 1930.

McNeile, A. H., *New Testament Teaching in the Light of St. Paul's.* New York: Macmillan Company, 1923.

Moffatt, James, *The Epistle of Paul to the Corinthians,* Moffatt New Testament Commentary. New York: Harper and Brothers Publishers, n.d.

————. *Grace in the New Testament.* New York: Richard Long and Richard R. Smith, 1952.

————. *Love in the New Testament.* New York: Richard R. Smith, 1930.

————. *The Approach to the New Testament.* London: Hodder and Stoughton, 1921.

Montefoire, Claude G., *Rabbinic Literature and Gospel Teachings.* New York: Macmillan and Company, 1930.

————. *Religious Teaching of Jesus.* London: Macmillan and Company, 1910.

————. *Judaism and St. Paul.* London: M. Goshen, 1914.

Moore, George Foote, *Judaism in the First Centuries of the Christian Era.* I. Cambridge: Harvard University Press, 1927.

218

Moore, Paul Elmer, *The Christ of the New Testament*. Princeton: Princeton University Press, 1924.

Morgan, William, *The Religion and Theology of Paul*. Edinburgh: T. and T. Clark, 1917.

Morris, Charles, *The Open Self*. New York: Prentice-Hall, 1948.

Moses, David G., and Others, "The Problem of Truth in Religion," *The Authority of Faith*. Vol. I The Madras Series. New York: International Missionary Council, 1939.

Moulton, James H. and George Milligan, *The Vocabulary of the Greek New Testament*. Grand Rapids: Eerdmans Publishing Company, 1950.

Niebuhr, Reinhold, *The Nature and Destiny of Man*. 2 vols. New York: Charles Scribner's Sons, 1941-43.

————. *Christian Realism and Political Problems*. New York: Charles Scribner's Sons, 1953.

————. *The Self and the Drama of History*. New York: Charles Scribner's Sons, 1955.

————. *Reflections on the End of an Era*. New York: Charles Scribner's Sons, 1934.

Neil, William, *St. Paul's Epistles to the Thessalonians*, Torch Bible Commentaries. London: SCM Press, 1957.

Nestle, D. Eberhard, (ed.), *Novum Testamentum Greece*. Stuttgart: Privilegierte Wurttembergische Bibelanstalt, 1948.

Nock, Arthur Darby, *St. Paul*. New York: Harper and Brothers Publishers, 1938.

Nygren, Anders, *Commentary on Romans*. Translated by Carl C. Rasmussen. Philadelphia: Muhlenberg Press, 1949.

Ogden, Charles and Ivor A. Richards, *The Meaning of Meaning*. New York: Harcourt, Brace and Company, (1923), 1936.

Oman, John W., *The Paradox of the World*. Cambridge: University Press, 1921.

————. *Grace and Personality*. New York: Macmillan Company, 1925.

Onions, C. T., (ed.), *A Shakespeare Glossary*. Oxford: Clarendon Press, 1941.

Papini, Giovanni, *The Life of Christ*. Translated by Dorothy Canfield Fisher. New York: Harcourt, Brace and Company, 1923.

Parkes, James W., *Jesus, Paul and the Jews*. London: Student Christian Movement Press, 1936.

Pascal, Blaise, *Pensées*. Edited by Louis Allard. Montréal: Les Editions Variétés, n.d.

Petry, Ray C., *Christian Eschatology and Social Thought*. New York: Abingdon Press, 1956.

Pfleiderer, Otto, *Primitive Christianity*. Translated by W. Montgomery. I. New York: G. P. Putnam's Sons, 1906.

————. *Lectures on the Influence of the Apostle Paul on the Development of Christianity*. Translated by J. Frederick Smith. London: Williams and Norgate, 1885.

Plato, *Epistles*, VII, 343A. Translated by R. G. Bury. New York: G. P. Putnam's Sons, 1929.

Ploeg, J. Van Der, *The Excavations at Qumran: A Survey of the Judean Brotherhood and Its Ideas*. Translated by Kevin Smyth. New York: Longmans, Green and Company, 1958.

Plummer, Alfred, *Second Epistle of St. Paul to the Corinthians*, ICC. Edinburgh: T. and T. Clark, 1956.

Porter, Frank C., *The Mind of Christ in Paul*. New York: Charles Scribner's Sons, 1930.

Poteat, Edwin McNeill, *The Dimension of Depth*. New York: Harper and Brothers Publishers, 1957.

Pringle-Pattison, A. Seth, *The Idea of God in Recent Philosophy*. New York: Oxford University Press, 1920.

Rahlfs, Alfred, (ed.), *Septuaginta*, 3rd ed. Stuttgart: Bibelanstalt (1935), 1949.

Rall, Harris Franklin, *According to Paul*. New York: Charles Scribner's Sons, 1947.

————. *Christianity*. New York: Charles Scribner's Sons, 1941.

Ramsay, William M., *The Teaching of Paul in Terms of the Present Day*. London: Hodder and Stoughton, 1913.

———. *The Cities of St. Paul*. New York: A. C. Armstrong and Son, 1908.

———. *Pauline and Other Studies*. New York: A. C. Armstrong and Son, 1906.

———. *St. Paul the Traveler and the Roman Citizen*. New York: G. P. Putnam's Sons, 1898.

Ridderbos, Herman, *Paul and Jesus*. Translated by David H. Freeman. Philadelphia: Presbyterian and Reformed Publishing Company, 1958.

Riddle, Donald Wayne, *Paul: Man of Conflict*. Nashville: Cokesbury Press, 1940.

Robertson, Archibald and Alfred Plummer, *The First Epistle of St. Paul to the Corinthians*, ICC. New York: Charles Scribner's Sons, 1925.

Robinson, Henry Wheeler, *The Christian Doctrine of Man*. Edinburgh: T. and T. Clark, 1911.

Rolfe, William James, (ed.), *The Poetic and Dramaitc Works of Alfred Lord Tennyson*, "De Profundis," Cambridge: Riverside Press, 1898.

Royce, Josiah, *Lectures in Modern Idealism*. New Heaven: Yale University Press, 1919.

———. *The Sources of Religious Insight*. New York: Charles Scribner's Sons, 1912.

———. *The World and the Individual*. New York: Macmillan and Company, 1901.

Russell, Bertrand, *An Inquiry into Meaning and Truth*. New York: W. W. Norton and Company, 1940.

Sabatier, Auguste, *The Apostle Paul*. Edited by George G. Findlay. Translator's name not stated. New York: James Pott and Company, 1891.

Salit, Charles R., *Man in Search of Immortality*. New York: Philosophical Library, 1958.

221

Sanday, William and Arthur C. Headlam, *The Epistle to the Romans*, ICC. New York: Charles Scribner's Sons, 1926.

Santayana, George, *"O World,"* Poems. Selected and revised by the author. New York: Charles Scribner's Sons (1901), 1923.

Schilpp, Paul Arthur, *The Quest for Religious Realism*. New York: Harper and Brothers, 1938.

Schweitzer, Albert, *Paul and His Interpreters*. Translated by William Montgomery. London: Adam and Charles Black, 1912.

————. *The Mysticism of Paul the Apostle*. Translated by William Montgomery. New York: Henry Holt and Company. 1931.

Scott, Charles A. A., *Living Issues of the New Testament*. Cambridge: University Press, 1933.

————. *New Testament Ethics*. Cambridge: University Press, 1930.

————. *Christianity According to St. Paul*. New York: Macmillan and Company, 1927.

————. *St. Paul, the Man and the Teacher*. Cambridge: University Press, 1936.

Scott, Ernest Findlay, *The Nature of the Early Church*. New York: Charles Scribner's Sons, 1941.

Scott, Ernest Findlay, *The Varieties of New Testament Religion*. New York: Charles Scribner's Sons, 1943.

————. *Paul's Epistle to the Romans*. London: SCM Press, 1947.

Sheldon, Henry C., *New Testament Theology*. New York: Macmillan and Company, 1911.

Slater, Robert Lawson, *Paradox and Nirvana*. Chicago: University of Chicago Press, 1950.

Smith, Walter Chalmers, "The Christian Paradox," *Masterpieces of Religious Verse*. Edited by James Dalton Morrison. New York: Harper and Brothers Publishers, 1948.

Sockman, Ralph Washington, *The Paradoxes of Jesus*. New York: Abingdon Press, 1936.

Somerville, David, *St. Paul's Conception of Christ*. Edinburgh: T. and T. Clark, 1897.

Sperry, Willard L., *The Paradox of Religion*. New York: Macmillan Company, 1927.

———. *Religion in America*. New York: Macmillan Company, 1946.

Stafford, Russell Henry, *The Paradoxes of the Kingdom*. Boston: Fort Hill Press, 1929.

Stamm, Raymond T., *Corinthians*, The Interpreter's Bible. X. New York: Abingdon-Cokesbury Press, 1953.

Steere, Douglas Van, *On Beginning from Within*. New York: Harper and Brothers, 1943.

Stendahl, Krister, Anton Fridrichsen and Others, *The Root and the Vine*. Introduction by A. G. Herbert. Dacre Press. London: Adam and Charles Black, 1953.

Stevens, George Barker, *The Pauline Theology*. New York: Charles Scribner's Sons, 1894.

Stewart, James S., *A Man in Christ*. New York: Harper Brothers Publishers, 1935.

Strachan, Robert Harvey, *The Second Epistle of Paul to the Corinthians*, Moffatt New Testament Commentary. New York: Harper and Brothers, 1931.

Streeter, Brunett Hillman, *The Primitive Church*. New York: Macmillan Company, 1930.

Sypherd, Wilbur Owen, *The Literature of the English Bible*. New York: Oxford University Press, 1938.

Thackeray, Henry St. John, *The Relation of Paul to Contemporary Jewish Thought*. London: Macmillan and Company, 1930.

Thompson, Francis, "The Hound of Heaven," *Masterpieces of Religious Verse*. Edited by James Dalton Morrison. New York: Harper and Brothers Publishers, 1948.

Tillich, Paul, *Systematic Theology*. I. Chicago: University of Chicago Press, 1951.

Titus, Eric Lane, *Essentials of New Testament Study*. New York: Ronald Press, 1958.

Trench, Richard Chenevix, *The Study of Words*. London: Macmillan and Company, 1876.

Troeltsch, Ernst, *The Social Teaching of the Christian Churches*. I. Translated by Olive Wyon. New York: Macmillan Company, 1938.

Underhill, Evelyn, *Worship*. New York: Harper and Brothers, 1937.

Walpole, Hugh R., *Semantic*. New York: W. W. Norton Company, 1941.

Wand, John W., *What St. Paul Said*. New York: Oxford University Press, 1952.

Watts, Allan W., *The Two Hands of God*. New York: Collier Books, 1963.

Watkinson, William L., *The Moral Paradoxes of St. Paul*. New York: Fleming H. Revell Company, n.d.

Weigle, Luther A., (ed.), *Bible Words That Have Changed in Meaning*. New York: Thomas Nelson and Sons, n.d.

Weiss, Johannes, *The History of Primitive Christianity*. 2 vols. Edited by F. C. Grant. Translated by R. Knopf, completed by four friends. New York: Wilson-Erickson, 1937.

————. *Paul and Jesus*. Translated by H. J. Chaytor. New York: Harper and Brothers, 1909.

Weizsäcker, Carl von, *Apostolic Age of the Christian Church*. I. Translated by James Millar. New York: G. P. Putnam's Sons, 1894.

Wernle, Paul, *Beginnings of Christianity*. I. New York: G. P. Putnam's Sons, 1903.

Whicher, George Frisbie, *This Was a Poet*. New York: Charles Scribner's Sons, 1939.

Whitehead, Alfred North, *Process and Reality*. New York: Macmillan Company, 1929.

Wieman, Henry Nelson, *The Source of Human Good*. Chicago: University of Chicago Press, 1946.

Wieman, Henry Nelson and Walter Marshall Horton, *The Growth of Religion*. New York: Willett, Clark and Company, 1938.

Wilder, Amos N., *New Testament Faith for Today*. New York: Harper and Brothers Publishers, 1955.

Wilder, Amos N., *The Language of the Gospel*. New York: Harper and Row, Publishers, 1964.

Wisdom, John, *Paradox and Discovery*. New York: Philosophical Library, 1965.

Wilkinson, William Cleaver, *St. Paul and the Revolt Against Him*. Philadelphia: Griffith and Roland Press, 1914.

Wilson, Thomas. *St. Paul and Paganism. Edinburgh*. T. and T. Clark, 1927.

Wrede, William D., *Paul*. Translated by Edward Lummis. London: Philip Green and Company, 1907.

———. *Paulus*. Halle: Gebauer-Schwetschke, 1904.

Zeitlin, Solomon, (ed.), *The Second Book of Maccabees*. Translated by Sidney Tedesche. New York: Harper and Brothers, 1950.

B.   *Articles*

Abelson, J., "Mysticism and Rabbinical Literature," *Hibbert Journal*, X (1911-1912), 426-477.

Andrews, Elias, "The Relevance of Paul for Preaching," *Canadian Journal of Religion*, II (1955-1956), 49-55.

Bartlet, J. Vernon, "The Life and Work of Paul," *Abingdon Bible Commentary*, (1929), 931-943.

Belkin, Samuel, "The Problem of Paul's Background," *Journal of Biblical Literature*, LIV (1935), 41-60.

Buckham, John Wright, "The Potency of Paradox," *Journal of Philosophy*, XLI (1944), 5-12.

Case, Shirley Jackson, "The Jewish Bias of Paul," *Journal of Biblical Literature*, XLVII (1928), 25-26.

Collingwood, R. G., "Reason is Faith Cultivating Itself," *Hibbert Journal*, XXVI (1927-28), 13-14.

Come, Arnold B., "Theology Beyond Paradox," *Religion in Life*, XXV (1955-56), 35-46.

Cross, Frank M., "The Scrolls and the New Testament," *Christian Century*, LXXII (1955), 968-971.

Cullmann, Oscar, "The Significance of the Qumran Texts for Research into the Beginnings of Christianity," *Journal of Biblical Literature*, LXXIV (1955), 213-226.

Davies, Paul E., "Paul's Missionary Message," *Journal of Bible and Religion*, XVI (1948), 205-211.

Enslin, Morton S., "Paul and Gamaliel," *Journal of Religion*, VII (1927), 360-375.

———. "The Place of Morality in the Thought of Paul," *Crozer Quarterly*, IV (1927), 159-170.

Fowler, Henry Thatcher, "Paul, Q and the Jerusalem Church," *Journal of Biblical Literature*, XLIII-XLIV (1924-1925), 9-14.

Hamilton, Clarence H., "Encounter with Reality in Buddhist Madhyamika Philosophy," *Journal of Bible and Religion*, XXVI (1958), 13-22.

Homrighausen, Elmer G., Review of Brunner, *The Divine-Human Encounter*, *Theology Today*, I (1944), 135.

Horton, Walter M., "Law and Grace," *Religion in Life*, XI (1941-42), 421-427.

Johnson, Paul W., "The Christian Concept of Freedom," *Religion in Life*, XIV (1944-45), 267-277.

Johnson, Sherman E., "Paul and the Manuel of Discipline," *Harvard Theological Studies*, XLVIII (1955), 157-165.

Knopf, Rudolph., "Paul and Hellenism," *American Journal of Theology*, XVIII (1914), 497-520.

Langer, Susanne K., "Form and Content: A Study in Paradox," *Journal of Philosophy*, XXIII (1926), 435-438.

McCormick, Virginia Taylor, "Paradox," *The Personalist*, (ed.), Ralph T. Flewelling. XVII (1936), 156.

Minkin, Jacob B., "Jewish Mysticism," *Journal of Religion,* XXIV (1944), 188-200.

Niebuhr, Reinhold, "Coherence, Incoherence, and Christian Faith," *Journal of Religion,* XXXI (1951), 167-168.

———. "The Contribution of Paul Tillich," *Religion in Life,* VI (1937), 574-581.

Niven, W. D., "New Testament Words," *The Expository Times,* LXVII (1955-1956), 136-137.

Riddle, Donald W., "The Jewishness of Paul," *Journal of Religion,* XXIII (1943), 240-244.

Shroyer, M., "Paul's Departure from Judaism to Hellenism," *Journal of Biblical Literature,* LIX (1940), 41-49.

Stewart, William K., "Christianity as Paradox," *Hibbert Journal,* XXVII (1928-29), 220-230.

Stewart, William K., "A Study of Paradox," *Hibbert Journal,* XXVII (1928-29), 1-14.

Thompson, Samuel "A Paradox Concerning the Relation of Inquiry and Belief," *Journal of Religion,* XXXI (1951), 91-93.

Tillich, Paul, "What is Wrong with Dialectical Theology?" *Journal of Religion,* XV (1935), 127-145.

Wilder, Amos N., "Paul Through Jewish Eyes," *Journal of Bible and Religion,* XII (1944), 181-188.

C. Encyclopedias

Bullinger, Ethelbert W., *A Critical Lexicon and Concordance,* 8th ed. London: Lamp Press, 1957.

Emry, H. G. and K. G. Brewster, (eds.), *New Century Dictionary.* New York: D. Appleton-Century Company, 1946.

Findlay, G. G., "Paul the Apostle," *Dictionary of the Bible,* edited by James Hastings and John Selbie. New York: Charles Scribner's and Sons, 1900, III, 696-731.

Ginzberg, L., "Cabala," *Jewish Encyclopedia.* Edited by Isidore Singer and Others. New York: Funk and Wagnalls Company, 1906, III, 456-479.

Jackson, Samuel Macauley, (ed.), "Parables of Jesus Christ, *New Schaff-Herzog Encyclopedia.* New York: Funk and Wagnalls Corporation, 1910, VIII, 344-348.

Jacob, Ernest I., "Paul," *Universal Jewish Encyclopedia.* Edited by Isaac Landman. New York: Universal Jewish Encyclopedia, 1942, VIII, 415-417.

Jenkinson, A. J., "Paradox," *Dictionary of Christ and the Gospels.* Edited by James Hastings and Others. New York: Charles Scribner's Sons, 1908, II, 319.

Kohler, Kaufmann, "Saul of Tarsus," *Jewish Encyclopedia.* Edited by Isidore Singer and Others. New York: Funk and Wagnalls Company, 1907, XI, 79-87.

Liddell, Henry George and Robert Scott, *A Greek-English Lexicon.* 2 vols. Oxford: Clarendon Press, (1843), 1948.

Lodge, Oliver, "Physics," *Encyclopaedia Britannica.* 14th ed. rev., 1942, XVII, 880-883.

MacCulloch, J. A., "Parable," *Encyclopedia of Religion and Ethics.* Edited by James Hastings and Others. New York: Charles Scribner's Sons, 1924, IX, 631-632.

Mackie, G. M., "Parable," *Dictionary of the Bible.* One Vol. Edited by James Hastings. New York: Charles Scribner's Sons, 1942, 679.

Mellone, S. H., "Paradox," *Encyclopedia of Religion and Ethics.* Edited by James Hastings. New York: Charles Scribner's Sons, 1924, IX, 632.

Moffatt, James, "Essenes," *Encyclopedia of Religion and Ethics.* Edited by James Hastings. New York: Charles Scribner's Sons, 1912, V, 396-401.

Moulton, W. J., "Parable," *Dictionary of Christ and the Gospels* Edited by James Hastings and Others. New York: Charles Scribner's Sons, 1908, II, 312-317.

Neilson, William Allan (ed. in Chief), *Webster's New International Dictionary.* Unabridged 2nd ed. Springfield: G. and C. Merriam Company, 1948, 859, 1769, 1771.

"Paradox," *Encyclopaedia Britannica.* 11th ed., 1911, XX, 752.

"Paradox," *Oxford English Dictionary.* Oxford: Clarendon Press, 1933, VII, 450-451.

Robertson, Nicoll W., (ed.), *Expositor's Greek Testament.* 3 vols. New York: George H. Doran, n.d.

Runes, Dagobert, (ed.), "Logical Paradox," *The Dictionary of Philosophy.* New York: Philosophical Library, 1942, 225.

Sanday, William, "Jesus Christ," *Dictionary of the Bible.* Edited by James Hastings. New York: Charles Scribner's Sons, 1902, II, 603-653.

Singer, Isidore and Others (eds.), "Parallelism in Hebrew Poetry," *Jewish Encyclopedia.* New York: Funk and Wagnalls Company, 1907, XI, 520-522.

Souter, A., "Roads and Travel," *Dictionary of the Apostolic Church.* Edited by James Hastings and Others. New York: Charles Scribner's Sons, 1918, II, 393-399.

FOOTNOTES

CHAPTER ONE

1. Rufus Jones, Harold Anson and Others, *Concerning Prayer* (London: Macmillan and Company, 1916), p. 107.
2. William L. Watkinson, *The Moral Paradoxes of Paul* (N. Y.: Fleming H. Revell Company, n.d.).
3. Ralph W. Sockman, *The Paradoxes of Jesus* (N. Y.: Abingdon Press, 1936).
4. *Encyclopedia of Religion and Ethics,* Vol. IX (1917), p. 632; *A Dictionary of Christ and the Gospels,* Vol. II (1908), p. 319.
5. Arnold B. Come, "Theology Beyond Paradox", *Religion in Life,* XXV (1955-1956), pp. 35-46.
6. Clarence H. Hamilton, "Encounter with Reality in Buddhist Madhyamika Philosophy," *Journal of Bible and Religion,* XXVI (1958), pp. 13-22.
7. Robert Lawson Slater, *Paradox and Nirvana* (Chicago: University of Chicago Press, 1950).
8. Erich Fromm, *The Art of Loving* (N. Y.: Harper and Brothers Publishers, 1956), p. 72ff.
9. Kermit Eby and June Greenlief, *The Paradoxes of Democracy* (N. Y.: Association Press, 1956).
10. William Ernest Hocking, *The Coming World Civilization* (N. Y.: Harper and Brothers Publishers, 1956), p. 45ff.
11. See I Cor. 5:9; Col. 4:16; Phil. 3:1.
12. II Cor. 10:10, *The Holy Bible* (N. Y.: Thomas Nelson and Sons, 1946 and 1952).

CHAPTER TWO

1. *Oxford English Dictionary,* Vol. VII (Oxford: Clarendon Press, 1933), p. 450.
2. James H. Moulton and George Milligan, *The Vocabulary of the Greek New Testament* (*Grand Rapids*: Eerdmans Publishing Company, 1950), p. 483. See also Lu. 2:20.
3. *Supra.,* p. 483. See Aristeas 175.
4. Lu. 5:26.

5. D. Eberhard Nestle (ed.), *Novum Testamentum Graece* (Stuttgart: Privilegierte Wurtembergishche Bibelanstalt, 1948), p. 156.

6. William K. Stewart, "A Study of Paradox," *Hibbert Journal*, XXVII (1928-1929), p. 2.

7. "Paradox," *Encyclopaedia Britannica*, 11th ed., Vol. XX, p. 752.

8. John Wright Buckham, "The Potency of Paradox," *Journal of Philosophy*, XLI (1944), p. 7.

9. André Lalande, *Vocabulaire de la Philosophie* (Paris: Librairie Felix Alcan, 1926), p. 566.

10. L. Harold DeWolf, *The Religious Revolt Against Reason* (N. Y.: Harper and Brothers Publishers, 1949), p. 141.

11. Henry Nelson Wieman and Walter Marshall Horton, *The Growth of Religion* (Chicago: Willet, Clark and Company, 1938), p. 256.

12. Dagobert D. Runes, (ed.), "Logical Paradox," *The Dictionary of Philosophy* (N. Y.: Philosophical Library, 1942), p. 225.

13. Josiah Royce, *The Sources of Religious Insight* (N. Y.: Charles Scribner's Sons, 1912), p. 103.

14. Gustaf Aulén, *The Faith of the Christian Church,* trans. Eric H. Wahlstrom and G. Everett Arden (Philadelphia: Muhlenberg Press, 1948), p. 103.

15. Lu. 14:25-33; Jn. 12:14-26, 32; 16:20, 33.

16. Lu. 10:29-37.

17. William Ernest Hocking, *The Coming World Civilization* (N. Y.: Harper Brothers Publishers, 1956), p. 90. See Matt. 10:39.

18. Edwin Lewis, *Great Christian Teachings* (N. Y.: The Methodist Book Concern, 1933), pp. 103-104.

19. Gustaf Adolf Deissmann, *St. Paul: A Study in Social and Religious History,* trans. William B. Wilson (N. Y.: George H. Doran and Company, 1926), p. 63, 65, 234.

20. Donald M. Baillie, *God Was in Christ* (N. Y.: Charles Scribner's Sons, 1948), p. 108.

21. Emil Brunner, *The Philosophy of Religion* (N. Y.: Charles Scribner's Sons, 1937), p. 55.

22. Gustaf Aulen, *The Faith of the Christian Church,* trans. Eric H. Wahlstrom and G. Everett Arden (Philadelphia: Muhlenberg Press, 1948), p. 103.

23. Paul Tillich, *Systematic Theology,* Vol. I (Chicago: University of Chicago Press, 1951), pp. 56-57.

24. L. Harold DeWolf, *The Religious Revolt Against Reason* (N. Y.: Harper and Brothers Publishers, 1949), p. 142.

25. I Cor. 12:10.

26. Mk. 4:28.

27. John Wright Buckham, "The Potency of Paradox," *Journal of Philosophy*, XLI (1944), p. 9.
28. Matt. 17:20; Mk. 10:25; Lu. 14:26; Matt. 8:22; 5:30.
29. Giovanni Papini, *The Life of Christ*, trans. Dorothy C. Fischer (N. Y.: Harcourt, Brace and Company, 1923), p. 93.
30. Phil. 4:13; 2:3.
31. Rom. 1:8; Col. 1:6; I Thess. 1:8.
32. Rom. 13:14.
33. I Cor. 11:11.
34. I Cor. 1:19; 2:4; 2:13; 1:20,21.
35. I Cor. 4:6-21.
36. Gal. 2:6,9.
37. Hos. 6:6.
38. Gen. 4:24; Jud. 5:19; Psa. 1:6; Prov. 10:1ff.
39. Matt. 7:24, 26; Ja. 1:21-25.
40. II Cor. 4:8-10; Compare Rom. 11:10-24; 2:13; 12:3-16; II Cor. 11:22-31.
41. Carl von Weizäcker, *The Apostolic Age of the Christian Church*, trans. James Millar (N. Y.: G. P. Putnam's Sons, 1894-1895), I, p. 137.
42. *Webster's New International Dictionary* (Unabridged, 2nd ed., Springfield: G. and C. Merriam Company, 1948), p. 859.
43. I Cor. 14:33.
44. Rom. 6:20-23.
45. I Cor. 13:13.
46. W. J. Moulton, "Parable," *Dictionary of Christ and the Gospels*, (eds.), James Hastings and others, II (1908), p. 314.
47. II Sam. 12:1-14; 14:16; I Ki. 20:39; Isa. 5:1-6; 28:24-28.
48. G. M. Mackie, "Parable," *Dictionary of the Bible*, One Vol., (ed.), James Hastings (1942), p. 679. See also comprehensive definition of parable by W. Sanday in his article "Jesus Christ" *Hastings Bible Dictionary*, Vol. II, p. 617.
49. Psa. 1.
50. Arthur J. Culler, Creative Religious Literature (N. Y.: The Macmillan Company, 1930), p. 123. See Wilbur Owen Sypherd, *The Literature of the English Bible* (N. Y.: Oxford University Press, 1938), pp. 92-95; Isidore Singer and others, "Parallelism in Hebrew Poetry," *The Jewish Encyclopedia*, Vol. XI (N. Y.: Funk and Wagnalls Company, 1906), pp. 520-522.
51. Rom. 1:14, 18-22; 5:12-21; 11:34; I Cor. 9:10; 15:35-49; II Cor. 9:6; Gal. 5:16.
52. II Cor. 4:5.

53. John Wright Buckham, "The Potency of Paradox," *Journal of Philosophy*, XLI (1944), p. 12.
54. Edward Chauncey Baldwin, *Types of Literature in the Old Testament* (N. Y.: Thomas Nelson and Sons, 1929), p. 44.
55. James Dalton Morrison, (ed.), *Masterpieces of Religious Verse*, "Rabbi ben Ezra" St. VII (N. Y.: Harper and Brothers Publishers, 1948), p. 78.
56. A. Seth Pringle-Pattison, *The Idea of God in Recent Philosophy* (N. Y.: Oxford University Press, 1920), p. 244.
57. George Frisbie Whicher, *This Was a Poet* (N. Y.: Charles Scribner's Sons, 1939), pp. 296-297.
58. Martha Dickinson Bianchi and Alfred Leete Hampson, (eds.) *Further Poems by Emily Dickinson* (Boston: Little, Brown and Company, 1929), p. 18.
59. James Dalton Morrison, (ed.), *Masterpieces of Religious Verse*, "A Free Nation" (N. Y.: Harper and Brothers Publishers, 1948), p. 481.
60. *Ibid.*, p. 356 "Stanzas on Freedom".
61. W. J. Rolfe (ed.), *The Poetic and Dramatic Works of Alfred Lord Tennyson*, "De Profundis" (Cambridge: The Riverside Press, 1893), p. 449.
62. James Dalton Morrison (ed.), *Masterpieces of Religious Verse*, "The Hound of Heaven" (N. Y.: Harper and Brothers Publishers, 1948), p. 60.
63. Virginia Taylor McCormick, "Paradox" *The Personalist*, (ed.), Ralph T. Flewelling, XVII (1936), p. 156.
64. William Hampson, *Paradoxes of Nature and Science* (N. Y.: E. P. Dutton and Company, 1907), Preface V.
65. *Ibid.*, pp. 98-99.
66. Sir Oliver Lodge, "Physics," *Encyclopedia Britannica*, 14th ed., Vol. XVII, pp. 880-883.
67. Lincoln Barnett, *The Universe and Dr. Einstein* (N. Y.: The New American Library, 1950), pp. 25-30.
68. David G. Moses and Others, "The Problem of Truth in Religion," *The Authority of Faith*, Vol. I. The Madras Series (N. Y.: International Missionary Council, 1939), p. 64.
69. Sir Oliver Lodge, *Modern Scientific Ideas* (London: Ernest Benn Publisher, 1927), p. 19.
70. Kermit Eby and June Greenlief, *The Paradoxes of Democracy* (N. Y.: The Association Press, 1956), p. 13. See Also p. 49.
71. Robert Lawson Slater, *Paradox and Nirvana* (Chicago: University of Chicago Press, 1950), p. 100.
72. I Ki. 8:27.

73. Job 11:7.
74. Job 13:3.
75. Job 16:2.
76. Psa. 10:1.
77. Psa. 42:9.
78. Psa. 118:22.
79. Isa. 6:9.
80. Isa. 42:8.
81. Isa. 55:1.
82. Isa. 55:8, 9.
83. Isa. 55:6.
84. Moses Hadas, (ed. and trans.), *The Third and Fourth Books of Maccabees* (N. Y.: Harper and Brothers, 1953), IV Macc. 2:14, p. 155. See Alfred Rahlfs', *Septuaginta* (Stuttgart: Wurttemberger Bibelanstalt, 3rd. ed. (1935)1949).
85. Solomon Zeitlin, (ed.), *The Second Book of Maccabees,* trans. Sidney Tedesche (N. Y.: Harper and Brothers, 1950), II Macc. 9:24, p. 187.
86. Edgar J. Goodspeed, *The Apocrypha* (Chicago: University of Chicago: University of Chicago Press, 1938), Wisdom of Sirach 43:25, p. 309.
87. *The Apocrypha,* Introd. Robert Pfeiffer (N. Y.: Harper and Brothers Publishers, n.d.), Judith 13:13, p. 100.
88. Russell Henry Stafford, *Paradoxes of the Kingdom* (Boston: The Fort Hill Press, 1929), p. 5.
89. Matt. 23:12.
90. Matt. 10:39.
91. Mk. 9:35.
92. Matt. 13:12.
93. Matt. 6:25, 34.
94. Mk. 10:43.
95. Matt. 5:44.
96. Matt. 19:30.
97. Jn. 8:36.
98. Matt. 13:13.
99. Jn. 16:32.
100. Lu. 23:34.
101. Matt. 19:26.
102. Jud. 12:6.
103. Luther A. Weigle, ed., *Bible Words That Have Changed in Meaning* (N. Y.: Thomas Nelson and Sons, n.d.), p. 3. See Richard C. Trench, *The Study of Words* (London: Macmillan and Company,

1876); James H. Moulton and George Milligan, *The Vocabulary of the Greek New Testament* (Grand Rapids: Eerdmans Publishing Company, 1950); Frederick Kenyon, *Our Bible and the Ancient Manuscripts* (N. Y.: Harper and Brothers, 1940).

104. Ronald Knox, *Trials of a Translator* (N. Y.: Sheed and Ward, 1949), p. 10-11.

105. W. D. Niven, "Words," *The Expository Times*, LXII (1956), p. 137. For further treatment see William Barclay, *A New Testament Wordbook* (N. Y.: Harper and Brothers).

106. C. T. Onions, ed., *A Shakespeare Glossary* (Oxford: Clarendon Press, 1941), p. 157. See Hamlet III, I, 116.

107. Augustus DeMorgan, *A Budget of Paradoxes*, Vol. I, ed., David Eugene Smith (Chicago: The Open Court Publishing Company, 1915), p. 2.

108. Paton James Gloag, *Introduction to the Pauline Epistles* (Edinburgh: T. T. Clark, 1874), p. 250.

109. Charles Grandison Finney, *Lectures in Systematic Theology*, (ed.), J. H. Fairchild (Oberlin: E. J. Goodrich, 1878), p. 375.

110. Hugh R. Walpole, *Semantics* (N. Y.: W. W. Norton Company, 1941), p. 150.

111. Alfred North Whitehead, *Process and Reality* (N. Y.: The Macmillan Company, 1929), p. 845.

112. Thomas Curtis Clark, (ed.), *1000 Quotable Poems*, "Ulysses" (Chicago: Willet, Clark and Company, 1937), p. 225.

113. Kirsopp Lake, *Paul: His Heritage and Legacy* (N. Y.: Oxford University Press, 1934), p. 72.

114. Gal. 1:13ff.

115. II Cor. 12:4.

116. Evelyn Underhill, *Worship* (N. Y.: Harper and Brothers, 1937), p. 113.

117. *Plato*, "Epistles," VII, 343E., trans. R. G. Bury (N. Y.: G. P. Putnam's Sons, 1929), p. 534. See also B. Jowett, *The Dialogues of Plato*, Vol. I (London: Oxford University Press, 1924), p. 385ff. "Cratylus" 438D.E. sourcebook for Plato's theory of language.

118. See "Theaetetus" 208Bff.

119. R. G. Collingwood, "Reason is Faith Cultivating Itself," *Hibbert Journal*, XVII (1927-1928), p. 14.

120. A. H. Johnson, *The Wit and Wisdom of Alfred N. Whitehead* (Boston: The Beacon Press, 1947), p. 57.

121. L. Harold DeWolf, *A Theology of the Living Church* (N. Y.: Harper and Brothers Publishers, 1953,) p. 364.

122. Paul Arthur Schilpp, *The Quest for Religious Realism* (N. Y.:

Harper and Brothers Publishers, 1938), p. 162. Quoting from Albert Schweitzer, *Out of My Life and Thought,* p. 275.

123. II Cor. 3:18.

124. Charles Grandison Finney, *Lectures in Systematic Theology,* ed., J. H. Fairchild (Oberlin: E. J. Goodrich, 1878), p. 378.

125. Mk. 4:2-20.

126. Edward Howe Cotton, ed., *Has Science Discovered God?* (N. Y.: Thomas Y. Crowell Company, 1931), pp. 96, 97.

127. Isa. 45:15.

128. Psa. 104:2.

129. George Santayana, "O World, Thou Choosest Not the Better Part," *Poems.* Selected and revised by the author. (N. Y.: Charles Scribner's Sons, (1901 , 1923), p. 5.

130. Mk. 4:11; See also Matt. 13:11; Lu. 8:10.

131. John Gassner, (ed.), *Twenty Best Plays* (N. Y.: Crown Publishers (1939 , 1941), p. 193.

132. II Tim. 1:12.

133. Rom. 8:38-39.

134. II Cor. 5:19-20.

135. Amelia Josephine Burr, "Certainty Enough," *Selected Lyrics* (N. Y.: Doubleday and Company, 1927), p. 21. Used by permission of the publisher.

136. Bertrand Russell, *An Inquiry Into Meanings and Truth* (N. Y.: W. W. Norton and Company, 1940), p. 215.

137. Susanne K. Langer, "Form and Content: A Study in Paradox" *The Journal of Philosophy,* XXIII (1926), p. 435.

138. Henry Nelson Wieman, *The Source of Human Good* (Chicago: University of Chicago Press, 1946), p. 33.

139. Henry Nelson Wieman and Walter Marshall Horton, *The Growth of Religion* (Chicago: Willett, Clark and Company, 1939), p. 256. Also see pp. 432-433.

140. Albert C. Knudson, *Basic Issues in Christian Thought* (N. Y.: Abingdon-Cokesbury Press, 1950), p. 163.

141. Albert C. Knudson, *The Principles of Christian Ethics* (N. Y.: Abingdon-Cokesbury Press, 1943), p. 155.

142. Henry Churchill King, *Reconstruction in Theology* (N. Y.: The Macmillan Company, 1901), p. 8.

143. Edwin McNeill Poteat, *Dimension of Depth* (N. Y.: Harper and Brothers Publishers, 1957), p. 92-93. See Webster's *New World Dictionary of the American Language,* World Publishing Company, 1954).

144. Soren Kierkegaard, *Philosophical Fragments,* trans. David Swenson (Princeton: Princeton University Press, 1946), p. 29.

145. *Ibid.,* p. 50.
146. Soren Kierkegaard, *Philosophical Fragments,* trans. David Swenson (Princeton: Princeton University Press, 1946), p. 66.
147. *Ibid.,* p. 37.
148. Soren Kierkegaard, *Sickness Unto Death,* trans. Walter Lowrie (Princeton: Princeton University Press, 1946).
149. Soren Kierkegaard, *Christian Discourses,* trans. Walter Lowrie (N. Y.: Oxford University Press, 1939), p. 375.
150. Soren Kierkegaard, *Philosophical Fragments,* trans. David Swenson (Princeton: Princeton University Press, 1946), p. 29.
151. Soren Kierkegaard, *Concluding Unscientific Postcript,* trans. David Swenson, completed by Walter Lowrie (Princeton: Princeton University Press, 1941), p. 504.
152. Soren Kierkegaard, *Concluding Unscientific Postcript,* trans. David Swenson, completed by Walter Lowrie (Princeton: Princeton University Press, 1941), p. 183.
153. Karl Barth, *The Knowledge of God,* trans. J. L. M. Haire and Iran Henderson (N. Y.: Charles Scribner's Sons, 1939), p. 72.
154. Karl Barth, *The Doctrine of the Word of God,* trans. G. T. Thompson (Edinburgh: T. T. Clark, 1936), sec. 6, 3 and 4.
155. Paul Tillich, "What is Wrong with Dialectical Theology?" *Journal of Religion,* XV (1935), p. 135.
156. Edwin Ewart Aubrey, *Living the Christian Faith* (N. Y.: The Macmillan Company, 1939), quoting Barth, p. 68.
157. Karl Barth, *Das Wort Gottes und die Theologie* (Munich: Kaiser, 1924), p. 399.
158. Karl Barth, *Der Romerbrief* (Munich: Kaiser, 1922), p. 371.
159. Karl Barth, *The Doctrine of the Word of God,* trans. G. T. Thompson (Edinburgh: T. T. Clark, 1936), p. 188.
160. Karl Barth, *Der Romerbrief* (Munich: Kaiser, 1922), p. 342.
161. Emil Brunner, *Der Mittler* (Tubingen: J. C. B. Mohr, 1927), p. 254.
162. *Ibid.,* pp. 122, 483.
163. Emil Brunner, *The Christian Doctrine of Creation and Redemption,* Vol. II. trans. Olive Wyon (London: Lutterworth Press, 1952), p. 171.
164. Emil Brunner, *Philosophie und Offenbarung* (Tubingen: Mohr, 1925). p. 34.
165. Emil Brunner, *The Philosophy of Religion* (N. Y.: Charles Scribner's Sons, 1937), p. 55.
166. Emil Brunner, *The Misunderstanding of the Church* (Philadelphia: The Westminster Press, 1953), p. 11.

167. *Ibid.*, p. 17.
168. Frederick C. Grant, *An Introduction to New Testament Thought* (N. Y.: Abingdon-Cokesbury Press, 1950), p. 78, 88.
169. *Ibid.*, pp. 302-303.
170. Donald M. Baillie, *God Was in Christ* (N. Y.: Charles Scribner's Sons, 1948), p. 108.
171. *Ibid.*, pp. 109-110.
172. Sergius Bulgakov, *The Wisdom of God*, p. 116. "Cited by" Donald M. Baillie, *God Was in Christ* (N. Y.: Charles Scribner's Sons, 1948), p. 109.
173. Reinhold Niebuhr, *Christian Realism and Political Problems* (N. Y.: Charles Scribner's Sons, 1953), p. 197.
174. Reinhold Niebuhr, *The Nature and Destiny of Man*, Vol. II, (N. Y.: Charles Scribner's Sons, 1943), p. 118.
175. Reinhold Niebuhr, "Coherence, Incoherence, and Christian Faith," *Journal of Religion*, XXXI (1951), pp. 167-168.
176. Reinhold Niebuhr, *The Self and the Drama of History* (N. Y.: Charles Scribner's Sons, 1955), p. 240.
177. Reinhold Niebuhr, *The Nature and Destiny of Man*, Vol. I, (N. Y.: Charles Scribner's Sons, 1941), p. 3, 262.
178. *Ibid.*, p. 125. See also p. 258, 263.
179. Reinhold Niebuhr, *Reflections on the End of an Era* (N. Y.: Charles Scribner's Sons, 1934), p. 296.
180. Gustaf Aulén, *The Faith of the Christian Church*, trans. Eric H. Wahlstrom and G. Everett Arden (Philadelphia: Muhlenberg Press, 1948), p 102.
181. Gustaf Aulén, *The Faith of the Christian Church*, trans. Eric H. Wahlstrom and G. Everett Arden (Philadelphia: Muhlenberg Press, 1948), p. 103. Also p. 166.
182. *Ibid.*, p. 102.
183. *Ibid.*, p. 294.
184. Paul Tillich, *Systematic Theology*, Vol. I (Chicago: University of Chicago Press, 1951), pp. 56-57.
185. *Ibid.*, p. 57.
186. *Ibid.*, p. 57.
187. Nicolas Berdyaev, *Freedom and the Spirit*, trans. Oliver F. Clarke (N. Y.: Charles Scribner's Sons, 1935), p. 18.
188. Nicolas Berdyaev, *Freedom and the Spirit*, trans. Oliver F. Clarke (N. Y.: Charles Scribner's Sons, 1935), p. 64ff. See also Elmer G. Homrighausen, a review of *The Divine-Human Encounter* by Brunner, *Theology Today*, I (1944), pp. 135ff.
189. Nicolas Berdyaev, *Slavery and Freedom*, trans. R. M. French (N. Y.: Charles Scribner's Sons, 1944), p. 12.

190. Nicolas Berdyaev, *Freedom and the Spirit,* trans. Oliver F. Clarke (N. Y.: Charles Scribner's Sons, 1935), p. 238.

191. L. Harold DeWolf, *The Religious Revolt Against Reason* (N. Y.: Harper and Brothers Publishers, 1949), pp. 136-137.

192. *Ibid.,* pp. 41-42.

193. L. Harold DeWolf, *The Religious Revolt Against Reason* (N. Y.: Harper and Brothers Publishers, 1949), p. 142.

194. Willard L. Sperry, *The Paradox of Religion* (N. Y.: The Macmillan Company, 1927), pp. 17-18.

195. *Ibid.,* p. 20.

196. Walter Marshall Horton, *Theism and the Modern Mood* (N. Y.: Harper and Brothers, 1930), p. 159.

197. *Ibid.,* p. 159.

198. Jack Finegan, *Beginnings of Theology* (N. Y.: Association Press, 1956), p. 11.

199. Jack Finegan, *Beginnings of Theology* (N. Y.: Association Press, 1956), p. 235. "Cited by" Jack Finegan.

200. Harris Franklin Rall, *According to Paul* (N. Y.: Charles Scribner's Sons, 1947), p. 237.

201. *Ibid.,* pp. 241-242.

202. Harris Franklin Rall, *Christianity* (N. Y.: Charles Scribner's Sons, 1941), p. 28. For a fuller treatment of his view of polarity see the entire chapter III.

203. Arnold B. Come, "Theology Beyond Paradox," *Religion in Life,* XXV (1955-1956), p. 37.

204. *Ibid.,* p. 42.

205. *Ibid.,* p. 43.

206. I John 4:1.

207. I Thess. 5:19.

208. Gal. 5:16.

209. Gal. 5:22, 23.

210. Matt. 7:20.

211. I Thess. 5:24.

212. I Cor. 12:7.

213. Gilbert Keith Chesterton, *Orthodoxy* (N. Y.: Dodd, Mead and Company, 1938), p. 177.

214. Gilbert Keith Chesterton, *Orthodoxy* (N. Y.: Dodd, Mead and Company, 1938), pp. 148, 149, 170, 171-172, 173-174. See algo Hugh Kenner, *Paradox in Chesterton* (N. Y.: Sheed and Wood, 1947), p. 3.

215. Gerald Kennedy, *The Lion and the Lamb* (N. Y.: Abingdon-Cokesbury Press, 1950), p. 8.

216. William Ernest Hocking, *Types of Philosophy* (N. Y.: Charles Scribner's Sons, 1929), p. 443.

217. William Ernest Hocking, *The Meaning of God in Human Experience* (New Haven: Yale University Press, 1912), p. 427. See also p. 494.

218. Josiah Royce, *Lectures in Modern Idealism* (New Haven: Yale University Press, 1919), p. 96.

CHAPTER THREE

1. James Iverach, *The Life and Times of St. Paul* (N. Y.: Anson D. F. Randolph, n.d.), p. 1ff. For more detailed information on Tarsus see Sir William Ramsay, *The Cities of St. Paul*, 1908), pp. 187-199.

2. John S. Howson, *The Metaphors of St. Paul* (London: Strahan and Company Publishers, 1869 (2nd ed.).

3. Shirley Jackson Case, "The Jewish Bias of Paul," *Journal of Biblical Literature*, XLVII (1928), pp. 25-26.

4. William David Davies, *Paul and Rabbinic Judaism* (Cambridge: The University Press, 1948), p. 2. See Henry St. John Thackeray, *The Relation of Paul to Contemporary Jewish Thought* (London: Macmillan and Company, 1930).

5. Morton S. Enslin, "Paul and Gamaliel," *Journal of Religion*, VII (1927), pp. 360-375.

6. Acts 22:3.

7. Samuel Belkin, "The Problem of Paul's Background," *Journal of Biblical Literature*, LIV (1935), p. 41. Gal. 1:4. A notable study on Paul's Jewish background has been made by William Sanday and Arthur C. Headlam, *Epistle to the Romans*, ICC, Preface VI, VII, (N. Y.: Charles Scribner's Sons, 1926).

8. Otto Pfleiderer, *Primitive Christianity*, Vol. I, trans. William Montgomery (N. Y.: G. P. Putnam's Sons, 1906), p. 436.

9. Albert Schweitzer, *Paul and His Interpreters*, trans. William Montgomery (London: Adam and Charles Black, 1912), p. 71.

10. Thomas Wilson, *St. Paul and Paganism* (Edinburgh: T. T. Clark, 1927), Preface VI.

11. James Moffatt, "Essenes," *Encyclopedia of Religion and Ethics*, V (ed.) James Hastings (1912), p. 400.

12. Charles Theodore Fritsch, *The Qumran Community: A Study of the History and Scrolls* (N. Y.: The Macmillan Company, 1956), p. 126. See also the survey of this Judean brotherhood and its ideas by J. Van Der Ploeg, *The Excavation at Qumran*, trans. Kevin Smyth (N. Y.: Longmans, Green and Company, 1956), pp. 217-223; Sherman E. Johnson, "Paul and the Manual of Discipline,"

Harvard Theological Review, XLVIII (1955), pp. 157-165.

13. Oscar Cullman, "The Significance of the Qumran Texts for Research into the Beginnings of Christianity," *Journal of Biblical Literature*, LXXIV (1955), p. 213.

14. Samuel Belkin, "The Problem of Paul's Background," *Journal of Biblical Literature*, LIV (1935), p. 41.

15. Gal. 2:18.

16. Auguste Sabatier, *The Apostle Paul,* trans. not given (N. Y.: James Pott and Company, 1891), pp. 69-70.

17. Donald W. Riddle, "The Jewishness of Paul," *Journal of Religion,* XXIII (1943), p. 240ff.

18. Gustaf Adolf Deissmann, *St. Paul: A Study in Social and Religious History,* trans. William E. Wilson (N. Y.: George H. Doran and Company, 1926), p. 98.

19. Wilfred Lawrence Knox, *St. Paul and the Church of the Gentiles* (Cambridge: The University Press, 1939), pp. 25-26.

20. Claude G. Montefoire, *Judaism and St. Paul* (London: M. Goshen, 1914), p. 93. See Joseph Klausner, *From Jesus to Paul,* trans. William F. Stinespring (N. Y.: Macmillan and Company, 1943).

21. Phil. 3:5ff.; II Cor. 11:22.

22. Martin Dibelius and Georg Kummel, *Paul,* trans. Frank Clarke (Philadelphia: Westminster Press, 1935), p. 32.

23. William Ramsay, *The Teaching of Paul in Terms of the Present Day* (London: Hodder and Stoughton, 1913), pp. 161, 162.

24. Henry Wheeler Robinson, *The Christian Doctrine of Man* (Edinburgh: T. T. Clark, 1911), p. 104.

25. Albert Schweitzer, *Paul and His Interpreters,* trans. William Montgomery (London: Adam and Charles Black, 1912), p. 238.

26. William Ramsay, *The Cities of St. Paul* (N. Y.: A. C. Armstrong and Son, 1908), p. 34.

27. William Ramsay, *The Cities of St. Paul* (N. Y.: A. C. Armstrong and Son, 1908), p. 233.

28. Joseph Barber Lightfoot, *Biblical Essays* (London: Macmillan and Company, 1893), p. 206.

29. Charles A. A. Scott, *Christianity According to St. Paul* (N. Y.: The Macmillan Company, 1927), pp. 127-129.

30. Arthur Darby Nock, *St. Paul* (N. Y.: Harper and Brothers, Publishers, 1938), pp. 136, 237.

31. Albert Schweitzer, *Paul and His Interpreters,* trans. William Montgomery (London: Adam and Charles Black, 1912), p. 87.

32. William David Davies, *Paul and Rabbinic Judaism* (Cambridge: The University Press, 1948), p. 320. See also William Sanday and

Arthur C. Headlan, *Romans,* I.C.C. Preface VI, VII (N. Y.: Charles Scribner's Sons, 1926).

33. Rudolf Karl Bultmann, *Theology of the New Testament,* Vol. II, trans. Kendrick Grobel, (N. Y.: Charles Scribner's Sons, 1955), p. 39.

34. Rudolf Karl Bultmann, *Theology of the New Testament,* Vol. I, trans. Kendrick Grobel (N. Y.: Charles Scribner's Sons, 1951), pp. 63, 187.

35. *Ibid.,* pp. 293-294.

36. Rudolf Karl Bultmann, *Primitive Christianity in its Contemporary Setting,* trans. Reginald H. Fuller (N. Y.: Thames and Hudson, 1956), p. 197.

37. Col. 1:25-27; 2:2; Compare I Tim. 3:9, 16.

38. Gustaf Adolf Deissmann, *St. Paul: A Study in Social and Religious History,* trans. R. M. Strachan (N. Y.: Hodder and Stoughton, 1912), pp. 305-307.

39. H. A. A. Kennedy, *St. Paul and the Mystery Religions* (N. Y.: Hodder and Stoughton, 1913), pp. 280-282.

40. William Ramsay, *Pauline and Other Studies* (N. Y.: A. C. Armstrong and Son, 1906), p. 5. See Samuel Dill, *Roman Society from Nero to Marcus Aurelius* (London: Macmillan Company, (rev. ed.), 1920). A good treatment of customs and habits of living as well as of history.

41. A. Souter, "Roads and Travel," *Dictionary of the Apostolic Church,* ed. James Hastings and Others, Vol. II (1918), pp. 393-399.

42. Gustaf Adolf Deissmann, *St. Paul: A Study in Social and Religous History,* trans. R. M. Strachan (N. Y.: Hodder and Stoughton, 1912), p. 88.

43. Franz Cumont, *Oriental Religions in Roman Paganism* (Chicago: The Open Court Publishing Company, 1911), pp. 2-3. See also Edith Hamilton, *The Roman Way* (N. Y.: W. W. Norton, 1932). A fine interpretation of the genius and weakness of Roman civilization.

44. Joseph Barber Lightfoot, *Biblical Essays* (London: Macmillan and Company, 1893), p. 203.

45. William M. Ramsay, *St. Paul the Traveller and the Roman Citizen* (N. Y.: G. P. Putnam's Sons, 1898), p. 31ff.

46. William M. Ramsay, *Pauline and Other Studies* (N. Y.: A. C. Armstrong and Son, 1906), p. 64.

47. Ludwig Friedlander, *Roman Life and Manners,* Vol. II, trans. J. H. Freese and Leonard A. Magnus (N. Y.: E. P. Dutton and Company, n.d.), p. 131ff.

48. Amos N. Wilder, "Paul Through Jewish Eyes," *Journal of Bible and Religion*, XII (1944), p. 185. See E. F. Scott, *The Varieties of New Testament Religion*, 1943, Chap. IV.

49. Kirsopp Lake, *Paul: His Heritage and Legacy* (N. Y.: Oxford University Press, 1934), p. 69.

50. Andrew Martin Fairbairn, *Philosophy of the Christian Religion* N. Y.: The Macmillan Company, 1902), p. 440.

51. Alexander Balmain Bruce, *St. Paul's Conception of Christianity* (N. Y.: Charles Scribner's Sons, 1909), pp. 132, 216, 302.

52. Paul Wernle, *Beginnings of Christianity*, Vol. I (N. Y.: G. P. Putnam's Sons, 1903), p. 224.

53. William Ralph Inge, *Christian Ethics and Modern Problems* (N. Y.: G. P. Putnam's Sons, 1930), p. 73. See also James S. Stewart, *A Man in Christ* (N. Y.: Harper Brothers Publishers, 1935).

54. W. J. Conybeare and J. S. Howson, *The Life and Letters of Saint Paul* (Hartford: S. S. Scranton and Company, 1899), Introduction XIII-XV.

55. R. Birch Hoyle, *The Holy Spirit in St. Paul* (N. Y.: Doubleday, Doran and Company, 1928), p. 178.

56. Philemon 19.

57. Rom. 16:22.

58. I Peter 5:12.

59. Rom. 1:1-7; I Cor. 3:21-23.

60. I Cor. 15:1, 2; Rom. 5:18; II Cor. 8:10-15; Gal. 2;6, the latter reference shows how a sentence begins in one way and ends in another.

61. See I Cor. 15:45-48; Col. 1:16.

62. Arthur Darby Nock, *St. Paul* (N. Y.: Harper and Brothers, Publishers, 1938), p. 237.

63. I Cor. 2:1; II Cor. 11:6.

64. Col. 2:4.

65. Henry Thatcher Fowler, "Paul, Q and the Jerusalem Church," *Journal of Biblical Literature*, XLIII-XLIV (1924-1925), p. 13.

66. II Thess. 3:17.

67. I Cor. 5:9; 7:1; II Cor. 2:3ff.; 7:8ff.

68. Heinrich Julius Holtzmann, *Lehrbuch der Neutestamentlichen Theologie*, Vol. II (Tubingen: J. C. B. Mohr, 1911), pp. 9-11.

69. *Ibid.*, p. 236.

70. James Freeman Clarke, *The Ideas of the Apostle Paul* (Boston: James R. Osgood and Company, 1884), pp. 10-11.

71. *Ibid.*, pp. 10-11.

72. James S. Stewart, *A Man in Christ* (N. Y.: Harper Brothers Publishers, 1935), p. 28.

73. See II Thess. 2:15; 3:6; I Cor. 11:2.
74. I Cor. 8:13.
75. Rom. 2:21; also verses 17-19.
76. I Cor. 13:11-12; Phil. 3:13-15.
77. Gal. 3:1, 3.
78. Rom. 2:3-4; 21-23; 26, 27; 3:1, 3, 5-9; 27-29, 31; Col. 1:28; I Cor. 9.
79. Rom. 3:5; 6:19.
80. I. Cor. 2:4.
81. Rudolf Knopf, "Paul and Hellenism," *American Journal of Theology,* XVIII (1914), p. 520.
82. Archibald M. Hunter, *Interpreting Paul's Gospel* (Philadelphia: Westminster Press, 1954).
83. Ernest F. Scott, *The Varieties of New Testament Religion* (N. Y.: Charles Scribner's Sons, 1943), p. 8. See also George B. Findlay, *The Epistles of the Apostle Paul* (London: C. H. Kelly, n.d.), p. 34.
84. Harry Bulcock, *The Passing and the Permanent in St. Paul* (London: Macmillan and Company, 1926), pp. 135-136. Citing Reinhold Seeberg, *Lehrbuch der Dogmengeschichte,* 2nd ed. 1908.
85. Jonathan Edwards, "Observations Concerning Faith," *Works,* Vol. II (N. Y.: Robert Carter and Brothers, 1844) p. 607.
86. Wilhelm Bousset, *Kyrios Christos* (Gottingen: Vandenhoeck, 1921), p. 143.
87. William Wrede, *Paul,* trans. Edward Lummis (London: Philip Green, 1907), p. 170ff.
88. *Ibid.,* p. 156ff.
89. Rudolf Bultmann, *Jesus and the Word,* trans. Louise Pettibone Smith (N. Y.: Charles Scribner's Sons, 1934), p. 8.
90. Rudolf Bultmann, *Theology of the New Testament,* Vol. I, trans. Kendrick Grobel (N. Y.: Charles Scribner's Sons, 1951), pp. 293-294.
91. Karl Barth, *The Doctrine of the Word of God,* trans. G. T. Thompson, 1936), p. 188.
92. L. Harold DeWolf, *A Theology of the Living Church* (N. Y.: Harper and Brothers Publishers, 1953), pp. 245-246.
93. Johannes Weiss, *Paul and Jesus,* trans. H. J. Chaytor (N. Y.: Harper and Brothers, 1909), pp. 41-56.
94. William Ramsay, *The Teaching of Paul in Terms of the Present Day* (N. Y.: Hodder and Stoughton, 1914), p. 21ff.
95. Charles A. A. Scott, *Christianity According to St. Paul* (N. Y.: The Macmillan Company, 1927), p. 11ff.
96. II Cor. 5:16; I Cor. 9:1.

245

97. Albert Schweitzer, *The Mysticism of Paul the Apostle,* trans. William Montgomery (N. Y.: The Macmillan Company, 1955), p. 245.

98. Johannes Weiss *The History of Primitive Christianity,* Vol. I, trans. R. Knopf (N. Y.: Wilson-Erickson, Inc. 1937), p. 188.

99. Gustaf Adolf Deissmann, *St. Paul: A Study in Social and Religious History,* trans. William E. Wilson (N. Y.: George H. Doran and Company, 1926), p. 197.

100. Frank C. Porter, *The Mind of Christ in Paul* (N. Y.: Charles Scribner's Sons, 1930), p. 16ff.

101. Gal. 1:18; I Cor. 11:23; 15:3-7.

102. Paul Wernle, *Beginnings of Christianity,* Vol. I (N. Y.: G. P. Putnam's Sons, 1903), p. 159.

103. Adolf Harnack, *What is Christianity?* (N. Y.: G. P. Putnam's Sons, 1901), p. 189.

104. Rom. 5:15; Rom. 1:3; 9:5; Gal. 4:4; Gal. 1:19; Rom. 15:8; I Cor. 15:5; I Cor. 11:23-26; II Cor. 13:4; I Cor. 15:4.

105. I Cor. 10:1; Rom. 5:19; II Cor. 5:21; Phil. 2:8; II Thess. 3:5; 8:9; Rom. 8:35; Rom. 1:1-4.

106. Gal. 5:21; I Cor. 6:9; 7:10; 9:14; 15:10; Rom. 12:14-21; I Thess. 2:15; 16; 4:15-17; 5:1-6; I Thess. 5:15; II Thess. 2:2.

107. Rom. 15:6; I Cor. 8-6.

108. Rom. 3:22, 29; 10:12; I Cor. 12:13; Gal. 3:23; Col. 3:11.

109. For an elaboration of this point see, Henry C. Sheldon, *New Testament Theology* (N. Y.: The Macmillan and Company, 1911), p. 190ff.

110. See Phil. 2; Col. 3.

111. Benjamin W. Bacon, *Jesus and Paul* (N. Y.: The Macmillan Company, 1921), p. 111.

112. I Cor. 7:10, 12, 25.

113. I Cor. 7:10; 9:14; 11:23-25; I Thess. 4:15-17.

114. Charles Harold Dodd, *The Epistle of Paul to the Romans,* Moffatt New Testament Commentary (N. Y.: Roy Long and Richard R. Smith, 1932), p. 208.

115. Rudolf Bultmann, *Jesus and the Word,* trans. Louise Pettibone Smith (N. Y.: Charles Scribner's Sons, 1934), p. 84.

116. For a fuller treatment of this examine Charles A. A. Scott, *New Testament Ethics* (Cambridge: The University Press, 1930, Lecture IV).

117. John Baillie, *The Place of Jesus Christ in Modern Christianity* (N. Y.: Charles Scribner's Sons, 1929), p. 101.

118. Compare: Matt. 22:21, Rom. 13:7; Matt. 5:44, Rom, 12:14, 17, 20; Matt. 24:36, 43, I Thess. 5:2-8; Matt. 17:20, I Cor. 13:2; Matt. 7:1-5, Rom. 14:4, 10, 13; Matt. 6:25, Phil. 4:6.

119. John Knox, *Christ the Lord* (N. Y.: Harper and Brothers, 1945), p. 23.
120. *Ibid.,* p. 56.
121. *Ibid.,* p. 56.
122. Joseph Klausner, *Jesus of Nazareth,* trans. Herbert Danby (N. Y.: The Macmillan Company, 1953), p. 376.
123. Gustaf Adolf Deissmann, *St. Paul: A Study in Social and Religious History,* trans. Lionel R. M. Strachan (N. Y.: Hodder and Stoughton, 1912), p. 3.

CHAPTER FOUR

1. Job 12:13-25; Psa. 46; 50:21; Dan. 2:46-47; 5:17-28.
2. I Chron. 8:1-10; Compare II Ki. 11:6; Isa. 45:9; 64-8; Jer. 8:1-10; Psa. 22:28; Eccles. 1:4.
3. Millar Burrows, *An Outline of Biblical Theology* (Philadelphia: The Westminster Press, 1946), p. 72.
4. Isa. 63:16; 64:8; Jer. 3:4, 14, 19; 31:9; Deut. 32:6; II Sam. 7:14; Psa. 68:5; 89:27; Mal. 1:6; 2:10.
5. Matt. 7:11.
6. Andrew Martin Fairbairn, *Studies in Religion and Theology* (N. Y.: The Macmillan Company, 1910), p. 15.
7. Albert C. Knudson, *The Doctrine of God* (N. Y.: The Abingdon Press, 1930), p. 328.
8. Rom. 8:15; Gal. 4:6; Compare Mk. 14:36.
9. I Thess. 1:3; 3:11, 13. Usually Paul speaks of "the Father of our Lord Jesus Christ" as in Rom. 15:6 which may be his way of saying Jesus revealed God as His Father and our Father.
10. Gal. 4:4-6.
11. William Newton Clarke, *The Christian Doctrine of God* (N. Y.: Charles Scribner's Sons, 1914), p. 155.
12. Gal. 3:26.
13. Gal. 1:15, 16.
14. Gal. 4:1, 7.
15. Rom. 8:14-17.
16. Gustaf Adolf Deissmann, *The Religion of Jesus and the Faith of Paul,* trans. William E. Wilson (N. Y.: George Doran Company, 1923), p. 54. See Gal. 4:6; Rom. 8:15.
17. Gerald R. Cragg, *Romans,* The Interpreter's Bible, Vol. IX, (eds.) Nolan B. Harmon and Others (N. Y.: Abingdon-Cokesbury Press, 1954), p. 515.

18. Jn. 8:44.
19. Jn. 1:2; Compare 16:3.
20. Col. 1:2.
21. Col. 3:3.
22. Col. 1:13.
23. Hosea 1:10; Compare II Cor. 6:18.
24. I Cor. 3:22, 23.
25. J. Scott Lidgett, *The Fatherhood of God* (Edinburgh: T. and T. Clark, 1902), p. 141.
26. Rom. 8:28-30.
27. Charles Harold Dodd, *The Meaning of Paul for Today* (London: The Swarthmore Press, 1937), pp. 36-37.
28. Rom. 8:28ff.
29. Phil. 1:6.
30. Ex. 9:12.
31. Ex. 9:34, 35.
32. Rom. 9:15; Compare Ex. 33:19.
33. Rom. 11:7.
34. Rom. 9:32; 10:3, 10-13, 21.
35. II Cor. 3:17.
36. Johannes Weiss, (ed.), Frederick C. Grant, *The History of Primitive Christianity,* Vol. II, trans. R. Knopf. Completed by four friends. (N. Y.: Wilson-Erickson, 1937), p. 557. See Gal. 5:17; Rom. 7:15; Phil. 2:13.
37. I Cor. 7:22.
38. Rom. 6:6.
39. Gal. 5:1.
40. Gal. 5:13; Compare I Cor. 6:19, also I Cor. 8, 9, 14.
41. Ernest DeWitt Burton, *The Epistle to the Galatians,* ICC, (N. Y.: Charles Scribner's Sons, 1920), p. 393. See Gal. 4:9; 5:1; Rom. 12: 14-21; I Cor. 11:25-33.
42. I Cor. 9:19.
43. Rom. 6:15-22.
44. Walter Lippmann, *A Preface to Morals* (N. Y.: The Macmillan Company, 1929), pp. 329-330.
45. Rom. 15:1.
46. John W. Oman, *The Paradox of the World* (Cambridge: The University Press, 1921), p. 124.
47. Gal. 5:6.
48. Ernest DeWitt Burton, *The Epistles to the Galatians,* ICC (N. Y.: Charles Scribner's Sons, 1920), p. 279.
49. Gal. 5:4.

50. I Cor. 7:18-19.
51. Ernest DeWitt Burton, *The Epistle to the Galatians,* ICC (N. Y.: Charles Scribner's Sons, 1920), p. 280.
52. William Adams Brown, *How to Think of Christ* (N. Y.: Charles Scribner's Sons, 1945), p. 117.
53. Gal. 4:6.
54. Raymond T. Stamm, *Corinthians,* The Interpreter's Bible, Vol. X (eds.) Nolan B. Harmon and Others. (N. Y.: Abingdon-Cokesbury Press, 1953), p. 528.
55. Gal. 4:5.
56. Gal. 4:4, 5, 7.
57. Phil. 4:13.
58. Gal. 2:4ff.
59. Rom. 6:18, 22.
60. II Cor. 3:17.
61. Rom. 1:18-25; 3:10-18.
62. Rom. 6:1, 15, 16; I Cor. 8:12; 15:34.
63. I Cor. 15:31.
64. Rom. 1:21-24; Gal. 5:16-17.
65. Rom. 5:21.
66. Rom. 6:23.
67. Rom. 7:7-24; Gal. 3:19, 21ff.
68. Charles A. Anderson Scott, *Christianity According to Paul* (N. Y.: The Macmillan Company, 1927), pp. 46, 47.
69. I Cor. 2:8; Rom. 8:38: Gal. 3:19; 4:9; Col. 2:18.
70. I Cor. 8:5.
71. I Cor. 10:20.
72. II Cor. 4:4.
73. Reinhold Niebuhr, *The Nature and Destiny of Man,* Vol. I (N. Y.: Charles Scribner's Sons, 1941), p. 256.
74. Henry St. John Thackeray, *The Relation of St. Paul to Contemporary Jewish Thought* (London: Macmillan and Company, 1930), p. 33.
75. Rom. 5:12, 19; See also I. Cor. 15:22.
76. Wisdom of Sirach 25:24; II Esdras 3:20; 4:30ff.; 7:11, 48; 9:11; IV Esdras 7:18-20; Apocalypse of Baruch 54:15-19.
77. William David Davies, *Paul and Rabbinic Judaism* (Cambridge: The University Press, 1948), pp. 34-35.
78. William Sanday and Arthur C. Headlam, *The Epistle to the Romans,* ICC (N. Y.: Charles Scribner's Sons, 1926), pp. 215-216.
79. Arthur C. Headlam, *Christian Theology* (London: Oxford University Press, 1940), p. 203.

249

80. Albert Schweitzer, *Paul and His Interpreters,* trans. William Montgomery (London: Adam and Charles Black, 1912), p. 160.

81. James W. Parkes, *Jesus, Paul and the Jews* (London: Student Christian Movement Press, 1936), p. 120.

82. D. William Wrede, *Paul,* trans. Edward Lummis (London: Philip Green and Company, 1907), p. 77. See *Paulus* (Halle: Gebauer-Schwetschke, 1904), p. 73.

83. Rom. 2:25; Compare Acts 18:18; 21:20-26.

84. Rom. 7:12; 7:14.

85. Rom. 9:4.

86. Rom. 2:18; 3:1-3.

87. Gal. 3:24.

88. Gal. 5:1; 3:10; Deut. 27:26.

89. Gal. 5:14.

90. Rom. 7:6; Gal. 4:4.

91. Rom. 5:20; Gal. 3:19.

92. Rom. 8:2.

93. Gal. 3:11-13; Lev. 18:5.

94. Rom. 10:4.

95. Rom. 3:31.

96. I Cor. 9:20-21.

97. Rom. 8:4; 13:9; Gal. 5:14; 6:2; I Cor. 9:21.

98. Hans Lietzmann, *The Beginnings of the Christian Church,* trans. Bertram Lee Woolf (N. Y.: Charles Scribner's Sons, 1952), p. 130.

99. Kaufmann Kohler, "Saul of Tarsus," *The Jewish Encyclopedia,* Vol. XI, (eds.), Isidore Singer and Others. (N. Y.: Funk and Wagnalls Company, 1907), p. 84. The interpolations cited, I Thess. 2:4b-16; I Cor. 15:56; II Cor. 3:6-4:4.

100. George Foote Moore, *Judaism in the First Centuries of the Christian Era,* Vol. I (Cambridge: Harvard University Press, 1927), pp. 481, 485, 490; See Claude G. Montefiore, *Rabbinic Literature and Gospel Teachings* (N. Y.: Macmillan and Company, 1930), p. 174.

101. Ernest DeWitt Burton, *Galatians, ICC,* (N. Y.: Charles Scribner's Sons, 1920), pp. lii-lxv.

102. Gal. 5:2; 6:15.

103. Gal. 3:24-25.

104. William Morgan, *The Religion and Theology of Paul* (Edinburgh: T. and T. Clark, 1917), p. 79.

105. Johannes Weiss, (ed.), Frederick C. Grant, *The History of Primitive Christianity,* Vol. I, trans. Rudolf Knopf. Completed by four friends. (N. Y.: Wilson-Erickson, 1937), p. 301.

106. James Moffatt, *The Approach to the New Testament* (London: Hodder and Stoughton, 1921), p. 141.

107. Gal. 3:21.

108. Gal. 2:19.

109. Gal. 3:13.

110. Rom. 2:15.

111. Gal. 3:14.

112. Gal. 3:17.

113. Rom. 7:6, 12, 14; 10:4.

114. Rom. 2:28-29.

115. Rom. 7:7, 13.

116. Rom. 8:2.

117. Rom. 7:10.

118. Rom. 7:9.

119. Rom. 8:3.

120. Alfred Ernest Garve (ed.), *Romans,* The New Century Bible (N. Y.: Oxford University Press, 1901), p. 142.

121. Rom. 1:18.

122. L. Harold DeWolf, *A Theology of the Living Church* (N. Y.: Harper and Brothers Publishers, 1953), p. 191.

123. Otto Pfleiderer, *Lectures on the Influence of the Apostle Paul on the Development of Christianity,* trans. J. Frederick Smith (London: Williams and Norgate, 1885), pp. 87-96.

124. Rom.. 5:20.

125. Rom. 9:4; 2:20; 7:10.

126. John Knox, *Christ the Lord* (N. Y.: Willett, Clark and Company, 1941), p. 116; W. M. Macgregor, *Christian Freedom* (N. Y.: Harper and Brothers, 1931), pp. 283-295.

127. Rom. 8:3, 4.

128. Matt. 5:20.

129. H. D. A. Major, T. W. Manson, and C. J. Wright, *The Mission and Message of Jesus* (N. Y.: E. P. Dutton and Company, 1938), p. 44.

130. Phil. 3:9.

131. Rom. 1:17.

132. Matt. 9:13.

133. Wilfred Lawrence Knox, *St. Paul and the Church of the Gentiles* (Cambridge: The University Press, 1939), p. 96.

134. Rom. 8:2.

135. II Cor. 5:2; Rom. 8:29.

136: Joseph Klausner, *From Jesus to Paul,* trans. William F. Stinespring (N. Y.: The Macmillan Company, 1943).

251

137. Auguste Sabatier, *The Apostle Paul,* trans. not given. (N. Y.: James Pott and Company, 1891), pp. 298-299. For a further discussion of the term "grace" see Charles H. Dodd,, *The Epistle of Paul to the Romans,* Moffatt New Testament Commentary (N. Y.: Roy Long and Richard R. Smith, 1932); Anders Nygren, *Commentary on Romans,* trans. Carl C. Rasmussen (Philadelphia: Muhlenberg Press, 1949).

138. Augustine Sabatier, *The Apostle Paul,* trans. not given. (N. Y.: James Pott and Company, 1891), p. 322.

139. Charles A. Anderson Scott, *St. Paul: The Man and the Teacher* (Cambridge: The University Press, 1936), p. 110.

140. Rom. 12:6.

141. Rom. 5:2; See also II Thess. 2:16.

142. William Manson, "Grace in the New Treatment," *The Doctrine of Grace,* (ed.), W. T. Whitley (London: Student Christian Movement Press, 1932), pp. 42-55.

143. Otto Pfleiderer, *Primitive Christianity,* Vol. I, trans. William Montgomery (N. Y.: G. P. Putnam's Sons, 1906), p. 436. See also James Moffatt, *Grace in the New Testament* (N. Y. Richard Long and Richard R. Smith, 1932), pp. 131-295.

144. Rom. 5:8.

145. I Cor. 15:10.

146. Donald M. Baillie, *God Was in Christ* (N. Y.: Charles Scribner's Sons, 1948), p. 114.

147. I Cor. 5:10.

148. II Cor. 6:1.

149. II Cor. 5:18-19; See also Rom. 5:10-11; Col. 1:20.

150. Donald M. Baillie, *God Was in Christ* (N. Y.: Charles Scribner's Sons, 1948), pp. 106-107.

151. William Ralph Inge, *The Things that Remain* (N. Y.: Harper and Brothers, Publishers, 1958), p. 9.

152. II Cor. 5:14-15.

153. James Moffatt, *Love in the New Testament* (N. Y.: R. R. Smith, 1930), p. 320.

154. I Cor. 1:23-24.

155. Ernest F. Scott, *The Nature of the Early Church* (N. Y.: Charles Scribner's Sons, 1941), p. 20.

156. L. Harold DeWolf, *The Religious Revolt Against Reason* (N. Y.: Harper and Brothers Publishers, 1949), p. 103.

157. II Cor. 6:8-10.

158. Lu. 12:32.

159. Matt. 6:33.

160. Phil. 2:12-13.
161. Joseph Barber Lightfoot, *Saint Paul's Epistle to the Philippians* (N. Y.: The Macmillan Company, 1903), p. 115.
162. Krister Stendahl, Anton Fridrichsen and Others, *The Root and the Vine* (London: A. and C. Black, 1953), p. 63. Citing P. Ewald, (ed.) D. Theodor Zahn, *Kommentar zum Neuen Testament,* Vol. XI (Lepzing: A. Deichert (1909) 1923, p. 136.
163. Phil. 2:8.
164. Rom. 14:5.
165. Matt. 7:17.
166. Rom. 14:10.
167. John Burnaby, *Christian Words and Christian Meanings* (N. Y.: Harper and Brothers Publishers, 1955), pp. 128-129.
168. Rom. 5:20.
169. Rom. 6:1-2, 11.
170. Gal. 5:22.
171. Gal. 6:9.
172. Rom. 6:4.
173. I Cor. 10:12-13.
174. Peter A. Bertocci, *Free Will, Responsibility and Grace* (N. Y.: Abingdon Press, 1957), p. 108.
175. Rom. 8:28.
176. Phil. 3:14.
177. John W. Oman, *The Paradox of the World* (Cambridge: Cambridge University Press, 1921), p. 111.
178. Rom. 10:16.
179. Rom. 11:14.
180. Rom. 11:12, 26.
181. II Cor. 2:15.
182. II Cor. 4:4.
183. Rom. 11:25.
184. Rom. 3:29; Compare Rom. 2:12-16; 10-12.
185. Rom. 4:17; Gal. 3:8.
186. Rom. 1:16, 17; 2:16.
187. Rom. 5:19.
188. Rom. 3:25, 29, 30; 2:2-16; 2:4.
189. I Cor. 15:45.
190. I Cor. 5:14.
191. Rom. 8:29;5;17.
192. Rom. 5:1-11.
193. Rom. 5:12-20.
194. Rom. 1:18-20, 21, 24, 26, 28.

195. Rom. 8:18-25.
196. I Cor. 15:24.
197. I Cor. 15:25; I Thess. 1:9.
198. Col. 1:20.
199. Phil. 2:9-11.
200. Reinhold Nebuhr, *The Nature and Destiny of Man,* Vol. II (N. Y.: Charles Scribner's Sons, 1943), p. 107.
201. I Cor. 6:12.
202. I Cor. 9:19.
203. Rom. 7:24-25.
204. Rom. 8:2.
205. Willard L. Sperry, *Religion in America* (N. Y.: The Macmillan Company, 1946), p. 193.
206. Charles R. Salit, *Man in Search of Immortality* (N. Y.: Philosophical Library, 1958), p. 11.
207. Douglas Van Steere, *On Beginning from Within* (N. Y.: Harper and Brothers, 1943), p. 119. See also Herman Feifel (ed.), *The Meaning of Death* (N. Y.: McGraw-Hill Book Company, 1959).
208. Walter Chalmers Smith, "The Christian Paradox" *Masterpieces of Religious Verse,* (ed.), James Dalton Morrison (N. Y.: Harper and Brothers Publishers, 1948), p. 413.
209. I Jn. 3:14; Compare Jn. 5:24.
210. Lu. 15:24.
211. Matt. 10:39.
212. I Thess. 4:15; I Cor. 15:45; Rom. 7:1.
213. I Thess. 1:19; II Cor. 3:3; 6:16; Rom. 14:11.
214. I Cor. 9:14.
215. I Thess. 3:8.
216. II Cor. 5:14-15; Rom. 6:12; 8:12-13; Col. 2:20; 3:7; Gal. 2:14, 19-20; 5:25.
217. Gal. 3:11-12; Rom. 1:17 (Hab. 2:4); Rom. 10:5 (Lev. 18:5); Rom. 12:1.
218. I Thess. 5:10; Rom. 6:10; 14:9; I Cor. 15:19.
219. I Cor. 5:14-15; Compare II Cor. 4:11-12.
220. II Cor. 6:9.
221. II Cor. 4:10; Compare Rom. 4:19.
222. Alfred Plummer, *Second Epistle of St. Paul to the Corinthians,* ICC (Edinburgh: T. and T. Clark, 1956), p. 129.
223. II Cor. 4:16; Compare I Cor. 15:31; Col. 1:24; Phil. 3:10.
224. Rom. 8:21.
225. Jn. 12:24.

226. Rom. 12:1. The Authorized Version uses "reasonable" service which is preferred here.
227. Gustaf Adolf Deissmann, *The Religion of Jesus and the Faith of Paul*, trans. William E. Wilson (N. Y.: George Doran Company, 1923), p. 234.
228. Rom. 5:1, 3, 5.
229. I Cor. 15:54.
230. Rom. 5:1, 3, 5.
231. Rom. 8:18.
232. Rom. 8:36; Compare Psa. 44:22.
233. Rom. 8:39.
234. Rom. 8:37.
235. Douglas Van Steere, *On Beginning from Within* (N. Y.: Harper and Brothers Publishers, 1943), p. 132.
236. Rom. 6:11; See the entire passage 6:3-11.
237. Rom. 6:12-14.
238. Gal. 6:14.
239. Gal. 2:19-20.
240. Ernest DeWitt Burton, *The Epistle to the Galatians*, ICC (N. Y.: Charles Scribner's Sons, 1920), p. 136.
241. II Cor. 5:15; Rom. 4:24, 25.
242. Phil. 3:10.
243. Rom. 8:17.
244. Phil. 1:20.
245. Phil. 1:21.
246. Rom. 14:7.
247. Rom. 6:4. See verses 1-11 for Paul's fuller treatment of baptism.
248. I Cor. 15:45; Compare Gen. 2:7.
249. I Cor.15:22.
250. Archibald Robertson and Alfred Plummer, *The First Epistle of St. Paul to the Corinthians*, ICC (N. Y.: Charles Scribner's Sons, 1925), p. 353.
251. Rom. 5:12.
252. Emil Brunner, *The Christian Doctrine of Creation and Redemption*, Vol. II, trans. Olive Wyon (London: Lutterworth Press, 1952), p. 104.
253. Rom. 5:18-19.
254. William Ernest Hocking, *Thoughts on Death and Life* (N. Y.: Harper and Brothers, 1937), p. 5.
255. I Cor. 15:50.
256. II Cor. 5:1-8.

257. I Cor. 15:35.
258. I Cor. 15:44.
259. I Cor. 15:37-38.
260. I Cor. 13:12.
261. II Cor. 3:18.
262. Phil. 3:20.
263. I Cor. 15:19.
264. Blaise Pascal, (ed.), Louis Allard, *Pensées* (Montréal: Les Editions Variétés, n.d.), 376, p. 187.
265. Gal. 1:15.
266. Archibald Joseph Cronin, *Adventures in Two Worlds* (N. Y.: Mc-Graw Hill, 1952).
267. II Cor. 12:10; Compare II Cor. 5:8; I Thess. 2:8; 3:1.
268. II Cor. 11:23-30.
269. II Cor. 12:9.
270. I Cor. 2:1-6.
271. II Cor. 12:9.
272. I Thess. 5:16-18.
273. I Thess. 5:25; Also II Thess. 3:1; 14:20.
274. Rom. 8:26.
275. I Cor. 14:15.
276. I Cor. 1:26-29.
277. I Cor. 2:8; 15:20.
278. II Cor. 13:4.
279. Rom. 5:6.
280. II Cor. 3:5-6.
281. Phil. 4:13.
282. Rom. 1:16.
283. Cor. 1:11-12.
284. II Cor. 4:8-10; Compare I Cor. 2:3-4. Other hardships are listed in II Cor. 4:7; 6:4, 10; 11:23-32; 12:10; I Cor. 4:9-13; 15:31; Rom. 8: 35-39; Phil. 1:29.
285. Floyd V. Wilson, *Corinthians,* The Interpreter's Bible, Vol. X, (eds.), Nolan B. Harmon and Others. (N. Y.: Abingdon Press, 1953), p. 319.
286. Permission to quote this poem was granted by the author in a personal letter.
287. Gal. 5:1.
288. Gal. 2:11.
289. II Thess. 3:1-2.
290. II Cor. 1:14.
291. Jer. 1:6.
292. Jer. 1:18.

293. II Cor. 11:30.
294. II Cor. 1:5; Phil. 3:10.
295. II Cor. 12:9.
296. I Cor. 1:30.
297. John W. Oman, *The Paradox of the World* (Cambridge: The University Press, 1921), p. 261.
298. Phil. 2:13.
299. Col. 1:27.
300. II Cor. 12:7.
301. Gal. 4:13-14.
302. II Cor. 10:10.
303. II Cor. 12:7.
304. II Cor. 12:9.
305. II. Cor. 5:1.
306. I Thess. 2:11; Rom. 16:13; I Cor. 4:14: 13; II Cor. 2:4; Phil. 3:18.
307. I Cor. 5:9; 7:1; 8; II Cor. 2:2-4; 7:8; 10:10; Rom. 14:1-15:13.
308. I Cor. 15:9ff.
309. Isa. 49:4.
310. I Cor. 1:18.
311. I Cor. 9:27.
312. Compare John 15:6.
313. Rom. 7:22-25.
314. Rom. 7:18.
315. Rom. 8:2.
316. Rom. 8:4.
317. James Arthur Hadfield, *The Spirit,* (eds.), Burnett Hillman Streeter, A. Seth Pringle-Pattison and Others. (N. Y.: The Macmillan Company, 1925), p. 84.
318. Jud. 15:1-20.
319. I Cor. 1:26.
320. Rom. 15:1-2.
321. I Cor. 10:24.
322. II Cor. 11:29; Compare Psa. 55:22.
323. Rom. 16; I Cor. 8.
324. Gal. 6:1.
325. Gal. 6:2.
326. Gal. 6:5.
327. Matt. 11:28-30.
328. Richard Burton, "Strength in Weakness," *Masterpieces of Religious Verse* (ed.), James Dalton Morrison (N. Y.: Harper and Brothers Publishers, 1948), p. 383.
329. Psa. 111:10.

330. Prov. 9:10.

331. Jer. 9:23-24.

332. Eccles. 1; 2.

333. Paul Elmer Moore, *The Christ of the New Testament* (Princeton: Princeton University Press, 1924), p. 102.

334. Edwin McNeill Poteat, *The Dimension of Depth* (N. Y.: Harper and Brothers Publishers, 1957), p. 36.

335. I Cor. 8:1-3; Compare Rom. 8:26.

336. I Cor. 3:18; 11:16; See also Rom. 12:16.

337. I Cor. 13:2.

338. I Cor. 13:12.

339. I Cor. 1:18.

340. Rom. 1:22-23.

341. I Cor. 2:1-2.

342. I Cor. 1:17-24.

343. I Cor. 1:23.

344. II Cor. 5:19.

345. Rom. 5:8.

346. Matt. 27:42; Compare Lu. 24:21.

347. Gal. 5:11; I Cor. 1:23.

348. I Cor. 1:25.

349. Gal. 3:12ff.

350. Jn. 14:9.

351. I Cor. 1:25.

352. Mk. 8:35; Matt. 10:39; Lu. 17:33; Jn. 12:35.

353. I Cor. 1:18-25; 15:14.

354. I Cor. 1:26-31.

355. II Cor. 2:4.

356. I Cor. 2:3-4.

357. James Moffatt, *The First Epistle of Paul to the Corinthians,* Moffatt New Testament Commentary (N. Y.: Harper and Brothers, n.d.), p. 16.

358. II Cor. 11:6.

359. Jn. 9:25.

360. II Cor. 12:8.

361. Clarence Tucker Craig, *Corinthians,* The Interpreter's Bible, Vol. X (eds.), Nolan B. Harmon and Others (N. Y.: Abingdon-Cokesbury Press, 1953), p. 31.

362. I Cor. 1:21.

363. I Cor. 1:18; See also I Cor. 2:14; 3:19.

364. I Cor. 1:22.

365. Isa. 29:14.

366. Psa. 33:10.

367. I Cor. 1:20.
368. I Cor. 11:25.
369. I Cor. 1:26-27.
370. Jer. 9:23.
371. I Cor. 1:28.
372. I Cor. 3:18-19; See also 4:10.
373. Job. 5:12-13.
374. Psa. 94:11.
375. I Cor. 1:31; Compare Jer. 9:24.
376. II Cor. 10:17-18.
377. I Cor. 1:20.
378. Matt. 5:14; 6:34; 9:12.
379. I Cor. 1:24; 30.
380. Col. 2:3; See also Col. 1:15-18.
381. Mk. 6:2.
382. II Cor. 2:7. Note Psa. 51:6.
383. Prov. 8; Compare Wisdom of Sol. 7:22-27; Eccles. 24:24-27.
384. I Cor. 2:8.
385. I Cor. 2:14; Note vs. 10-13 also.
386. II Cor. 105; II Cor. 1:12.
387. I Cor. 8:4.
388. I Cor. 4:10.
389. I Cor. 3:18.
390. Cor. 11:16.
391. II Cor. 12:11.
392. II Cor. 12:11.
393. I Cor. 3:3-9.
394. Gal. 5:7-12; 6:12-13; II Cor. 11:3-4, 13-15, 20.
395. Gal. 6:7; Compare I Cor. 6:9.
396. I Cor. 15:33; Probably a quote from Meander's "Thais".
397. I Cor. 1:30.
398. I Cor. 2:13.
399. I Cor. 1:9.
400. I Cor. 2:14.
401. Jude 19.
402. Lu. 12:16-21.
403. Archibald Robertson and Alfred Plummer, *The First Epistle of St. Paul to the Corinthians,* ICC (N. Y.: Charles Scribner's Sons, 1925), p. 49.
404. Col. 3:2.
405. Phl. 3:15.
406. Rom. 1:16-17.
407. Rom. 1:20. See also Isa. 40:25, 28.

408. Rom. 1:21-23.
409. Rom. 2:14-16.
410. Rom. 3:21-22.
411. Rom. 6:1, 15, 16; 8:1-17.
412. Rom. 14:1-19.
413. Rom. 14:20-22; I Cor. 8:12; Compare I Cor. 15:34.
414. I Cor. 8:9.
415. John Masefield, "Good Friday," *Verse Plays* (N. Y. The Macmillan Company, 1925), p. 52. Used by permission of the publisher.
416. Col. 1:9.
417. Col. 1:28-29.

CHAPTER FIVE

1. William Kilbourne Stewart, "Christianity as Paradox," *Hibbert Journal*, XXVII (1928-1929), p. 223.
2. Lu. 5:26.
3. L. Harold DeWolf, *The Religious Revolt Against Reason* (N. Y.: Harper and Brothers Publishers, 1940), p. 134.
4. Mandell Creighton, *Life and Letters of Mandell Creighton*, Vol. II, (ed.), Louise Creighton (N. Y.: Longmans, Green and Company, 1904), p. 504.
5. *Ibid.*, p. 505.
6. G. G. Findlay, "Paul the Apostle," *Dictionary of the Bible*, Vol. III, (ed.), James Hastings (N. Y.: Scribner's and Sons, 1900), p. 696.
7. James S. Stewart, *A Man in Christ* (N. Y.: Harper and Brothers, Publishers, 1935), p. 29.
8. Arthur Darby Nock, *St. Paul* (N. Y.: Harper and Brothers, Publishers, 1938), p. 239.
9. Amos N. Wilder, *New Testament Faith for Today* (N. Y.: Harper and Brothers Publishers, 1955), pp. 111-112.
10. Phil. 4:11.
11. Marcus Tullius Cicero, *Paradoxes of the Stoics*, Vol. II, Book III, trans. H. Rackham (Cambridge: Harvard University Press, 1942), p. 257.
12. *Ibid.*, p. 285.
13. Henry J. Cadbury, *Jesus: What Manner of Man* (N. Y.: Macmillan and Company, 1947), p. 123.
14. John Oman, *Grace and Personality* (N. Y.: The Macmillan and Company, 1925), pp. 63-64.

15. Rom. 12:1; I Thess. 5:21; Col. 1:9; I Cor. 1:5; Phil. 1:9.
16. I Cor. 1:23; 12:2; Rom. 1:15; 15:20.
17. Robert Newton Flew, *The Idea of Perfection* (London: Oxford University Press, 1934), p. 59.
18. Phil. 1:6; 4:13; Gal. 3:27; I Thess. 5:23.
19. Phil. 3:12-15.
20. Rom. 14:10; II Cor. 5:10.
21. I Thess. 5:8, 21; II Thess. 2:17; 3:10-11.
22. Morton Scott Enslin, *The Ethics of Paul* (N. Y.: Harper and Brothers, 1930), p. 63. Mary Edith Andrews, *The Ethical Teaching of Paul* (Chapel Hill: University of North Carolina, 1934), p. 25ff.
23. Gal. 5:22-23.
24. Rom. 7:4; 9:30; 11:6; Gal. 6:7-10; Col. 1:6, 10; Phil. 4:17.
25. Phil. 4:8.
26. II Cor. 514; Note also I Cor. 13.
27. I Cor. 5:9; I Cor. 9:1; 10:9; Gal. 6:11; Phil. 3:1; Col. 4:16.
28. Percy Gardner, *The Religious Experience of St. Paul* (N. Y.: G. P. Putnam's Sons, 1911), p. 139.
29. Ernest Troeltsch, *The Social Teaching of the Christian Churches,* Vol. I, trans. Olive Wyon (N. Y.: The Macmillan Company, 1938), pp. 84-85.
30. *Ibid.,* p. 85.
31. Ray C. Petry, *Christian Eschatology and Social Thought* (N. Y.: Abingdon Press, 1956), p. 78.
32. Emile Durkheim, (ed.), George E. G. Catlin, *The Rules of Sociological Method,* trans. Sarah A. Solovay and John H. Mueller (Chicago: University of Chicago Press, 1930), p. 46ff.
33. Phil. 2:5.
34. I Cor. 2:16; Compare Matt. 11:29; 20:28.
35. William Ralph Inge, *Christian Mysticism* (N. Y.: Charles Scribner's and Sons, 1899), p. 39.
36. Jacob B. Minkin, "Jewish Mysticism," *Journal of Religion,* XXIV (1944), pp. 188-200; J. Abelson, "Mysticism and Rabbinical Literature," *Hibbert Journal,* X (1911-1912), pp. 426-477; L. Ginzberg, "Cabala," *Jewish Encyclopedia,* III (1906), pp. 456-479.
37. Albert Schweitzer, *The Mysticism of Paul the Apostle,* trans. William Montgomery (N. Y.: Henry Holt and Company, 1931), p. 5.
38. Rom. 8:14.
39. Gal. 2:20.
40. Rufus M. Jones, *Studies in Mystical Religion* (N. Y.: Macmillan and Company, 1909), Introd. XV.
41. Jacques Maritain, *Ransoming the Time* (N. Y.: Charles Scribner's Sons, 1941), p. 85.

42. II Cor. 5:17-20; Gal. 6:7-10; Col. 3:12-25.
43. II Cor. 1:13.
44. I Cor. 14:19.
45. Gal. 2:13-14.
46. Rom. 16:17; II Cor. 11-13; Gal. 1:7, 9; Phil. 1:15.
47. I Cor. 3:3-6.
48. Elias Andrews, "The Relevance of Paul for Preaching," *Canadian Journal of Theology,* I (1956), p. 51. See also Halford E. Luccock, *Preaching Values in the Epistles of Paul,* Vol. I. Romans and Corinthians (N. Y.: Harper and Brothers, 1959).
49. John W. Oman, *Grace and Personality* (N. Y.: The Macmillan Company, 1925), pp. 142-143.
50. Walter R. Matthews, *God in Christian Thought and Experience* (London: Nisbet and Company, 1930), pp. 25-26.
51. Eric Lane Titus, *Essentials of New Testament Study* (N. Y.: The Ronald Press, Company, 1958), p. 125.
52. William Cleaver Wilkinson, *Paul and the Revolt Against Him* (Philadelphia: The Griffith and Rowland Press, 1914), p. 42.
53. I Cor. 9;16.
54. Gal. 1:14.
55. Jer. 1:5.
56. I Cor. 1:26.
57. Gal. 1:14.
58. Ernest DeWitt Burton, *Galatians,* ICC (N. Y.: Charles Scribner's Sons, 1920), p. 46.
59. Phil. 3:14.
60. I Cor. 2:1-5; II Cor. 7:15.
61. II Cor. 4:7-9.
62. Gal. 2:19, 20.
63. II Cor. 4:10-12.
64. Psa. 116:10.
65. II Cor. 4:14.
66. II Cor. 4:16.
67. Ernest Findlay Scott, *Paul's Epistle to the Romans* (London: S. C. M. Press, 1947), p. 90.
68. George B. Findlay, *The Epistles of the Apostle Paul* (London: C. H. Kelly, n.d.), p. 34.
69. II Cor. 5:11.
70. Rom. 8:24; I Ccr. 13; II Cor. 7:10; Col. 3:12-14.
71. Rom. Chapters 3-8.
72. Rom. 12:1.
73. Ethelbert Stauffer "Hina und das problem des theologischen Den-

kens bei Paulus," *Theologische Studien und Kritiken,* 1930, p. 102.
See Krister Stendahl, *The Root and the Vine* (Dacre Press. London: Adam and Charles Black, 1953), p. 66.
74. Matt. 17:2.
75. Rom. 12:2.

CHAPTER SIX

1. Hans Lietzmann, *The Beginnings of the Christian Church,* trans. B. L. Woolf (N. Y.: Charles Scribner's Sons, 1937), p. 27.